Leading in Complex Worlds

Leading in Complex Worlds

Edited by

JoAnn Danelo Barbour

and

Gloria J. Burgess, Lena Lid Falkman, and
Robert M. McManus

A Volume in the International Leadership Series
Building Leadership Bridges

International Leadership Association

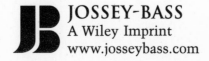

JOSSEY-BASS
A Wiley Imprint
www.josseybass.com

Published by Jossey-Bass
A Wiley Imprint
One Montgomery Street, Suite 1200, San Francisco, CA 94104-4594—www.josseybass.com

Jossey-Bass books and products are available through most bookstores. To contact Jossey-Bass directly call our Customer Care Department within the U.S. at 800-956-7739, outside the U.S. at 317-572-3986, or fax 317-572-4002.

Wiley also publishes its books in a variety of electronic formats and by print-on-demand. Some material included with standard print versions of this book may not be included in e-books or in print-on-demand. If the version of this book that you purchased references media such as CD or DVD that was not included in your purchase, you may download this material at http://booksupport.wiley.com. For more information about Wiley products, visit www.wiley.com.

ISBN: 978-1-118-26699-1

Printed in the United States of America
FIRST EDITION
PB Printing   10 9 8 7 6 5 4 3 2 1

Contents

List of Contributors

Pedram Alaedini is the president and CEO of Primapax Group, a life sciences management and technology firm with offices in Princeton and Shanghai that specializes in the integration of technical, process, and organizational skills in pharmaceutical development and manufacturing. He is a chemical engineer and lives in Princeton, New Jersey.

Scott J. Allen is an assistant professor of management at John Carroll University, University Heights, Ohio. Scott is the coauthor of the *Little Book of Leadership Development* (AMACOM) and *Emotionally Intelligent Leadership: A Guide for College Students* (Jossey-Bass). Along with writing and speaking, Scott blogs (www.centerforleaderdevelopment.net), consults, facilitates workshops, and leads retreats across industries.

JoAnn Danelo Barbour is professor of education administration and leadership at Texas Woman's University. Her research interests include critical and experiential, multidisciplinary, and artistic approaches to leading and teaching. Her publications include ten entries in *Sage Encyclopedia of Educational Leadership and Administration*, several journal articles, and chapters in leadership texts, most recently "Critical Policy/Practice" in *Sage Handbook of Educational Leadership*. Former ILA Leadership Education Member Interest Group Chair, Barbour was chief editor of *Academic Exchange Quarterly* and coeditor of *Building Leadership Bridges* in 2008, *Global Leadership: Portraits of the Past, Visions for the Future* and in 2010, *Leadership for Transformation*.

Richard Bergeon is a principal of Bergeon, Fu and Associates. He holds a BBS in general management (Wayne State University, Detroit), an MA in whole systems design (Antioch University, Seattle, Washington), and certification as an organization systems renewal consultant. He has been employed as manager, director, and executive leadership consultant in banking, public utilities, transportation, manufacturing, pharmaceutics, and telecommunications. His specialties are adoption of new technologies and staff development.

Gloria J. Burgess is professor of leadership and organization systems renewal at Seattle University and an affiliate faculty member in leadership at the University of Washington in Seattle. Her research interests include the intersection of the arts and leadership, spirituality and leadership, gender and leadership, and intercultural praxis and leadership. Frequently invited to keynote events, she has published journal articles, three volumes of poetry, and several books, including her most recent, *Dare to Wear Your Soul on the Outside*.

Patricia Carr is an assistant professor in the doctoral program in organizational learning and leadership at Gannon University, Erie, Pennsylvania. She also teaches for Duquesne University, Pittsburgh, and in its masters program for women religious, Rome, Italy. She is a consultant in organizational development and leadership. Her interests include organizational design, organizational learning, and sustainable human resources. She holds a PhD from the University of Pittsburgh in administrative and policy studies. She can be reached at drpatcarr@msn.com.

Paul B. Carr is a Beta Phi Scholar and a professor in the School of Global Leadership and Entrepreneurship at Regent University, Virginia Beach. He is also director of the PhD program in human resource development. He is the director of the Autonomous Learning World Caucus, which is held annually at Oxford University. His research interests include learner autonomy, resourcefulness intentions in the adult autonomous learner, human agency, and creating environments conducive to learning and success.

Jeri Darling is vice president of EnCompass LLC and directs the global practice for leadership and organizational effectiveness. She has more than twenty-five years of experience working with diverse organizations in the areas of learning strategy, leadership, talent management, and organizational development. She holds an MA from George Washington University, Washington, DC; an MBA from Case Western Reserve University, Cleveland; a BA in international relations from the University of Wisconsin, Madison; and a certificate in leadership coaching from Georgetown University.

Deanne de Vries has spent the past seven years with Agility—a Kuwait-based global logistics company—where she is currently Vice President Africa. Her passion, global mind-set, and extensive cross-cultural leadership have helped people and companies grow by turning chaos into clarity in the global marketplace. She speaks many languages; has worked on five continents; received her MBA from Thunderbird School of Global Management, Glendale, Arizona; and is a doctoral student at Eastern University, Philadelphia.

Lena Lid Falkman (Andersson) is a scholar at Stockholm School of Economics, Sweden. Lid Falkman's interest is value-based leadership, global leadership, rhetoric, and communication. Her doctoral thesis dealt with leadership in the United Nations and has received European and American awards. Lid Falkman has fifteen years of experience teaching master's and executive level education, and she is an often-invited lecturer to organizations, businesses, and governmental institutions. Lid Falkman's research blog http://lenalidfalkman.se has been awarded prizes, and her personal passion is traveling the world.

Caroline Fu is assistant professor of the doctoral program in leadership studies at Gonzaga University, Spokane, Washington. She holds a PhD in leadership and change from Antioch University, Yellow Springs, Ohio, and an MA in whole systems design from Antioch University, Seattle, Washington. Her MS in computer sciences and BS in applied mathematics, engineering (EE), and physics are both from University of Wisconsin, Madison. She has a certificate of completion in system dynamics advanced study from the Sloan School of Management, Massachusetts Institute of Technology.

Lori N. H. Guasta holds a PhD in leadership studies from Gonzaga University, Spokane, Washington, and a master's in clinical sociology from the University of Northern Colorado, Greeley. Lori is the Director of Organizational Behavior and Emerging Markets for Safety Solutions International, Inc. and teaches sociology, communication, and business courses at the University of Colorado (Colorado Springs) and at Regis University, Colorado Springs. Her research interests are in the areas of community and social capital, safety leadership, and occupational ethnography.

Juanita Johnson-Bailey, who holds the Josiah Meigs Distinguished Teaching Professorship, is the director of the Institute for Women's Studies and a professor in the Department of Lifelong Education, Administration and Policy at the University of Georgia, Athens. She is the author of *Sistahs in College: Making a Way Out of No Way* (Krieger Press, 2001), coeditor of *Flat-Footed Truths: Telling Black Women's Lives* (Henry Holt, 1998), and *The Handbook of Race in Adult Education* (Jossey-Bass, 2010).

Michael S. Lane holds a PhD in organizational leadership from Regent University, Virginia Beach. He currently is the general manager of Foresight Culture and Business Consulting Ltd., located in the People's Republic of China. Since the 1990s, he has led multicultural teams in complex, cross-cultural environments. He also conducts seminars and enjoys writing and research regarding cross-cultural adjustment, innovation, spirituality in the workplace, and uncertainty management. He can be reached at laneforesight@psmail.net.

Greg Laudeman develops and manages innovative, technology-oriented economic development programs for Georgia Institute of Technology's Enterprise Innovation Institute, Atlanta, focusing on how information and communications technologies make communities and organizations more competitive and productive. Currently pursuing a doctorate in learning and leadership at the University of Tennessee at Chattanooga, he has diverse experience in academia and business. Greg can be reached at laudeman@gatech.edu or 706-271-5521.

Nigel Linacre is a cofounder of Extraordinary Leadership, which enables leadership development in Europe and America, Asia and Africa. He is the coauthor with Jefferson Cann of *An Introduction to 3-Dimensional Leadership*. Nigel's books include *The Successful Executive*, *Recipes for Happiness*, *Why You Are Here—Briefly*, and *Knock, Knock, Who's God?* Nigel is a founding trustee of WellBoring, a membership-based charity that provides sustainable water solutions to African schools and communities.

Beth Ann Martin is a professor at John Carroll University in Cleveland, Ohio, and holds a PhD in industrial and organizational psychology from Purdue University, West Lafayette, Indiana. Her research interests are in the areas of performance management systems, leadership, and goal setting. She has published her research in several journals including *International Journal of Occupational Behavior*, *Personality and Individual Differences*, *Academy of Educational Leadership Journal*, *Human Performance*, *Journal of Managerial Issues*, *Journal of Management*, and *Organizational Behavior and Human Performance*.

Jeanne Martinson is a principal of Martrain Corporate and Personal Development. She holds an MA in leadership from Royal Roads University, Victoria, British Columbia, Canada. Since 1992 she has focused on leadership development in government and the private sector, where she assists leaders and human resource professionals in understanding diversity issues so they may attract, retain, and engage an effective workforce. Martinson is the author of three books on leadership and diversity. She is the recipient of the EMCY Award, Canada's business award for excellence in diversity issues.

Robert M. McManus is the McCoy Associate Professor of Leadership Studies and Communication at the McDonough Center for Leadership and Business at Marietta College, Ohio. He offers courses on the foundations of leadership, organizational leadership, theories and models of leadership, and global leadership. His research interests center on the connections among liberal arts, leadership studies, and communication.

Kimberly Nehls is executive director of the Association for the Study of Higher Education (ASHE). She also serves as a visiting assistant professor of higher education at UNLV and teaches classes for UNLV's interdisciplinary minor in leadership and civic engagement. Kim earned her doctorate in educational leadership and her master's and bachelor's degrees in speech communication.

Georgia Pappas is a leadership trainer, executive coach, and educator. She has worked in the nonprofit sector for more than twenty years and currently works with leaders to help them reach their highest potential as change agents for the common good. She is a faculty member at Regis University, Denver, in the Global Nonprofit Leadership Department. She holds a PhD in human development from Fielding Graduate University in Santa Barbara, California. She can be reached at gpappas@regis.edu.

Kathleen Patterson currently serves with the School of Global Leadership & Entrepreneurship at Regent University. She is noted as an expert on servant leadership and coordinates an annual servant leadership roundtable where scholars and practitioners engage in servant leadership discourse. She also co-coordinated the first Global Servant Leadership Research Roundtable in the Netherlands with Dirk van Dierendonck, with whom she also coedited the recent book *Servant Leadership: Developments in Theory and Research*.

Dionne Rosser-Mims is assistant professor in the College of Education at Troy University, Alabama. She has taught in the adult education field for more than twelve years, and her main areas of teaching and research include adult learning and development, higher education administration, and leadership studies. She is the author of *How and Why Black Women Are Elected to Political Office: A Narrative Analysis of Nine Cases in Georgia*.

Eli Sopow is director of continuous improvement at the Royal Canadian Mounted Police (RCMP), Pacific Region, and professor of management at University Canada West, Vancouver, Canada. He holds a PhD in human and organizational systems from Fielding Graduate University, Santa Barbara, California. He is the recipient of the international Howard Chase Award for outstanding issues management as well as three national awards from the RCMP for management strategies. He can be reached at www.elisopow.com.

Elisebeth VanderWeil works as the director of undergraduate leadership programs at Mountain State University, Beckley, West Virginia, and holds a PhD in leadership studies from Gonzaga University, Spokane, Washington. Her seemingly disconnected yet thematic work experience—including drop-in centers, Microsoft, environmental research, and academia—has provided her with the skills and experience to continually exploit opportunities for people to be wonderful.

Introduction

JoAnn Danelo Barbour

> At moments of wonder, it is easy to avoid small
> thinking, to entertain thoughts that span the
> universe, that capture both thunder and tinkle,
> thick and thin, the near and the far.
> —Yann Martel, *Life of Pi*

To live in complex worlds, leaders live in the balance between moments of wonder as noted in the epigraph and moments of routine. In one sense, grand thoughts, ideas, or plans are warranted; in another sense, tedious repetitive tasks, mind-numbing operations, or daily rituals are needed. Anthropologists suggest cultures need rituals and ceremonies to survive; politicians talk about progressive and conservative ideologies; biologists give us information from the level of DNA to the interaction of brain, eye, and hand coordination needed to throw a ball. Michelangelo used thousands of brush strokes to paint the Sistine ceiling, Leonardo drew hundreds of sketches before building models of his war machines, and although Prokofiev took only four days to write his symphony for children, it took the rest of the world another several years to appreciate *Peter and the Wolf*. Leaders live in the place between the practice and the performance, the molecules and the muscle movements, the idea and the construction, and the constructed idea and its acceptance. We live at the place of negotiation, the point just before a board meeting begins, just before the decision is finalized, or in the middle of a crisis when life slows down and speeds up at the same time.

Physicists and organizational theorists (Gleick, 1987; Lewin, 1993; Lorenz, 1993; Nicolis & Prigogine, 1989; Pascale, Millemann, & Gioja, 2000; Waldrop, 1992; Wheatley, 1999) suggest the places described, the places or spaces in-between, are unpredictable yet somewhat predictable systems. Complexity, "a chaos of behaviors in which the components of the system never quite lock into place, yet never quite dissolve into turbulence either" (Cowan & Wolfram, cited in Waldrop, 1992, p. 293), is also the ability of a system "to switch between different modes of behavior as the environmental conditions are varied" (Nicolis & Prigogine, 1989, p. 218). This is to say, if complex worlds adapt to their environments, by implication, leaders in complex worlds must be adaptable. In the adventure novel *Life of Pi* (Martel, 2001), shipwrecked castaway Pi Patel, the character quoted in the epigraph at the beginning of this Introduction, survived 227 days in a lifeboat by living in that in-between place, with a Bengal tiger no less. To be adaptable, it might be extrapolated, leaders, like Pi, live life caught in the tension between order and disorder, on the edge of chaos, the place in which there is enough disorder for creativity but enough order for appropriate patterns to endure. Too much order or stability and there is no room for creativity or the new to develop. Too much disorder and nothing can last long enough for the usefully creative to occur; the chaos is a jumble that destroys the lot before it can get started.

Because leading in complex worlds involves adaptability, flexibility, and the ability to change, leaders must be willing and able to approach life within and through many lenses of sight, hearing, touch, and thinking. Leaders live lives of leading that are grounded, based, or positioned in multiple disciplines, multiple frames of reference, and multiple philosophies. With a sense of the multidisciplinarity of life, leaders need practices and approaches that are multidisciplinary, multimodal, often multitasked, multirelational, and so on.

With this book, we attempted to garner submissions that were multiperspective in scope and focused on leading and leadership, and that would be appropriate for helping leaders develop the understanding needed to live and lead in complex worlds. We sought submissions that blended the theory and practice of leading and leadership and were complex in their multiperspectives: multigrounded, multiframed, multidisciplinary, multimodal, multidimensional, multi-intelligent, and multilogical, for example.

For this book, the International Leadership Association (ILA) added three associate editors who, with the lead editor, culled through eighty-five submissions, narrowed them to thirty-two, and then to the selections contained herein. To assemble these selections into parts, we followed a naturalistic process; that is, we grouped parts into a likely fit and then gave each fit set a thematic title. The editors in this book introduce their parts, which include Part One, "The Complexity of Leader Development," Robert M. McManus, editor; Part Two, "The Complexity of Leadership Practice," Gloria J. Burgess, editor; and Part Three, "The Complexity of Leading in a Globalized World," Lena Lid Falkman, editor.

Although this book would not be possible without the contributions of the authors, we would especially like to express our appreciation to others who partnered with us in this effort, helping in the complex organization that is ILA. We are grateful for the work of Debra DeRuyver, ILA director of publications and special initiatives, who gently facilitated but strongly supported the process from individually submitted manuscripts to this book of essays, and for Joanne Ferguson, a copyeditor whose diligence makes the most complex editing appear simple. Additionally, we thank Cynthia Cherrey and Shelly Wilsey, respectively ILA's president and director, who, in keeping with the mission of the ILA, support our efforts to share with the reader contemporary thinking about leadership from a diverse range of scholars, practitioners, and educators working in the field of leadership studies across cultures, over time, and around the world. We also thank the ILA board of directors for their continuing support and encouragement of our attempts to understand and lead in complex worlds, to adapt in ways we hope will better serve all who study, practice, teach, and care about leadership in the world.

We invite the reader now to begin journeying in the "thick and thin, the near and the far" with the poem "Infusion," written by Elisebeth VanderWeil, who suggests leaders in complex worlds must "journey down to go up" and "go in to break out."

References

Gleick, J. (1987). *Chaos: Making a new science.* New York: Penguin Books.

Lewin, R. (1993). *Complexity: Life at the edge of chaos.* New York: Macmillan.

Lorenz, E. N. (1993). *The essence of chaos.* Seattle: University of Washington Press.

Nicolis, G., & Prigogine, I. (1989). *Exploring complexity: An introduction.* New York: W. H. Freeman.

Martel, Y. (2001). *Life of Pi.* Orlando, FL: Harcourt.

Pascale, R., Millemann, M., & Gioja, L. (2000). *Surfing the edge of chaos: The laws of nature and the new laws of business.* New York: Crown Business.

Waldrop, M. M. (1992). *Complexity: The emerging science at the edge of order and chaos.* New York: Simon & Schuster.

Wheatley, M. (1999). *Leadership and the new science: Discovering order in a chaotic world* (2nd ed.). San Francisco: Berrett-Koehler.

Infusion

Elisebeth VanderWeil

When the sun shines I become restless.

Standing on the precipice of then-now-then
I gulp gale force winds that threaten to blow me back,
suck me down.

I'm running in circles chasing my tale.
The paradox calls—
I must journey down to go up; I must go in to break out.

The wind scourges my eyes, mouth, throat, heart

rushing into me with suffocating ferocity.

Violence accompanies birth more often than death.

I must tear to emerge.

I must breathe.

    Why do I care?

Does a leap into the wind constitute moving forward
  when you are blown back?

What if . . .

    I swallow the wind

(June 2005)

Leading in Complex Worlds

Part One

The Complexity of Leader Development

Robert M. McManus

Educators in the area of leadership studies are careful to qualify what they promise. We can provide students with a body of knowledge surrounding the critical and analytical study of leadership and be a part of crafting experiences to help students develop skills that ultimately may be helpful to them in leading people and organizations. The development of a *leader*, however, is a complex process that calls for time and reflection. One can teach leadership studies; one cannot teach someone to "be a leader." This part of this book recognizes this complexity and provides valuable insight into this process.

We begin with Pedram Alaedini's short story in Chapter One, "Discovering Leadership and Winning Friends." In it, Alaedini reflects on a turning point early in his own development as a leader. He reminds us that the process of leadership development requires risk and continual contemplation. Alaedini shares with the reader a moment of personal vulnerability that led to a better understanding of his followers and of himself.

Alaedini's story is followed by Lori N. H. Guasta's chapter in which she articulates the importance of leaders developing with others through dialogue. In her chapter, "Deepening Self-Awareness Through Dialogue: A Theoretical Framework for Leading in Complex Worlds," Guasta employs the wisdom of philosophers such as Martin Buber and David Bohm to articulate the significance of authentic interpersonal connection as a way for leaders to develop the capacity to interact and relate in complex worlds. Like Alaedini, Guasta reinforces the importance of engaging "the other" as one seeks to develop as a leader.

Guasta's ephemeral concept is materialized in Eli Sopow's chapter, "Communications, Ethics, and Vision Trump Experience," wherein he provides compelling, quantitative evidence for the importance of interpersonal connections. The diverse humanistic, qualitative, and quantitative approaches featured in this chapter bear witness to the complexity of leadership development.

We then take a turn to examine a more systematic study of leader development with Greg Laudeman's "Leading Learnership: The Transformation of Leadership via Convergence with Learning," in which he links leadership and learning theory. Laudeman echoes the call of thinkers such as Wheatley and Heifetz to abandon outdated paradigms of "command and control" in exchange for more evolved ways of engaging in a complex world.

Kimberly Nehls next puts Laudeman's call into action and provides a pedagogical tool to help educators teach leadership in a way that better facilitates student learning in "Leadership Education: The Power of Storytelling." She helps us understand that when a story or a book touches leaders profoundly, they can use that meaning to make leadership connections.

Finally, Scott J. Allen and Beth Ann Martin tie Laudeman's call and Nehls's action into their discussion of developing an extensive curriculum designed to teach leadership studies—and to develop young leaders—by drawing on disciplines found throughout the liberal arts. Titled "Developing Leaders for a Complex World: Mapping ILA's Guiding Questions to an Undergraduate Interdisciplinary Minor in Leadership," their chapter shares an application of ILA's guidelines. For each of the five ILA guidelines areas, they provide a brief description of the guideline and how they developed their program using ILA's framework.

For those who hope to play a part in developing young leaders, these authors—Alaedini, Guasta, Sopow, Laudeman, Nehls, Allen, and Martin—and their work serve to remind that not only is leadership a complex process, but so is the development of a leader.

Chapter One

Discovering Leadership and Winning Friends

Pedram Alaedini

After I graduated from university with a degree in engineering, I took a job as a production supervisor at a large factory in northwest Ohio. It was a big plant in a small town with about 2,500 employees in a community of only about 4,000 people—most with the same half-dozen German last names. At the time of graduation, I really wanted to work as an engineer, not as a production supervisor, but I thought it would be fine as a first job. The town wasn't *that* bad, and it was less than a two-hour drive to Columbus, so I still could spend the weekends with my college friends. It was the highest-paying offer I had received anyway, so I accepted the job.

Supervising twenty-five union workers can be quite challenging for someone fresh out of college. But my manager, Bert, was always there to step in every time he felt I needed help. From the first day on the job, Bert, who was less than a year away from retirement, consistently reminded me that I was supervising hourly, unionized employees, and it was important that they worked *all the time*. He meant that if there was any downtime—and with the plant being old, downtime happened often—I had to keep the workers busy doing something. *Anything*. Whatever I could think of: wiping walls, moving things around and putting them back where they first were, scrubbing the floor, storing things, unstoring things, *whatever*. The most important factor was that the employees did not sit idle.

One early afternoon, about six months into my employment, the plant lost power. We still had a couple of hours until the end of our shift. The lines stopped running and the emergency lights came on. Fifteen minutes after the initial outage, Bert came over to say that the plant would be without electricity for the rest of the day. Second-shift operators were being called and told not to show up. He also said that because we were paying them for the whole day anyway, I should keep my operators busy until the end of their shift. "Make sure they don't hide in the restroom or sneak out to smoke," he said to me.

So I went to find my operators, who were mostly sitting or, rather, hiding throughout the plant behind pieces of equipment. I quickly started assigning them to different duties, careful not to assign the more senior operators to less-senior-sounding tasks. The last issue I wanted to deal with was to have an argument with the shop steward.

Then I saw Cliff. Cliff was one of the most senior operators. He was sitting on a turned-over bucket behind a large piece of equipment and chatting with John, who had started work a few months earlier and was sitting on another bucket. Cliff had started working at the plant when he was sixteen and had worked in that factory for close to forty years. Because of his seniority, he could bid on better-paying jobs (those that were a few cents more per hour), but he did not want to. Cliff was a relief-utility operator, and his job essentially was to relieve other operators during lunch and bathroom breaks. When he wasn't doing that, his job was to move production material from station to station. He was not tied to any specific workstation and he was able to move around at will, so Cliff was difficult to keep track of and hard to supervise.

I had had my problems with Cliff in the past. I always thought he was lazy. There were times that I looked for him but could not find him anywhere; I had given him various tasks but I was not happy with his work. I could tell, also, that he was not happy with me . . . and probably not happy with my work either.

The moment I saw them sitting on their buckets, my brain went into overdrive trying to think of something for them to do. I was sorry that I had already assigned the least desirable jobs to other operators. And I was in no mood to hang around keeping an eye on Cliff. I was anxious to go upstairs to the office because I hoped to get a chance to chat with Karen, the attractive new administrative assistant.

At first, Cliff and John met my stumbling on them with disappointment. Then, for a moment, our mutual stares turned to defiance. I told Cliff that there was no second shift coming in and we had to stay until the end of ours. "Can you think of anything important that needs to be done except sitting here? I don't want Bert to see you guys back here, and I don't have any work for you except sweeping the floor," I said to both of them. He was a little taken aback with my openness and honesty. Leaning over and still sitting on the bucket behind the large piece of equipment, he looked down the long wide corridor at the two dozen people sweeping, polishing, and scraping the shiny floor and said, "Look, Boss." (He often called me *Boss* but I was not sure why. No one else called me that.) "There's no need for more people sweeping." He went on, "John has been here for almost a year now but hasn't learned anything, and he still wants to become a utility operator on the graveyard shift. If he bids on it, he'll probably get it. But I don't want him to be working around machinery without knowing the process. It's not safe." By now, I was getting impatient waiting for the punch line. He continued, "Now that the lines are down we can walk around them. I want to teach him about the process and the equipment."

The "process" that Cliff was talking about was a complex chemical process involving around thirty stages that took an hour for each production unit to complete. This process included a dozen or so chemicals and more than fifty pieces of equipment in an area the size of a large banquet room. Additionally, I had no idea that Cliff knew anything about that stuff. In fact, I was sure that he didn't.

By now I was thinking to myself how typical it was of Cliff to try to find the easy way out of work. Still thinking about how to get to talk to Karen, I said, "Alright, what else do you want to do after that? We've still got two hours to go until the end of the shift." Although Cliff was delighted with my agreement, it was obvious that he did not want to reveal any more information as to what his thoughts were. Still, he looked at me and after a pause said, "There are a lot of expired chemicals in drums and cabinets in the chemical storage room. If they are still there when we have the next environmental and safety audit, you'll get in real trouble. I'll take John and we'll sort them out and transfer the expired stuff to the disposal room." I thought for a second and said, "Okay. Just make sure Bert doesn't see you guys."

Climbing up the stairs to go to the office, I almost bumped into Bert, who immediately asked me if I had everyone working. I said, "Yes, they're all sweeping and mopping the floor." Then I forced myself to say that I had asked Cliff to go over the equipment and manufacturing process with John to make sure he had a good understanding of it before transferring to third shift. Bert looked at me a little surprised and, with an uncharacteristic smile, said, "Good thinking. He's the right guy to do that; he knows a lot about that stuff. You know, twenty years ago Cliff and I went to Holland together to do the factory acceptance test for this same equipment before it was paid for and shipped to us." "I had no idea," I almost said, but I didn't. Instead, encouraged by his approval, I said, "After that, they'll go through the chemical storage and dispose of the expired chemicals." He thought for a second and said, "Good. Good. Yes, that needs to be done." And then, instead of going down to the shop floor to check on things, Bert went back to his office, apparently assured that everything was under control.

Two hours later I was sitting at my desk finishing the shift report. Someone knocked on the door and opened it. I was surprised that Cliff and John were standing there because I was sure

I would not see them until the next day. Cliff said, "Chief, we're done." Noticing that he had called me "Chief" this time, I said, "Thanks, I'll go down to look at it when I finish with what I'm doing." It was obvious that they were both a little disappointed with my lack of enthusiasm, but still, Cliff asked if there was anything else I wanted them to do before they left for the day. I said, "No, it's almost the end of the shift, let's clean up and go home." He said, "Okay, see you tomorrow."

Before going home, I went on the floor to make sure everything was in order and stopped at the chemical storage room. I was shocked! That place probably had not looked as orderly and clean since the day it was built! I knew it was impossible for Cliff and John to have cleaned up the place and sorted things out in less than two hours. Looking at the overstuffed garbage can outside the room and seeing a pile of dirty rags, I could tell that Cliff had recruited more of the operators to do the job. I guess he knew that the corridor did not need any more polishing and the walls did not need any more wiping . . . and so did the other operators. The story does not end here, however.

When I was driving home later, I decided to stop at the local watering hole, hoping to see Karen. Instead, when I walked in I saw Cliff sitting at the counter with a couple of guys I did not know. He saw me too, smiled, and pushed a stool slightly toward me and said "Sit here, Chief, this one's on me."

Several hours later, after finally going home, I was thinking about Cliff and thinking about what I had learned about his past, his family, and his trip to Holland twenty years earlier. I was also thinking about what I had learned about myself. I still do.

Chapter Two

Deepening Self-Awareness
Through Dialogue

A Theoretical Framework for Leading
in Complex Worlds

Lori N. H. Guasta

"In dialogue people become observers of their own thinking" (Senge, 1990, p. 242). Senge is correct in acknowledging the reflective nature in dialogue. In the spirit of reflection, I examine the power of dialogue in the process of deepening self-awareness, which may be considered a characteristic of effective leadership. In response to metanarrative decline, I argue that leaders can exercise choice, freedom, and responsibility using dialogue to inspire self-awareness and positive growth in the spirit of coherence and the greater good.

Simply attempting to understand the meaning of self-awareness is highly complex and multifaceted. Self-awareness may be considered to be personal and subjective, although equally connected to relationship and community. The importance of examining self-awareness in relation to dialogue is significant. I argue that self-awareness develops through dialogue, representing a process of growth on individual and communal levels. In fact, Buber (1958) suggests that the true personal self can only become known through "entering into relations" (p. 28). The relational nature of dialogue can be considered personally transformational. Bohm (1996) describes a product of dialogue as collective participation or "a harmony of the individual and collective, in which the whole constantly moves toward coherence" (pp. 32–33).

Courage and Vulnerability

It takes a significant amount of courage to deconstruct our attachment to self and exist with presence and care for others. Bohm (1992) discusses the importance of noticing our natural reflex to resist that which is unfamiliar and potentially disturbing through dialogue. In fact, a lack of courage can be used to explain individuals' failure to engage in authentic and constructive dialogue (Cayer, 2005). The value of developing self-awareness is clearly represented in the need for courage and vulnerability. Isaacs (1999) suggests that one form of suspending involves becoming "aware of the processes that generate . . . thought" (p. 143). Perhaps through suspending our inner voice and underlying assumptions, we can become more aware of what restricts our courage and vulnerability and prevents us from engaging authentically in dialogue and developing self-awareness. Essentially, perhaps courage and vulnerability are what allow dialogue and their absence is what restricts dialogue.

According to Friedman (2005), "One of the most terrible responsibilities in the world is that of really being present, of being a *presence* for the other" (p. 235). In dialogue, respect for the other involves active listening by suspending our internal voice and assumptions to gain a deeper understanding of individual thought processes. Underlying thoughts and feelings may be revealed and objective patterns may be identified regarding the philosophical nature of thought. Isaacs (1999) argues that by examining our thought processes, we gain the ability to transform them. The reflective nature of being present for the other through dialogue represents the power and significance involved in developing and deepening self-awareness. This power is cultivated when we reflect on another's presence, which can help us to become more fully and deeply aware of our own presence.

Gaining self-awareness can also create tremendous confusion and feelings of anxiety. A deep level of courage and vulnerability are essential in the practice of dialogue and within a commitment to develop self-awareness. This process of developing self-awareness may prove to be emotionally overwhelming and create personal discomfort. However, Wheatley (1999) suggests that "*disorder* can be a source of new *order*, and . . . growth appears from disequilibrium, not balance" (p. 21). Deetz and Simpson (2004) further offer, "*The way to feeling comfortable begins with being uncomfortable*" (p. 156). Fundamentally, courage toward vulnerability is required in dialogue and the development of self-awareness. The strength needed to assume courage and vulnerability is made possible through freedom, choice, and responsibility.

Freedom, Choice, and Responsibility

Frankl (1997) describes being human as having an "awareness of freedom and responsibleness" (p. 33). With freedom, naturally, comes choice. We are mostly free to choose how we act, behave, or conduct ourselves. On personal and social levels, choice is the gift of freedom. However, Bohm (1996) encourages us to identify and analyze our own assumptions when declaring freedom. "Doing what you like is seldom freedom, because what you like is determined by what you think and that is often a pattern which is fixed" (p. 27). Still, freedom entails our power to choose, to choose a journey toward self-awareness and coherent thought with others. With choice, however, comes a sense of responsibility, which Frankl (1997) contends to be one of three virtues in life. Responsibility, courage, and objectivity are three important virtues according to Frankl, which each relate to one's ability to be responsible for self and community.

Choice is considered a constructive function of dialogue, which involves "exploring the nature of choice" (Isaacs, 1999, p. 45). Choice entails exploring alternatives and gaining insight.

Exercising choice to engage in genuine dialogue represents courage and vulnerability and the readiness to explore new ways of thinking. Exploring the underlying assumptions that guide our thinking and behavior allows us to develop self-awareness and gain insight regarding human relations. Dialogue allows us to use freedom and choice and modify our thought processes to match our behavior coherently.

"Man has to answer to life by answering for life; he has to respond by being responsible; in other words, the response is necessarily a response-in-action" (Frankl, 1997, p. 29). By embracing the power of choice, individuals are able to exercise freedom and responsibility to seek coherence and develop self-awareness through dialogue. Our response-in-action is associated with a concern for subjectivity and objectivity. We must always consider our individual role within a larger whole, and consider as well the influences that communal contexts have on the individual.

Balance is essential in taking responsibility for the self in a context of complexity and relation with others. If one is truly self-responsible, a concern for the larger community is naturally assumed. In dialogue, it is important to maintain a healthy balance of suspension of self and integration into a larger mode of thought. Gadamer (1975) argues that we should be concerned less with "self-expression and the successful assertion of one's point of view," and more with "a transformation into communion" (p. 341).

Exercising freedom of choice involves responding to life in action. I consider Frankl's (1997) notion of response-in-action to be very similar to a response-in-care. Noddings (1984) contends that "goodness is felt, and it guides our thinking implicitly" (p. 49). By becoming more deeply aware of the feelings that guide our thought and actions, especially those associated with goodness, we are able to capitalize on the freedom of choice. It is possible for humans to choose to act with respect to goodness and care. Exercising this freedom of choice involves a responsibility to respond to life in action and in care. Such practices are not always the easiest to follow. Responding to life with care requires acceptance, patience, and a solid dignity in the potential of one's self and in humanity. Clearly, it is possible for us to choose to respond in care to all that we encounter in life. Practicing this response, however, requires a tremendous amount of courage and vulnerability to take responsibility and respond accordingly. Succeeding in vulnerability and humbleness represents the great courage and strength required in dialogue and is represented through an ethic of care.

Ethic of Care and Intuition

Caring must be conducted out of a regard for the general goodness of others, not only for one's self. Humans are relational and dependent on the mutuality involved in communication and interaction. Buber (1958) asserts, "The *I* is real in virtue of its sharing in reality. The fuller its sharing the more real it becomes" (p. 63). As awareness of self or *I* develops on a personal level, a reciprocal function is presented on a group level. A dialogue circle represents "a symbol of wholeness, and a setting in which creative transformation can take place" (Isaacs, 1999, p. 243). The relational nature of human interaction serves to generate creative and collective thought processes and reflectively encourages a deeper understanding of self. These functions are produced through dialogue and are also characteristic of an ethic of care.

A "fundamental aspect of caring from the inside" involves shifting concern from self to care for others (Noddings, 1984, p. 14). "Caring involves stepping out of one's own personal frame of reference into the other's. . . . Our attention, our mental engrossment is on the cared-for, not on ourselves" (p. 24). Authentic care or concern for others is a key value or quality for contemporary leaders to develop. In the context of this chapter, care could be considered a form of tacit knowledge that leaders can embrace and use to promote self-awareness and creative transformation through dialogue. The nature of care in leaders is sharpened as we engage in authentic dialogue. The reflective function involved in dialogue is represented when we successfully suspend our thinking, attempt to be present for others, and realize the commonalities that exist between our self and others.

Embracing an ethic of care as a form of tacit knowledge is a complex task. Even attempting to describe tacit knowledge can be problematic. Isaacs (1999) argues that tacit knowledge "*cannot* be turned into explicit knowledge. . . . [it] is defined precisely by the fact that *we have no words for it*. Yet we can't ignore it because it affects the way we act" (p. 51). Whether or not the notion of care may be considered tacit knowledge, it remains a responsibility among leaders to embrace freedom and choice and apply an ethic of care. Embracing freedom and consciously applying an ethic of care are possible through dialogue, which allows for collective participation and the generation of creative transformation in thought, with care, and in action.

Friedman (2005) suggests that an "intuitive awareness of ourselves grows in listening and responding . . . [and] hearing not just how the other responds but also how we ourselves respond" (pp. 236–237). Using dialogue to exercise the power of choice and responsibility with an ethic of care allows us to respond to the dialogic metanarrative decline that currently works to reinforce our fragmented and incoherent reality. By committing to an ethic of care and the art and practice of dialogue, a person becomes "assured of the freedom both of his being and of Being. Only he who knows relation and knows about the presence of the *Thou* is capable of decision" (Buber, 1958, p. 51). Dialogue helps to develop self-awareness as well as the relational connection that exists among all humans. An ethic of care enhances the development of self-awareness through dialogue by reminding us to suspend our assumptions, focus less on our self, and attempt to be truly present for the other. The practice of dialogue can subsequently encourage communal transformation and a deepened understanding of self.

Self-Awareness and Coherence

Incoherence involves "contradiction, confusion, and . . . self-deception in order to cover it up" (Bohm, 1996, pp. 88–89). Although coherence, a sense of order, peace, and harmony are desired, incoherence and fragmentation persist in society. Still, Bohm reminds us that incoherence "*is the road to coherence*" (p. 89). Connecting the notion of coherence and self-awareness can lead to a discussion of tacit knowledge and innate care. If humans naturally seek order and harmony, coherence may be regarded as an innate quality or even a form of tacit knowing. Through dialogue, I argue that self-awareness develops and we become more conscious of the incoherence that exists in society. Responding with an ethic of care and engaging in dialogue with others can similarly develop transformational awareness on personal and communal levels.

In dialogue, an individual and a collective mind exist (Bohm, 1996). The shared meaning and generative energy that is created in between subjective and objective thought can be transformational. Creativity and new order may be produced on a group level, and a more personal self-awareness may be deepened in the process. By thinking of subjectivity and objectivity as inter-related or interdependent concepts, it is possible to recognize the importance of self-awareness in dialogue with others. Bohm argues that shared meaning on individual and communal levels is essential. He suggests that "there is the possibility for a transformation of the nature of consciousness, both individually and collectively" (p. 54). Dialogue can be used to generate this collective consciousness that represents coherence and deeper holistic understanding.

Conclusion

Self-awareness is a fluid process. It is a journey involving courage, vulnerability, confusion, reflection, relation, discovery, and deepened awareness. Through dialogue, we become open to the realm of possibility that exists in discovering and rediscovering the true nature of our self, humanity, and the relation in between, which may lead us closer to what Bohm (1992) describes as a search for ultimate knowledge (p. 177). Through the practice of being present for others, dialogue can produce self-awareness and collective participation on one's journey toward transformation and coherence.

It is important to identify the influence that our thought has on communication, interaction, relationships with others, and dialogue. "The way you think determines the way you're going to do things" (Bohm, 1992, p. 16). This social constructivist perspective can be related to the organizational perspective of appreciative inquiry, which presents the heliotropic influence of communication. Appreciative inquiry argues that organizations "will turn in the direction to that dialogue which inspires action" (Sugarman, 2002, ¶7). Similarly, the transformational influence of dialogue is portrayed through an unspoken collective voice or communal process of thought that senses coherence, deepened self-awareness, and insight into the relationship between self and others.

"Through dialogue we learn how to engage our hearts" (Isaacs, 1999, p. 47). Transformational dialogue is a powerful method of reflection and discovery of relation, care, balance, and coherence. Along my own journey toward self-awareness, I have learned that my pursuit of subjective happiness represents my perception of truth. It is "easy to recognize the impracticality of getting all men to agree upon ultimate truths" (Greenfield, 1980, p. 30); however, through dialogue I have been reminded that a higher level objective notion of relation and coherence exists. Using dialogue to engage our hearts, a more holistic state of being may be recognized. As one of my leadership professors at Gonzaga University remarked, "I can love the mind with my heart—I can know the heart with my mind" (C. Francovich, personal communication, March 19, 2005). This statement represents a dialogic balance between heart and mind, subjective and objective, personal and communal. By learning to suspend our own assumptions, the power of dialogue as a vehicle for self-awareness can advance leaders' ability to interact and relate in complex worlds with presence and care for others and in the spirit of coherence and the greater good.

References

Bohm, D. (1992). *Thought as a system.* New York: Routledge.

Bohm, D. (1996). *On dialogue.* New York: Routledge.

Buber, M. (1958). *I and thou* (2nd ed.). (R. G. Smith, Ed.). New York: Charles Scribner's Sons.

Cayer, M. (2005). The five dimensions of Bohm's dialogue. In B. H. Banathy & P. M. Jenlink (Eds.), *Dialogue as a means of collective communication* (pp. 161–191). New York: Kluwer Academic/Plenum.

Deetz, S., & Simpson, J. (2004). Critical organizational dialogue: Open formation and the demand of "otherness." In R. Anderson, L. Baxter, & K. Cissna (Eds.), *Dialogue: Theorizing difference in communication studies* (pp. 141–158). Thousand Oaks, CA: Sage.

Frankl, V. E. (1997). *Man's search for ultimate meaning.* New York: Plenum.

Friedman, M. (2005). Becoming aware: A dialogical approach to consciousness. In B. H. Banathy & P. M. Jenlink (Eds.), *Dialogue as a means of collective communication* (pp. 217–239). New York: Kluwer Academic/Plenum.

Gadamer, H. G. (1975). *Truth and method.* (G. Barden & J. Cummings, Eds. & Trans.). New York: Seabury.

Greenfield, T. B. (1980). The man who comes back through the door in the wall: Discovering truth, discovering self, discovering organizations. *Educational Administration Quarterly, 16*(3), 26–59.

Isaacs, W. (1999). *Dialogue and the art of thinking together.* New York: Currency.

Noddings, N. (1984). *Caring: A feminine approach to ethics and moral education.* Berkeley: University of California Press.

Senge, P. M. (1990). *The fifth discipline: The art and practice of the learning organization.* New York: Doubleday/Currency.

Sugarman, H. C. (2002). *Appreciative inquiry (AI) more than a methodology: Practitioners' framing for successful transformation.* Appreciative Inquiry Commons website. Retrieved from http://appreciativeinquiry.case.edu/practice/bibAiArticlesDetail.cfm?coid=6478

Wheatley, M. J. (1999). *Leadership and the new science: Discovering order in a chaotic world.* San Francisco: Berrett-Koehler.

Chapter Three

Communications, Ethics, and Vision Trump Experience

Eli Sopow

By its nature, the work of policing can regularly present leaders with situations of uncertainty, crises, very high levels of public scrutiny, stressful situations, and constant change. In fact, these characteristics, external to the milieu of policing, can also be used to define the changing environments and pressures felt by many organizations, ranging from corporations and not-for-profit agencies to religious and governmental institutions. In the face of such external environments, however, policing in Canada has consistently achieved levels of public confidence and trust above 80 percent (Royal Canadian Mounted Police, 2010). In this chapter, I argue that the lessons from policing, and specifically factors associated with trust in leaders and job satisfaction, offer valuable lessons for all organizations facing change. If uncertainty and turbulence are now a constant, then a study of professions long experienced with such pressures on a daily basis may yield valuable lessons for complexity leadership.

Experiential and Theoretical Underpinnings

In the face of rapid change and increased public scrutiny of organizational behavior, those in charge of guiding major corporations and institutions have in recent years identified the urgency for a new paradigm of leadership that is attuned to the unpredictability, ambiguity, and uncertainty that faces the world today. There are many recent examples of leaders being adaptive and inclusive in the face of tremendous challenges to change. In the early 1990s, for example, IBM chairman and chief executive officer Louis Gerstner dramatically reversed the failing fortunes of an $86 billion corporation by practicing "decentralized decision-making with central strategy and common customer focus" (Gerstner, 2003, p. 22). Gerstner advocated management "by principle, not procedure" and "no committee decision-making" among his many management philosophies (Gerstner, 2003, pp. 22, 23). In an address to West Point cadets, General Electric chairman and chief executive officer Jeff Immelt stated that "it takes courage to rethink your leadership paradigm" (Immelt, 2009, p. 3) and offered five traits to assist with such rethinking: better listening skills; being systems thinkers and "comfortable with ambiguity"; building competency "and mov[ing] with speed"; "motivat[ing] with vision, but win[ning] through execution"; and "must like and respect people" (Immelt, 2009, pp. 4, 5). Equally instructive is the example of former General Motors (GM) chief executive officer Fritz Henderson who in 2009 undertook what many traditionalists at the giant automaker saw as radical actions to save the corporation. At GM, Henderson's principles of change included "speed, risk-taking and accountability" (Smerd, 2009, ¶5, An Opportunity in Bankruptcy). Those principles translated into far greater employee empowerment and decision making, greater transparency in all actions, dismantling of the matrix management model, and "'zero tolerance' for leaders who do not demonstrate the new cultural priorities" (Smerd, 2009, ¶9, The Aztek Lesson).

As leadership evolves to meet the challenges and ambiguities of constant change, even traditionally very hierarchical command-and-control organizational structures are adapting to the needs of shifting external environments. An example of such evolution is the venerable United States Marine Corps (USMC) and its acceptance of the principles of complex adaptive systems—systems and processes far more aligned with organic than mechanistic models of organizational behavior. As a USMC (1996) training manual on leadership states, "Like a living organism, a military organization is never in a state of stable equilibrium but is instead in a continuous state of flux continually adjusting to its surroundings . . . command and control is not so much a matter of one part of the organization getting control over another as it is something that connects all the elements together in a cooperative effort . . . this view recognizes that it is unreasonable to expect command and control to provide precise, predictable, and mechanistic order to a complex undertaking like war" (pp. 46, 47). Schwandt and Szabla (2007) add that integration is critical for an organization to function. "[Integration] comprised acceptable collective norms and actions, coordination, control, and communications. [Integration] reflected a rational orientation to systems, but acknowledged the individual cognitive and cathectic (emotional) influences on the actor's orientation to the system" (p. 48).

What the most recent and popular theories of leadership seem to have in common is the *relationship* built between a leader and followers. This relationship building is what contributes to a healthy development of organizational culture, to a sense of employee empowerment, and to successful collaboration and adaptability. The relationship between a leader and follower shapes the organization's internal environment and workplace climate and its ability to deal with changes in the external environment. Value is seen in treating employees as important, contributing individuals whose emotional needs and well-being play a major role in creating a healthy, productive, and engaging workplace (Ettner & Grzywacz, 2001; Fambrough & Hart, 2008; Fineman, 2000; Fischer & Manstead, 2008; Northrup, 1989; Rafaeli & Worline, 2001; van Knippenberg, van Knippenberg, Kleef, & Damen, 2008). Northouse (1997) suggests that leaders build credibility with their constituents as they encourage and enable others to engage in collaborative, team-oriented decision making. The importance of leaders' trustworthiness has a rich body of research (Barber, 1983; Butler, 1991; Garsten, 2001; Kramer & Tyler, 1996; Lewis & Weigert, 1985; Misztal, 1998; O'Hara, 2004). As Butler (1991) found, employees' perception of the trustworthiness of their leader was strongly influenced by the presence of availability, competence, consistency, fairness, integrity, loyalty, openness, promise fulfillment, and receptivity to new ideas.

A departmental annual survey (Royal Canadian Mounted Police, 2009; $N = 464$) showed very high ratings of employee job satisfaction with 86 percent of respondents agreeing they were proud of the work done by their unit, 80 percent agreeing the Royal Canadian Mounted Police (RCMP) was a good place to work, 89 percent agreeing that they were proud to be an employee, and 74 percent agreeing that they found their work fulfilling. Additionally, a 2009 public opinion survey by the police service ($N = 498$) showed that within the province, 91 percent of respondents agreed that the RCMP placed an emphasis on quality service, 89 percent agreed the RCMP was responsive to community needs, and 84 percent agreed the police service was an organization with integrity and trust (Royal Canadian Mounted Police, 2009). Follow-up surveys in 2010 by the RCMP found similar findings not only in the province of Nova Scotia but also throughout all provinces in Canada served by the RCMP.

Based on the current findings of research related to leadership trust and adaptability, and high employee job satisfaction with the RCMP, a research study was designed to test how the important attributes of change leadership manifested in a workplace facing an environment of constant change and often highly volatile external environments. The intent of this research was to explore further what correlations existed among several factors acknowledged in the engagement literature as contributing to high levels of job satisfaction. By delving further into the opinions of employees at the police service, it could be possible to draw conclusions about factors most strongly linked to trusted leadership in an environment of not only constant but frequently very demanding change. My guiding question is, "What can organizations that are facing increasingly complex leadership challenges learn from an organization that maintains high levels of public trust and employee engagement within an external environment of constant change, volatility, and violence?"

Research Design and Process

A two-set, twenty-one-item, Likert-scaled questionnaire was designed by the author to survey employee opinions. The RCMP was interested in the importance of key workplace factors related to employees' immediate leadership (as found in their supervisor or manager) as well as the performance of their immediate leader on each identified factor.

Research Participants

Participants in the research study were civilian employees and sworn police officers of the RCMP within the province of Nova Scotia. Within Nova Scotia, the RCMP polices rural areas and several municipalities with a total provincial population of 944,251 (Bureau of Statistics, Provincial Government of Nova Scotia, April 2011). Through its unique structure, the RCMP provides policing at the local and federal levels.

Survey Instrument

The questions in the survey were designed following a review of several commonly used job satisfaction and employee engagement instruments recognized as having high reliability and high validity. The job satisfaction surveys reviewed included the Job in General Scale, the Job Satisfaction Survey, the Minnesota Satisfaction Questionnaire, and the Job Satisfaction Inventory. A further review of employee engagement surveys included a wide range of instruments used in academia and with various consulting and research organizations (BlessingWhite, 2008; Buckingham & Coffman, 1999; Conference Board, 2006; Gallup, 2010; Schmidt & Marson, 2007; Vance, 2006).

The first set of twenty-one questions asked employees to rate the *importance* of workplace measures and the second set of questions asked employees to rate the *performance* of the measures. The five-point Likert scales provided respondents a range from *not very important* to *very important* for the importance ratings and from *very poor* to *very good* for the performance ratings. Measuring importance and performance, rather than only performance as is commonly practiced in employee surveys, enabled the calculation of importance or performance gaps showing the level of congruity between what employees valued the most in their workplace and their rating of the actual performance on those measures. This approach also served to meet Wright and Kim's (2004) definition of job satisfaction as being a measure of congruence between what employees want and actually receive from their jobs.

Policing is a profession with many specialized characteristics. The final set of questions used in the survey reflect the author's long and direct experience with policing and the unique culture and climate of the profession. Creation of a customized survey instrument for police personnel has been recognized by other researchers as necessary to capture the unique nature of the profession (Dantzker, 1997).

Data Collection

In addition to the two sets of twenty-one workplace climate questions, the following demographic data were collected: gender, years of service, category of employee, rank, and primary location of work. A review of results showed that the profile of respondents accurately represented the demographic weightings within the population of employees studied.

An invitation to participate in an online survey was sent by the commanding officer to all 1,266 employees. The employees were invited to link to an Internet-based survey where final results could only be accessed through use of a password by the researcher. Employees were advised in advance that their individual responses were anonymous but that the overall results of the survey would be shared with all employees.

Data Analysis

The survey instrument used a five-point Likert scale to rate two identical sets of twenty-one questions culled from an original set of thirty-one questions after tests for reliability. Cronbach's alpha coefficient of internal reliability showed a very high coefficient of internal consistency ($\alpha = .96$) for the twenty-one questions. All items also correlated with the total scale to a good degree (lowest $r = .53$ with all twenty others above $r = .60$, range being from .60 to .84). Responses to the survey were analyzed by means of Pearson product-movement correlations with all 210 variables showing a strong statistical significance (below $p < 0.01$).

Results

Six hundred twenty employees responded to the survey ($N = 620$) representing an overall response rate of 39 percent. Of the respondents, 69 percent were sworn police officers, 31 percent were civilian personnel in administrative and management roles, 65 percent were male, and 35 percent were female. A review of results showed that the profile of survey participants accurately represented the demographic weightings within the population of employees surveyed.

Table 3.1 presents the importance of the twenty-one variables to employees as well as their rating of leadership performance on each variable. It shows that the strongest rating of importance was afforded to treating all employees fairly ($M = 4.87$), having a leader with good listening skills ($M = 4.81$),

Table 3.1. Importance and Performance Rating of Leadership Factors

Leadership Factors	Importance Mean	Importance SD	Performance Mean	Performance SD	Importance Performance Gap
Treating all employees fairly	4.87	.385	3.80	1.16	-1.07
Good listening skills	4.81	.446	3.92	1.20	-0.89
Leader can be trusted	4.79	.520	3.87	1.33	-0.92
Very strong ethics	4.75	.490	4.03	1.16	-0.72
Excellent overall communication skills	4.75	.514	3.90	1.16	-0.85
Employees know expectations	4.75	.520	3.91	1.10	-0.84
All employees are held accountable	4.72	.528	4.16	.939	-0.56
Very knowledgeable about their area	4.70	.522	4.14	1.11	-0.56
Encourages teamwork	4.69	.565	4.01	1.14	-0.68
Mistakes are quickly admitted and corrected	4.66	.571	3.50	1.20	-1.16
Important information being quickly shared	4.65	.567	3.51	1.20	-1.14
There's a chance to offer feedback	4.64	.588	3.72	1.19	-0.92
Workplace conflicts are quickly resolved	4.63	.609	3.43	1.24	-1.20
A clear vision for action	4.60	.600	3.83	1.18	-0.72
Accessibility to the leader	4.58	.572	4.24	1.05	-0.34
Recognition for a job well done	4.49	.686	3.50	1.27	-0.99
New thinking is encouraged	4.47	.652	3.60	1.21	-0.87
Creative thinking	4.38	.688	3.79	1.16	-0.59
Seeks broad input on decisions	4.30	.792	3.57	1.24	-0.73
Formal training in leadership and management	3.98	1.01	3.58	1.06	-0.40
A long work history	3.96	.981	3.97	1.10	+0.01

Note: SD equals standard deviation.

having a trusted leader (M = 4.79), and being a leader with strong ethics, good communication skills, and having employees know what is expected of them in the workplace in terms of duties and accountability (each with a mean rating of 4.75). The least important leadership variable to employees was having a leader who has received formal training in leadership and management (M = 3.98) and a leader with a long work history in operational policing (otherwise known as tenure or experience within an organization—rated here at a mean of 3.96). In all cases the gap between what employees rated as important in terms of leadership attributes and the actual performance was marginal (at most a minus 1.20 for having workplace conflicts quickly resolved, with the range being from minus 1.20 to a plus 0.01 and the average gap being a minus 0.76).

Table 3.2 presents 210 statistically significant ($p < .01$) correlations involving the twenty-one variables. The very strongest correlations among the variables included being a good listener and an excellent communicator ($r = .85$), having a clear vision and being creative ($r = .83$), having a clear vision and being knowledgeable ($r = .77$), encouraging collaboration and having strong listening skills ($r = .77$), being a good listener and seeking feedback on decision making ($r = .76$), being creative and seeking input ($r = .76$), and being a creative thinker and encouraging collaboration ($r = .76$).

Employees in the study rated fairness as the most important quality in leadership (M = 4.87) with actual performance rated at a moderately high mean rating of 3.80. Although there is substantial literature on the definition, application, and meaning of workplace fairness, this study suggests that fairness to employees may achieve its dominance as a very important factor because of strong correlations to other important workplace factors. In this case, the research shows a strong correlation between having all employees treated fairly and having a trusted leader ($r = .65$), having workplace mistakes quickly admitted and corrected ($r = .64$), having a chance to offer feedback ($r = .63$), and

Table 3.2. Correlation of Workplace Leadership Factors

	1	2	3	4	5	6	7	8	9	10	11	12	13	14	15	16	17	18	19	20	21
1. Treated fairly	—																				
2. Know expectations	.63	—																			
3. Job recognition	.62	.59	—																		
4. Info sharing	.55	.57	.53	—																	
5. Trusted supervisor	.65	.67	.60	.54	—																
6. Chance for feedback	.63	.61	.65	.61	.57	—															
7. Accountability	.51	.59	.44	.46	.53	.48	—														
8. Conflict resolution	.60	.62	.57	.55	.69	.56	.55	—													
9. Open to new ideas	.56	.55	.59	.54	.52	.68	.50	.55	—												
10. Mistakes corrected	.64	.58	.57	.56	.56	.59	.52	.60	.59	—											
11. Easily accessible	.51	.54	.48	.47	.60	.52	.46	.53	.41	.47	—										
12. Excellent communicator	.54	.59	.50	.52	.72	.53	.51	.62	.53	.51	.69	—									
13. Good listener	.57	.63	.55	.50	.76	.57	.51	.63	.53	.52	.68	.85	—								
14. Very knowledgeable	.50	.55	.47	.48	.70	.47	.54	.59	.50	.52	.62	.71	.68	—							
15. Collaborative	.59	.59	.55	.54	.69	.59	.50	.63	.59	.54	.62	.73	.77	.68	—						
16. Very strong ethics	.54	.54	.47	.48	.70	.51	.50	.58	.47	.50	.60	.69	.72	.66	.70	—					
17. Creative	.53	.60	.54	.51	.70	.59	.49	.63	.61	.54	.59	.74	.75	.73	.76	.68	—				
18. Clear vision	.55	.62	.51	.52	.72	.54	.52	.64	.55	.54	.59	.73	.73	.77	.74	.72	.83	—			
19. Seeks broad input	.54	.57	.51	.52	.65	.59	.49	.60	.53	.51	.59	.69	.72	.58	.70	.66	.76	.70	—		
20. Long work history	.33	.33	.27	.31	.47	.32	.33	.41	.34	.31	.41	.50	.47	.52	.46	.46	.47	.52	.46	—	
21. Leadership or management training	.36	.39	.40	.38	.46	.43	.37	.46	.39	.38	.44	.50	.51	.50	.52	.48	.56	.56	.53	.51	—

knowing what leaders expect of employees ($r = .63$). Far weaker correlations were found between fairness and a leader having a long work history ($r = .33$) and having formal training in leadership and management ($r = .36$).

On the important matter of trust—rated as number three on the importance scale to employees ($M = 4.79$)—the results show that employees' trust in their immediate leader had a far weaker correlation to leaders having a long work history ($r = .47$) and having leadership and management training ($r = .46$) than to them being a good listener ($r = .76$), having a clear vision for action ($r = .72$), displaying very strong ethics ($r = .70$), and being very knowledgeable about their area of responsibility ($r = .70$). In fact, out of twenty correlations to having a trusted supervisor, the variables of long experience and specializing training in leadership and management ranked nineteenth and twentieth.

In the face of rapid change and chronic uncertainly facing many organizations, the ability to be creative, to be good at team building and collaboration, and to encourage new thinking from all employees would logically appear to be very useful leadership attributes. Findings from this study demonstrate that indeed employees rated such variables as high in importance to good leadership (creativity $M = 4.38$, team building $M = 4.69$, and new thinking $M = 4.47$). Additionally, the analysis shows that the attributes are also strongly correlated with trusted leadership (creativity at $r = .70$, encouragement of teamwork and collaboration at $r = .69$, and encouraging new thinking at $r = .52$). Table 3.2 shows the strength of positive correlations between the measures (anything above .40 is a strong correlation, anything above .70 is *very* strong).

Conclusion

The research in this study was guided by a question, "What can organizations facing increasingly complex leadership challenges learn from an organization that maintains high levels of public trust and employee engagement within an external environment of constant change, volatility, and violence?" The results of the research yielded several answers to the question.

An employee survey that asked participants to rate the importance *and* performance of twenty-one workplace factors found congruity between many of the measures that employees rated as most important to their workplace and the performance on those factors (the average importance-performance gap being minus 0.76). As other researchers have noted, congruity between what employees want from their workplace and what they in fact receive can be one gauge of employee job satisfaction. One conclusion to be drawn, then, is that organizations seeking to establish successful complexity leadership efforts may be well served by ensuring that measurements are taken not only of performance related to certain workplace factors but also of the importance of those measures to employees.

The correlation of all statistically significant performance measures also allowed for a determination of which factors were most strongly linked together. This analysis yielded information showing the strong importance of having a leader with a clear vision, creativity, and communication skills—competencies with far stronger interrelationships than experience or formal leadership and management training.

The results related to the twenty-one measures in this study show that one measure in particular—having a clear vision—has the greatest number of statistically significant *very* strong correlations to other workplace factors (eight altogether). Of the eight very strong correlations, three involve communication skills (seeking broad input on decisions, being an excellent communicator, and having good listening skills); three others include being creative, collaborative, and knowledgeable; and two of the very strong correlations are between having a clear direction and being seen as trustworthy and ethical.

Although more study is needed to replicate the findings noted in this chapter, what is particularly revealing is that having a long work history, though still statistically significant, has a weaker correlation to many of the variables than other measures, including a leader who is very knowledgeable about his or her workplace responsibility. The results suggest that having leaders who know what they are doing *and* who are adaptable *and* who are excellent communicators are more desirable in leading complexity than leaders who are steeped in experience but who do not have other leadership strengths. In short, employees understood that having a leader with many years of experience did not mean the leader was also knowledgeable in the context of today's unique challenges. Knowledge *may* be derived from experience but the lessons of yesterday can also be woefully inadequate in today's complex and turbulent world. Simply stated, findings from this research seem to suggest that employees have discovered just because a boss has been on the job for twenty-five years, he or she may have stopped learning about twenty years earlier.

Additionally, study results demonstrate that formal leadership and management training, though again showing statistically significant values, did not correlate as strongly with as many other measures as did a leader who had a clear vision, good communication skills, and was creative. These results also invite more research into the correlation between the competencies taught in leadership development programs and the actual needs of the workplace.

The research provides evidence that in today's often turbulent and uncertain world, complexity leadership requires skills and competencies that are wide ranging and interconnected, much like the interconnected nature of the forces of external and internal change facing organizations. This suggests that leadership models and training programs that focus on a narrower range of competencies, based on designs and conditions from the past, may be found wanting when it comes to the needs of those leading complexity today. In an increasingly changing world, paradigms of leadership rooted in the Industrial Age, which played a role in times of far greater certainty and less public scrutiny, are being found wanting as organizations strive to remain adaptable and nimble, accountable and responsible. Results from this study reveal that years of long experience and even specialized training are not enough for leaders to build trust with employees and, by extension, deal with the vagaries and vicissitudes of a changing internal and external environment. At a time when public trust in many institutions is low and attitudes toward corporate and government leaders is suffering a crisis in confidence, the successful change leader may benefit from modeling the attributes that entwine ethics and trust, open and honest communications, and a willingness to challenge the status quo.

References

Barber, B. (1983). *The logic and limits of trust*. New Brunswick, NJ: Rutgers University Press.

BlessingWhite. (2008). *The state of employee engagement 2008: North American overview*. Princeton, NJ: Author.

Buckingham, M., & Coffman, C. (1999). *First break all the rules*. New York: Simon & Schuster.

Bureau of Statistics, Provincial Government of Nova Scotia. (2011). Halifax, N.S., Canada.

Butler, J. (1991). Toward understanding and measuring conditions of trust. Evolution of a conditions of trust inventory. *Journal of Management, 17*(3), 643–663.

Conference Board. (2006). *Employee engagement: A review of current research and its implications*. New York: The Conference Board.

Dantzker, M. L. (1997). Police officer job satisfaction: Does agency size make a difference? *Criminal Justice Policy Review, 8*(2–3), 309–322.

Ettner, S. L., & Grzywacz, J. G. (2001). Workers perceptions of how jobs affect health: A social ecological perspective. *Journal of Occupational Health Psychology, 6*(2), 1–24.

Fambrough, M., & Hart, R. (2008). Emotions in leadership development: A critique of emotional intelligence. *Advances in Developing Human Resources, 10*(5), 740–758.

Fineman, S. (2000). *Emotion in organization*. Thousand Oaks, CA: Sage.

Fischer, A. H., & Manstead, A.S.R. (2008). Functions of emotion from an organizational perspective. In N. M. Ashkanasy & C. L. Cooper (Eds.), *Research companion to emotion in organizations* (pp. 605–616). Cheltenham, UK: Edward Elgar.

Gallup. (2010). National poll of Americans conducted November 19–21, 2010. Retrieved from www.pollingreport.com

Garsten, C. (2001). Trust, control, and post-bureaucracy. *Organization Studies*, 26(3), 24–37.

Gerstner, L. V. (2003). *Who says elephants can't dance?* New York: HarperCollins.

Immelt, J. (2009, December 9). *Renewing American leadership*. Presentation to the United States Military Academy at West Point. Retrieved from http://files.gereports.com/wp-content/uploads/2009/12/90304–2-JRI-Speech-Reprint1–557.qxd_8.5x11.pdf

Kramer, R., & Tyler, T. (1996). *Trust in organizations*. Thousand Oaks, CA: Sage.

Lewis, J., & Weigert, A. (1985). Trust as a social reality. *Social Forces*, 63(4), 967–985.

Misztal, B. A. (1998). *Trust in modern societies*. Cambridge, MA: Polity Press.

Northrup, T. (1989). The dynamic of identity in personal and social conflict. In L. Kriesberg, T. Northrup, & S. Thorson (Eds.), *Intractable conflicts and their transformation*. Syracuse, NY: Syracuse University Press.

Northouse, P. G. (1997). *Leadership: Theory and practice*. Thousand Oaks, CA: Sage.

O'Hara, K. (2004). *Trust: From Socrates to spin*. Cambridge, MA: Icon Books.

Rafaeli, A., & Worline, M. (2001). Individual emotion in work organizations. *Social Science Information*, 40(1), 95–123.

Royal Canadian Mounted Police. (2009). *National public opinion survey*. Ottawa: Survey Centre, RCMP Headquarters.

Royal Canadian Mounted Police. (2010). *National public opinion survey*. Ottawa: Survey Centre, RCMP Headquarters.

Schmidt, F., & Marson, B. (2007, February). Employee engagement: A foundation for organizational performance. *Canadian Government Executive Magazine*. www.networkedgovernment.ca

Schwandt, D. R., & Szabla, D. B. (2007). Systems and leadership: Co-evolution or mutual evolution towards complexity? In J. Hazy, J. Goldstein, & B. Lichtenstein (Eds.), *Complex systems leadership theory: New perspectives from complexity science on social and organizational effectiveness* (pp. 35–60). Mansfield, MA: ISCE Publishing.

Smerd, J. (2009, November 9). Can a new corporate culture save General Motors? *Workforce Management*. Retrieved from www.crainsdetroit.com/article/20091109/EMAIL01/911099979/can-a-new-corporate-culture-save-general-motors#

United States Marine Corps. (1996). *Command and control MCDP 6.* Washington, DC: Department of the Navy, USMC Headquarters. Retrieved from www.dtic.mil/doctrine/jel/service_pubs/mcdp6.pdf

Vance, R. (2006). *Employee engagement and commitment: A guide to understanding, measuring and increasing engagement in your organization.* Alexandria, VA: Society for Human Resource Management.

van Knippenberg, D., van Knippenberg, B., Kleef, G. A., & Damen, F. (2008). Leadership, affect, and emotions. In N. M. Ashkanasy & C. L. Cooper (Eds.), *Research companion to emotion in organizations* (pp. 465–475). Cheltenham, UK: Edward Elgar.

Wright, B. E., & Kim, S. (2004). Participation's influence on job satisfaction: The importance of characteristics. *Review of Public Personnel Administration, 24*(1), 18–40.

Chapter Four

Leading Learnership

The Transformation of Leadership via Convergence with Learning

Greg Laudeman

Leadership, as is often pointed out, has many meanings. Simply put, I define leadership as achieving through others, the ability or quality to cause people to pursue some valued outcome, and the class of persons who can do this. Note that *leadership* is commonly used as a noun. It is a *thing* or a *state of being*. My purpose in this chapter is to argue that leadership is evolving into a highly cooperative and distributed form, which I refer to as *leading learnership*. To adapt to the increasing complexity of society, leadership is increasingly about effectively developing and mobilizing human capabilities. I review the grand narrative of leadership and the parallel evolution of learning, each with a discussion of how leadership and learning are converging. Then I provide examples of leading learnership and discuss its practical and theoretical implications.

Talking About Leadership: Grand Narrative of Leadership

There are many stories about leadership, what it means, and how it functions. The substance of these narratives has changed, from classical prototypical leadership, through modern official leadership, to postmodern social leadership. We see evidence of the changing nature of leadership around the globe, most notably in citizen revolutions from the fall of the Berlin Wall and Tiananmen Square to the "Arab Spring," but also in profound changes in the way goods are produced and problems solved.

Classical, Prototypical Leadership

The classical, prototypical version of leadership integrates the man—it was almost invariably men whom history remembers as leaders—and the function. Alexander the Great epitomized classical leadership, as did Henry the Eighth, Julius Caesar, Xerxes, and most all notable leaders from history. Their leadership inevitably involved coercion and exploitation, armies and weapons. Even the most positively beneficial classical leader led via force and violence. Generally, for these leaders, someone had to lose for them and their followers to win. Classical leadership was seen as conferred by heritage—directly or via some supernaturally conferred trait—or by shear cunning and strength. *The Art of War* (Sun Tzu, 1910/2003) and *The Prince* (Machiavelli, 1961/2004) speak to prototypical leaders. Great minds and many backs supported them, but the leaders rose above and separate from their advisors and followers. Followers of prototypical leaders are little more than pawns or tools. Prototypical leadership is a single "fated" individual using coercion and force, leveraging identity, to exploit others for his personal glory and self-aggrandizement. The classical form of leadership can be seen in modern autocratic regimes, dictators, and presidents-for-life.

Modern, Official Leadership

Aristotle laid the foundation for the modern, official version of leadership that emerged in the nineteenth century in the guise of the self-made man—the capitalist, the politician, the scholar, and the visionary operating via the bureaucracy, the marketplace, the press, and the pulpit. Where classical leaders are largely products of their fated nature, heritage, cunning, ruthlessness, and strength, modern leaders are products of personal traits that make others want to follow them; followership is voluntary rather than coerced or forced. Official, modern leaders are self-consciously identified as such, and leadership becomes a widely discussed phenomenon attributed to contemporary people. Modern leadership consists of a few individuals with "leadership traits" using ideas and persuasion, again leveraging identity, to mobilize people for the greater good as they define it. This is the "great man" model of leadership.

The modern, official version of leadership arose coincidentally in literature about classical leaders, about modern leaders as powerful individuals who change others by force of will (rather than coercion or deception), and about rugged individualists who achieve and overcome by shear determination and intelligence, with honor and integrity. Mason Lockes Weems's *Life of George Washington*, published in 1800, exemplifies such literature (Ellis, 2004) as do Frederick Douglass's *Self-Made Men* from 1859 (1992), and the works of Horatio Alger, Jules Verne, and Sherlock Holmes, which was first published in 1892 (Doyle, 1906/1930). Victor Hugo's *Napoleon le Petit* (1852/1909) simultaneously champions modern leadership, derides autocratic classical leadership, and hints at the possibility of postmodern leadership. Although any man could hypothetically become an official leader, in practice, only a few have what it takes to fill the leader role.

The Transition to Postleadership

Leadership studies prior to the late twentieth century focused on what Rost (1993) calls the periphery and content of leadership. The characteristics and traits of a leader that make up the periphery and content of leadership is what they must know to be effective. The content and periphery were distilled and then commoditized for sale in books and workshops. The social consciousness of the mid-twentieth century ushered in new thinking about leadership, such as Greenleaf's concept of servant leadership (1977) and Burns's transformational leadership (1978), which focused on what Rost (1993) saw as essential but ignored: leadership as a process and a dynamic relationship. Bennis and Nanus (1985) presented the "new theory" of leadership, which posits that leaders *"empower others to translate intention into reality and sustain it"* (p. 80, emphasis in original). Deming (1986) suggested that the key to organizational efficacy is to transform supervisors into leaders: "The aim of leadership should be to improve the performance of man and machine, to improve quality, to increase output and simultaneously to bring pride of workmanship to people. Put in a negative way, the aim of leadership is not to find and record failures of men, but to remove the causes of failure: to help people do a better job with less effort" (p. 248).

Bennis (1989) promoted an even more accommodating and collaborative model of leadership that encourages dissent, embraces error, and manages the dream, along with more traditional leadership behaviors. Luke (1998) presented a similar model focused on bringing together groups of diverse persons to solve complex problems. Leadership is still about being in charge, but it is more collaborative, personable, and more of an activity or function than a thing: helping others to be successful. Northouse (2007) reviewed approaches to the practice and theories of leadership, all of which implicitly involve the "great man" in a one-to-many influence: only a few can be leaders. From a synthesis of the literature, Northouse (2007) argues that "leadership is a process whereby *an individual influences a group* of individuals to achieve a common goal" (p. 3, emphasis added).

The modern is implicit in official definitions of leadership: rational action can achieve any objective. Postmodernists maintain that objectivity and rationality are social constructions arbitrarily created by some to dominate and exploit others. Heidegger (1927/1996) rejected objectivity; Kuhn (1962/1996) laid bare the process by which scientific paradigms are constructed and supplanted. Derrida (1967/1998) and Foucault (1972) maintained that language is a tool for oppression. Lyotard (1979/1984) pointed out the impossibility of generalization, which provides the foundation for science and, by extension, the official model of leadership, and questioned the validity of universal "metanarratives." Habermas (1984) and Giddens (1986) argued that rationality and social structure are continually redefined as people communicate with each other. Similarly, scientists themselves were discovering how ambiguous reality could be. Einstein's theory of relativity (1920), Heisenberg's uncertainty principle (1930), Gödel's incompleteness theorem (1931/2000), and Arrow's impossibility theorem (1970) are examples. These theories blossomed into recognition of inherent limits to expertise-oriented approaches to problem solving (Rittel & Webber, 1973) and offered a totally new way of thinking about complex phenomena (Waldrop, 1992).

Postmodern, Social Leadership

A new generation of leadership thinkers has combined the postmodern perspective with complexity theory to suggest an approach to leadership in which *everyone* is a leader (Barker, 2002; Hock, 1999; Hurley & Brown, 2009; Nielsen, 2004; Wheatley, 1994). Others have documented the technology-enabled emergence of postmodern leadership in new approaches to production: social production of knowledge goods (Brafman & Beckstrom, 2006; Gladwell, 2002, 2009; Godin, 2008; Shirky, 2008; Surowiecki, 2004; Tapscott & Williams, 2006). Of special importance is the concept of *openness*, sharing and using information without bias or restraint and allowing individuals to make decisions at their own discretion, in conjunction with others, based on openly available information (Chesbrough, 2006; Tapscott & Ticoll, 2003; Tapscott & Williams, 2006). Openness applies to technology—as in open source software—and is facilitated by technology. Li (2010) applies openness to leadership to show how technology can enable leaders who are collaborative, curious, humble, and optimistic, starting with the realization that "the fundamental rules that have governed how *relationships* work are being rewritten, because of easy, no-cost information sharing" (p. xiv, emphasis in the original). Open leadership means ceding control to others via technologies that reduce transaction costs and enable collective action.

There are three salient characteristics of this new, "postleadership" perspective on leadership. First, everyone, not just a few lucky or special individuals, can be a leader; indeed, as many people as possible *must* be leaders for society to be effective, efficient, and equitable. Second, leadership is an activity—*leading*—engaged in collectively or in turn by multiple individuals rather than an existential state of an individual, a generalized identity for the powerful, or a one-to-many phenomenon. Third, "postleaders" are constantly learning, particularly *from* and *with* their followers, engaging in critical reflection and continuous improvement, and helping others learn. Generally, postleadership can be summed up in Hurley and Brown's (2009) catch phrase for what they call conversational leadership: "thinking together for a change" (p. 3). Compared to the leadership definitions previously discussed, there is no "other" and no concern with influence. In the postmodern world, leading is about contributing to collective cognition and enabling shared sensemaking.

Thinking About Learning: The Sociocognitive Evolution of Learnership

Learning, with some variation in meaning, can be defined as the act or process of acquiring capabilities, knowledge, or skills. More generally, learning is the process of changing one's own behavior. Where leadership is focused outward, toward others, learning focuses inward on the self. Where leadership is a characteristic of exclusive individual entities—even when it refers to a group, such as "the leadership team"—learning can occur at various levels of aggregation: individuals learn, but so do communities and economies, groups, organizations, regions, and whole societies. Where leadership is a thing—characteristics or a phenomenon—learning is an action and a process.

Classical, Prototypical Learning

Prehistorically, learning was natural and social. Education was "one of the prominent features of primitive life; although apparently unconscious process" (Woody, 1949, p. 3). As people became more civilized, this natural, social learning evolved into formal and specialized education for priests, scribes, and soldiers. Relatively few were needed for these roles, whereas many craft workers, farmers, and laborers were needed to support them; education, therefore, became a means of exclusion, of selecting and sorting. There were academies of some sort in most all cultures (Woody, 1949) but education was the domain of the elites— even in Greek and Roman societies where it was reserved for "citizens." Education was a way to enhance the elites' capabilities to control and exploit others in support of aristocratic, military, and religious hierarchy. Students were privileged and the teacher was as often exploited as revered. Prototypical learning was a means of filtering and qualifying persons to join the elite, to serve their leaders, to enable coercion, force, and exploitation.

Modern, Official Learning

Thomas Aquinas planted the seeds for modern, official learning when, during the late Medieval period, he insisted that because all truths come from God, and God gave mankind the power of reason, it is our responsibility to use reason to resolve truths and solve intellectual problems (Gwynne-Thomas, 1981). Taking this proposition further, some teachers began recruiting students to *studium generale*, "places of study open to all without restriction" (Gwynne-Thomas, 1981, p. 60), where there were no teaching qualifications or diplomas. Eventually, students formed *universitas* styled after craft guilds and established residential colleges for their mutual benefit and protection (Gwynne-Thomas, 1981). As colleges and universities evolved, some became bastions of humanism, realism, and scientism, whereas others developed as extensions of churches, new and old. Although prominent thinkers of the age—including Martin Luther—encouraged people to get educated, education required significant leisure time and privilege, so it remained the domain of the elite through the eighteenth century (Cubberley, 1922).

Standardized, universal education was justified first by the Protestant imperative for all people to read the Bible, then by democratization and industrialization (Bagley, 1937). But the earliest systems of compulsory education, in nineteenth-century Prussia, taught submission to authority first and foremost (Bagley, 1937; Cubberley, 1922). The common school movement, beginning in the mid-nineteenth century, was intended to mitigate the cultural pluralism that resulted from US immigration as a way to mold children into "the perfect political citizen, the perfect moral person, the perfect worker" (Spring, 1997, p. 28). Universal education was essentially developed as ideological management—"the control of ideas and cultures as a source of power" (Spring, 1997, p. 406)—a natural extension of colonialism, imperialism, and the belief in cultural superiority. Modern learning, treating students as objects to be indoctrinated and manipulated, and making teachers into rote disciplinarians, is a process of ideological management and social integration supporting the elites and their definition of the greater good.

Concurrent with school becoming compulsory for children, higher education was undergoing two profoundly modern transformations that led to the current, official version of learning. First was the rise of the research university during the late nineteenth century (Christensen & Eyring, 2011; Kronman, 2007). Second was the emergence of standardized testing early in the twentieth century (Smith, 1998). The latter was a product of the former, particularly of the scholarly drive to quantify human behavior (that is, behaviorism) and the drive for college admissions to be based on intellectual merit rather than social standing (Christensen & Eyring, 2011). Behaviorism exemplifies modernism in its glorification of objectivity and devaluation of beliefs and values. The educational application of behaviorism promoted rigid, standardized programs over those based on student interests and needs (Spring, 1997). The behaviorist model of education developed with standardized testing, which developed from the military's efforts to assess recruits' capabilities during the world wars and was adopted by education and other enterprises for assessing the intelligence of applicants as soldiers returned to the classroom and workforce (Christensen & Eyring, 2011; Smith, 1998). The modern approach makes education an artificial and even painful undertaking based on the concept of command-and-control and on nonsensical (literally) methods of measuring learning, according to Smith (1998), and it divorces learning from experience and interests.

Postmodern, Social Learning

In contrast to the modern, official form of learning, technological change is facilitating a participative view of cognition that can be summed up as "we participate, therefore we are" (Brown & Adler, 2008, p. 18). (Note how this view complements Hurley and Brown's [2009] definition of leading.) Brown and Adler shift the focus from the content to the learning activities and human interactions necessary for learning. Kohn (1993) provides a comprehensive review of empirical research and scientific knowledge that effectively debunks behaviorism with its mechanistic view of learning as simply a function of stimulus and response, positive and negative reinforcement, punishments and rewards. In its place, Kohn suggests the combination of collaboration and choice, with content, which he applies to managing people and raising children as well as running schools. Unfortunately, note these authors, the failures of the official approach to education are blamed on the least empowered: students and teachers.

Based on an extensive and thorough empirical review, the editors of *How People Learn* recommend educational approaches that "recognize the importance of building on the conceptual and cultural knowledge that students bring with them to the classroom" (National Research Council, 2000, p. 122) and are based on "what each student knows, cares about, is able to do, and wants to do" (p. 124). Scholars further recommend a postmodern approach to education: "When students who are motivated to improve have opportunities to assess their own and others' learning, they become more capable of managing their own educational progress, and there is transfer of power from the teacher to learner. On the other hand, when formative feedback is 'owned' entirely by the teacher, the power of the learner in the classroom is diminished, and the development of active and independent learning is inhibited" (National Research Council, 2001, pp. 237, 240).

Essentially, the National Research Council (2001) holds that all people are predisposed to learning and there are multiple paths that individuals follow to learning. Learning builds on prior knowledge via observation, practice, and feedback and is transferred from one topic to another via similar means. Learners must have responsive and supportive social contexts and must be able to assess their own thinking for learning and transfer to occur. These points are extended and supported by research into applications of cognitive science to education (such as Mayberry, Crocker, & Knoeferle, 2009; Richland, Bjork, Finley, & Linn, 2005; and Tytler & Prain, 2010).

Postmodern education is based on empirical knowledge of how people learn. "Postlearning," like "postleadership," has several significant qualities. As discussed previously, we learn actively and socially. Learners are not passive objects to be taught; rather, they are individuals actively and continually producing their knowledge. Learning is a state of being—*learnership*—that is simultaneously collective and individual. The individual learns most effectively when he or she is helping others learn, when enabling the success of others, acting as a leader. As with post-modern, social leadership, such learning uses new information and communications technologies to enable what Thomas and Brown (2011) call *collective indwelling*: "[Students] turn diversity into strength and build their own networked communities based on interest and shared passion and perspective. . . . Until now, we have lacked the ability, resources, and connections to make this kind of learning scaleable and powerful. . . . [T]oday, however, learning that is driven by passion and play is poised to significantly alter and extend our ability to think, innovate, and discover in ways that have not previously been possible" (p. 89).

Talking and Thinking Together: Leading Learnership

New, integrated models of leadership and learning are being created—and are needed—in our postmodern world. Information and communications technologies act as megaphone and mirror, facilitating human social tendencies. These technologies were developed via interactive learning driven by power relationships but increasingly require more of the former and restructuring of the latter so innovators can collaborate as peers. Leadership and learning are, more than ever, one and the same in an ever tighter self-reinforcing loop with technology, ulti-mately increasing human capabilities and meaning. Leadership is losing its exploitive qualities as it becomes more active, dis-tributed, and engaged. Learning no longer allows students to be treated as passive vessels to be filled and shaped, as it becomes a persistent characteristic, quality, or state of being.

So, talking and thinking together become *leading learnership*. Learnership—the state of constantly acquiring knowledge, con-tinually improving capabilities, reflecting, and learning to learn—is necessary to leading. Leading—making it easy for others to develop and use their knowledge and capabilities—is evidenced in learnership of others. Leading learnership can occur at any and across all levels, from individual through organizational to societal. The integration of postleadership and postlearning into a single practice multiplies power and value as it enables others, in direct contrast to classical and official versions of leadership and learning: leadership restricted to a few extraordinary and lucky individuals and learning limited to standardization via the classroom.

Classical and modern leadership and learning have a fundamental moral shortcoming because others are treated as means rather than ends, as objects rather than beings. Because previous versions of leadership are inherently self-centered, they naturally resist empowering others. Because previous versions of learning are constrained to certain places and times, they miss much of the serendipitous learning that occurs when people connect. Both fall short of realizing individuals' full potential because they disallow autonomy. Collective potential can only be maximized by giving individuals control over and responsibility for their actions and their minds. In contrast, leading learnership is active and reflective, contextual and social, and integrated yet distributed. It resolves the moral issues with prototypical and official learning and leadership and eliminates their practical limitations.

Evidence and Examples of Leading Learnership

Leading learnership is evident in much of the literature from the late twentieth century (Bandura, 1977, 1986, 1997; Becker, 1964, 1996; Berger & Luckmann, 1966; Burt, 1997; Coleman, 1988; Granovetter, 1973, 1985; Papert, 1980; Papert & Harel, 1991; Piaget, 1970, 1954/1999; Sen, 1988, 1999; Weick, 1995). A theory synthesized from the literature predicts that human capabilities will increase when connected via social networks due to lower transaction costs and better collective choice, sensemaking, and social construction for active, constructive, social learning; that is, *maximum value is created when each person works to increase the capabilities of others*. Humanity seems to be reinventing its primordial collaborative tendencies via technology, which is itself socially constructed. Leading learnership is not new but it is a transformation of fundamental human tendencies. We see evidence of it in various domains, as an increase in interactive knowledge acquisition, creation, search, transfer, and use that increases others' capabilities as well as one's own capabilities.

Active, Social Learning. The profound movement in education from the "sage on the stage" to the "guide on the side" (King, 1993) is still in progress. As discussed previously, the National Research Council (2000, 2001) has urged the practice to move beyond modernistic approaches. Postmodern learning has emerged in diverse forms, including active learning (Bonwell & Eison, 1991), constructivist-constructionist learning (Papert, 1980, Papert & Harel, 1991; Piaget, 1970, 1999), learner-centered curriculum and teaching (Dolence, 2003; Weimer, 2002), student-centered learning (Barr & Tagg, 1995; Farnes, 1975), and self-directed learning (Brookfield, 1986).

The paradigm shift is from education and instruction to learning and facilitation, based on the realization that learning is a natural, social process (Brown & Adler, 2008; Smith, 1998). The role of the educator and the educational enterprise is threefold: to make this process as easy as possible, to facilitate it particularly by structuring educational content, and to provide feedback. The role of the learner is to learn, which necessarily involves contemplating the "ways in which they can transform their personal and social worlds" (Brookfield, 1986, p. 47). This does not mean allowing the student to abdicate responsibility for her or his learning—quite the opposite: a primary role for educator as facilitator is to *make it easy for learners to take full ownership of their learning*.

Leaderless Organizations. Hock (1999) describes the creation of a "leaderless organization" as much more than rejecting the modern views of leadership and learning, and connects it to a fundamental rejection of rationalism and scientism. Wheatley (1994) and Barker (2002) echo these themes but they provide few practical examples; neither does Nielsen (2004), even as he presents a blueprint for leaderless organizations. Rather, it falls to Gladwell (2002, 2009), Brafman and Beckstrom (2006), Tapscott (Tapscott & Ticoll, 2003; Tapscott & Williams, 2006), Godin (2008), Shirky (2008), and Surowiecki (2004) to tell us tales of leaderless organizations. They provide numerous examples of achieving valued outcomes by connecting and leveraging diverse capabilities and knowledge without centralized, hierarchical, command-and-control leadership structures. Not coincidentally, these authors are generally trying to discover what makes enterprises and individuals successful in the postmodern world. Their answers involve unprecedented levels of openness and technology use, but also something more fundamental and profound: a culture of continual learning dedicated to enabling others—leading learnership.

Participative Management. The traditional model of production management is simple: "don't think, just do what you are told." Some time after World War II management thinkers began to realize the deficiencies of this approach. Drucker (1945/1993) began questioning command-and-control management and continued throughout his career, emphasizing the importance of being entrepreneurial and innovative (1985/2007), developing talent (2002), and using information technologies (1999). Crosby, Deming, and Juran (Martínez-Lorente, Dewhurst, & Dale, 1998) all focused more narrowly on production quality, but came to many of the same conclusions: employees must be actively engaged in production, valued for their ideas, and developed as assets (Hartman, 2002). These concepts have come to be called participative (or participatory) management (Participative Management, n.d.) and post-Fordism (Amin, 1994). The former emphasizes the participation of employees in making business decisions; the latter emphasizes the broader processes, means, and results, particularly flexible specialization, knowledge content and work, small-batch production, and extensive use of information technologies. More generally, participatory management involves nested, reiterated, and self-referential loops of collective learning that allow fundamental changes in organizational structure rather than just adaptive, incremental adjustments to particular functions (Argyris & Schön, 1978; Senge, 2006). These practices have enabled numerous organizations to become market leaders through greater productivity, higher quality, and more innovation (Dimancescu, Hines, & Rich, 1997; Hartman, 2002; Liker, 2004; Womack & Jones, 2003). Liker notes that continuous improvement and critical reflection that undergirds the quality revolution requires support from executives but depends on active buy-in by frontline employees; the role of middle management is to facilitate change.

Dialogical Planning. Unintended consequences are a perennial challenge for learning and leadership: "solving" one problem can create other problems, often worse and more intractable than the original. Such "wicked problems" (Rittel & Webber, 1973) can be impossible for professional experts to solve because they simply have no definitive, single-best solution, and so must be repeatedly solved or re-solved. Resolution must be systemic, Rittel and Webber maintain, and, because different people "own" different pieces, resolutions must be inclusive. Each wicked problem is essentially unique but interrelated with other such problems. The nature of wicked problems requires loosely coupled systems in which each participant's work enables others so that all can attack their aspects in a coordinated but independent manner.

Sustainability, or sustainable development that "meets the needs of the present without compromising the ability of future generations to meet their own needs" (World Commission on Environment and Development, 1987, p. 1), is a general, large-scale wicked problem. It requires simultaneous optimization of environmental, economic, and social factors—the "triple bottom line" of sustainability—to achieve development that is bearable, equitable, and viable (Elkington, 1998). The fundamental challenge is to develop all the three factors in a complementary manner rather than as mutually exclusive trade-offs (Adams, 2006). As with continuous improvement (Liker, 2004), sustainability simply is not possible without active buy-in of grassroots citizens; each person owns a piece of sustainability, and sustainability requires citizens of diverse backgrounds to learn together.

Harper and Stein (2006) present dialogical planning as an approach to resolving wicked problems. Planning should "focus on the *free, equal, and autonomous individual person* as the basic unit of society, the ultimate object of moral concern, and the ultimate source of value" (p. 7, emphasis in original). In the dialogical approach, the planner's job is to empower others—citizens—to plan collaboratively rather than planning for the citizens and to approach implementation as a learning process. Harper and Stein advocate decision making via true consensus during which ends and means coevolve, beliefs are modified based on practice, and change occurs via trial and error. In practice, dialogical planning means fair principles, collaborative leadership, consensus building, and, ultimately, peace making; it means promoting awareness of power and trust. The elements of dialogical planning, how it resolves wicked problems and avoids unintended consequences, is evident in planning methods used for sustainable development.

Scenario Planning. Dialogical planning first allows participants to reflect critically on current concepts and practices (Harper & Stein, 2006). Scenario planning (Schwartz, 1996) taps the collective intelligence of a group in ways that get participants to reconsider their assumptions and think differently about possibilities (Niles, 2009). Although scenario planning was developed for corporate strategic planning, it has been adapted to effectively plan conservation (Peterson, Cumming, & Carpenter, 2003), landscape (Tress & Tress, 2003), and transportation planning (Arampatzis, Kiranoudis, Scaloubacas, & Assimacopoulos, 2004).

Appreciative Inquiry and Community Visioning. Dialogical planning also generates alternative concepts and practices or at least allows participants to become familiar with those proposed by others. Appreciative inquiry and community visioning generate alternative concepts and practices by engaging participants in large-scale dialogues about ideal outcomes. Appreciative inquiry is based on the presumption that "as made and imagined, organizations are products of imagination and social constructions rather than some anonymous expression of an underlying natural order" (Cooperrider, Barrett, & Srivastva, 1995, p. 157). Rather than focusing on problems, appreciative inquiry seeks to develop new generative metaphors (Barrett & Cooperrider, 2001). Community visioning provides a means to engage citizens in creating action plans for their "leaders" to deal with complex and unique issues, particularly related to economic revitalization (Walzer & Deller, 1996). Both tap the intelligence of "regular" people to create new, more sustainable possibilities and essentially reverse the roles of followers and leaders: the followers set the direction and the leaders follow it.

World Café. World Café is a simple method for tapping collective knowledge to accomplish the third element of dialogical planning: evaluating new theories, vocabularies, or language games (Harper & Stein, 2006). The method involves convening a large group, seating them in multiple small groups, having each small group explore a few compelling questions, then sharing the insights of each small group with the large group (Hurley &

Brown, 2009; World Café, n.d.). World Café combines all of the elements of dialogical planning, as do the other examples and many other methods used in planning, but it is particularly powerful for vetting new concepts and practices, such as sustainable development.

Summary: Thinking, Talking, and Acting Together

Dialogical planning allows "owners" of the components of wicked problems to participate in the conversation with planners and others in traditional leadership roles and to act together as catalysts for shared problem resolution. Participants all lead at various points and in unique ways, constantly learning and creating new knowledge in the process, which is also true of active social learning, leaderless organizations, and participative management. Such approaches to learning, managing, organizing, and planning were undoubtedly possible, and have almost surely been used in the past. Today, though, the techniques are clearly more developed and widely used than ever before. They are critical to our collective future for dealing with wicked problems of unprecedented scale and scope. Yet, as educators, managers, planners, and other practitioners have begun to exploit the social technologies discussed by Tapscott and Williams (2006), Surowiecki (2004), Brafman and Beckstrom (2006), Li (2010), Thomas and Brown (2011), and others, we are left with a question: how might leading learnership progress as these technologies continue to develop and are diffused more widely, enabling more people to think, talk, and act together?

Conclusion

In the last few decades, leadership has been redefined as an enabling collective action, and learning has been reconceived as a state of continual improvement and critical reflection. The changes in leadership and learning are more inclusive and better for all, as the increasing prevalence of women as leaders and learners during the last century exemplifies. Everyone can lead others to higher levels of development, fulfillment, and success by practicing learnership, based on the recognition that each of us holds valid knowledge but none of us is perfect in our knowing. This understanding overcomes the moral and practical failings of modern, official models of learning and leadership by not treating people as means or objects. When leaders deployed education in the past to advance their personal agendas, the focus of leading is to enable others rather than to control and dominate. When hierarchical bureaucracies promoted leadership as "I win, you lose," learnership involves succeeding by helping others succeed.

It is no longer meaningful to conceptualize leadership without including learning. Nor can we practice or theorize about learning without incorporating leadership. The complexity of today's world demands the integration and transformation of leadership and learning. Leading *enhances* learnership and learnership *enables* leading.

Leading learnership is not a normative supposition; it is a positive proposition and metanarrative about the natural movement of humanity toward greater individual contributions, fulfillment, and meaning. The progression from classical leadership and learning, through modern versions, to leading learnership is sociocognitive evolution. Leading learnership posits that we are evolving from coercion and force as means to success, through reason and persuasion to collaborative sensemaking. The definition of success, of human meaning and what it means to be human, is evolving from heroic conqueror through magnanimous elites to interdependent yet unique equals, potentially achieving a social denouement in which economic imperatives align with moral imperatives.

Leading learnership is a "postpositive" theory that can generate practical and testable hypotheses while recognizing the inherent limits of the scientific approach to knowledge creation. It translates esoteric concepts of the postmodern into meaningful, useful ideas. Hypothetically, leading learnership creates greater aggregate value creation and is the result of socioeconomic evolution, emerging in conjunction with information and communications technologies. Hypothetically, with leading and learnership feeding into and mutually reinforcing each other, leading learnership will propagate at increasing rates. Recent developments in education, organization, planning, and production support these contentions, but the theory needs further development and testing in each of these contexts. Thus, leading learnership provides abundant opportunities for academic research. Leading learnership also provides practical hypotheses about how to reorganize, empower employees, engage customers, and improve processes by making them more equitable and open. So it should be useful to entrepreneurs, executives, and others who seek to create successful organizations.

As much as there is evidence of the emergence of leading learnership, however, there is ample evidence that official, modern learning and leadership persists. The same appears to be true of classical, prototypical leadership and learning. They have self-perpetuating power based on desire to belong, control, dominate, and exclude. The hypothetical question becomes whether leading learnership will continue to grow, eventually crowding out earlier forms of learning and leadership or whether learning and leadership will live on. The drives that undergird classical and modern approaches to leadership and learning will undoubtedly remain, but I argue that those drives will be diverted into norms of success through the success of others rather than by using others as means to success.

Practically, there is the challenge of fostering leading learnership in a world that takes official leadership and learning as givens, as the natural order. The answer to this challenge may simply be to practice leading learnership. Those who do practice leading learnership, I argue, will be collectively and individually more successful and prosperous than those who do not. Natural selection will cull those who cannot get beyond disintegrated leadership and learning and promote those who practice leading learnership. Thus, the grand narrative of leadership and the sociocognitive evolution of learning will converge and continue as leading learnership, as thinking, talking, and acting together for the betterment of all.

References

Adams, W. M. (2006). *The future of sustainability: Re-thinking environment and development in the twenty-first century. Report of the IUCN Renowned Thinkers Meeting, January 29–31.* The World Conservation Union. Retrieved from cmsdata.iucn.org/downloads/iucn_future_of_sustanability.pdf

Amin, A. (1994). *Post-Fordism: A reader.* Oxford, UK: Blackwell Publishing.

Arampatzis, G., Kiranoudis, C. T., Scaloubacas, P., & Assimacopoulos, D. (2004). A GIS-based decision support system for planning urban transportation policies. *European Journal of Operational Research, 152,* 465–475.

Argyris, C., & Schön, D. (1978). *Organizational learning: A theory of action perspective.* Reading, MA: Addison-Wesley.

Arrow, K. J. (1970). *Social choice and individual values* (3rd ed.). New Haven, CT: Yale University Press.

Bagley, W. C. (1937). *A century of the universal school.* New York: Macmillan.

Bandura, A. (1977). *Social learning theory.* Englewood Cliffs, NJ: Prentice Hall.

Bandura, A. (1986). *Social foundations of thought and action: A social cognitive theory.* Englewood Cliffs, NJ: Prentice Hall.

Bandura, A. (1997). *Self-efficacy: The exercise of control.* New York: W. H. Freeman.

Barker, R. A. (2002). *On the nature of leadership.* Lanham, MD: University Press of America.

Barr, R. B., & Tagg, J. (1995). From teaching to learning: A new paradigm for undergraduate education. *Change, 27*(6), 12–25.

Barrett, F. J., & Cooperrider, D. L. (2001). Generative metaphor intervention: A new approach for working with systems divided by conflict and caught in defensive perception. In D. L. Cooperrider, P. F. Sorensen Jr., T. F. Yaeger, & D. Whitney (Eds.), *Appreciative inquiry: An emerging direction for organization development.* Champaign, IL: Stipes Publishing. Retrieved from www.stipes.com/aichap7.htm

Becker, G. S. (1964). *Human capital: A theoretical and empirical analysis, with special reference to education.* Chicago: University of Chicago Press.

Becker, G. S. (1996). *Accounting for tastes*. Cambridge, MA: Harvard University Press.

Bennis, W. (1989). *On becoming a leader*. Reading, MA: Addison-Wesley.

Bennis, W., & Nanus, B. (1985). *Leaders: The strategies for taking charge*. New York: Harper and Row.

Berger, P. L., & Luckmann, T. (1966). *The social construction of reality: A treatise in the sociology of knowledge*. Garden City, NY: Anchor Books.

Bonwell, C. C., & Eison, J. A. (1991). Active learning: Creating excitement in the classroom. *ERIC Digest*. Washington, DC: ERIC Clearinghouse on Higher Education. Retrieved from www.oid.ucla.edu/about/units/tatp/old/lounge/pedagogy/downloads/active-learning-eric.pdf

Brafman, O., & Beckstrom, R. A. (2006). *The starfish and the spider: The unstoppable power of leaderless organizations*. New York: Penguin Portfolio.

Brookfield, S. (1986). *Understanding and facilitating adult learning*. San Francisco: Jossey-Bass.

Brown, J. S., & Adler, R. P. (2008). Minds on fire: Open education, the long tail, and learning 2.0. *EDUCAUSE Review*, *43*(1), 16–32.

Burns, J. M. (1978). *Leadership*. New York: Harper and Row.

Burt, R. S. (1997). The contingent value of social capital. *Administrative Science Quarterly*, *42*, 339–365.

Chesbrough, H. (2006). *Open innovation: The new imperative for creating and profiting from technology*. Boston: Harvard Business School Press.

Christensen, C. M., & Eyring, H. J. (2011). *The innovative university: Changing the DNA of higher education from the inside out*. San Francisco: Jossey-Bass.

Coleman, J. (1988). Social capital in the creation of human capital. *American Journal of Sociology*, *94*(Supplement), S95–S120.

Cooperrider, D. L., Barrett, F., & Srivastva, S. (1995). Social construction and appreciative inquiry: A journey in organizational theory. In D. Hosking, P. Dachler, & K. Gergen (Eds.), *Management and organization: Relational alternatives to individualism* (pp. 157–200). Farnham, Surrey, UK: Ashgate Publishing.

Cubberley, E. A. (1922). *A brief history of education: A history of the practice and progress and organization of education*. Boston: Houghton Mifflin.

Deming, W. E. (1986). *Out of the crisis*. Cambridge, MA: MIT Press.

Derrida, J. (1998). *Of grammatology* (G. C. Spivak, Trans.). Baltimore: Johns Hopkins University Press. (Original work published 1967)

Dimancescu, D., Hines, P., & Rich, N. (1997). *The lean enterprise: Designing and managing strategic processes for customer-winning performance*. Saranac Lake, NY: AMACOM.

Dolence, M. G. (2003). The learner-centered curriculum model: A structured framework for technology planning. *ECAR Research Bulletin* (Vol. 17). Boulder, CO: EDUCAUSE.

Douglass, F. (1992). Self-made men. In J. Blassingame & J. McKivigan (Eds.), *The Frederick Douglass papers* (Series 1, Vol. 4, pp. 545–575). New Haven, CT: Yale University Press. (Original work published 1859)

Doyle, A. C. (1930). *The complete Sherlock Holmes.* New York: Doubleday. (Original work published 1906)

Drucker, P. F. (1993). *Concept of the corporation.* Piscataway, NJ: Transaction Publishers. (Originally published 1945)

Drucker, P. F. (1999). *Management challenges for the 21st century.* New York: HarperBusiness.

Drucker, P. F. (2002). They're not employees, they're people. *Harvard Business Review, 80*(2), 70–77.

Drucker, P. F. (2007). *Innovation and entrepreneurship: Practice and principles.* Oxford, UK: Butterworth Heinemann. (Originally published 1985)

Einstein, A. (1920). *Relativity: The special and general theory* (R. W. Lawson, Trans.). London: Methuen and Company.

Elkington, J. (1998). *Cannibals with forks: The triple bottom line of 21st century business.* Gabriola Island, BC, Canada: New Society Publishers.

Ellis, J. J. (2004). *His excellency George Washington.* New York: Alfred A. Knopf.

Farnes, N. (1975, May). Student-centered learning. *Teaching at a Distance, 3,* 2–6.

Foucault, M. (1972). The discourse on language (A.M.S. Smith, Trans.). *Archeology of knowledge* (pp. 215–237). New York: Pantheon.

Giddens, A. (1986). *The constitution of society: Outline of the theory of structuration.* Berkeley: University of California Press.

Gladwell, M. (2002). *The tipping point: How little things can make a big difference.* New York: Little, Brown.

Gladwell, M. (2009). *Outliers: The story of success.* New York: Little, Brown.

Gödel, K. (2000). *On formally undecidable propositions of Principia Mathematica and related systems* (M. Hirzel, Trans.). (Original work published 1931) Retrieved from www.research.ibm.com/people/h/hirzel/papers/canon00-goedel.pdf

Godin, S. (2008). *Tribes: We need you to lead us.* New York: Portfolio.

Granovetter, M. S. (1973). The strength of weak ties. *American Journal of Sociology, 78,* 1360–1380.

Granovetter, M. (1985). Economic action and social structure: The problem of embeddedness. *American Journal of Sociology, 91,* 481–510.

Greenleaf, R. K. (1977). *Servant leadership: A journey into the nature of legitimate power and greatness.* Mahwah, NJ: Paulist Press.

Gwynne-Thomas, E. H. (1981). *A concise history of education to 1900 A.D.* Washington, DC: University Press of America.

Habermas, J. (1984). *The theory of communicative action. Vol. 1: Reason and the rationalization of society* (T. McCarthy, Trans.). Boston: Beacon Press.

Harper, T. L., & Stein, S. M. (2006). *Dialogical planning in a fragmented society: Critically liberal, pragmatic and incremental.* New Brunswick, NJ: Center for Urban Policy Research, Rutgers University.

Hartman, M. G. (2002). *Fundamental concepts of quality improvement.* Milwaukee: American Society for Quality.

Heidegger, M. (1996). *Being and time* (J. Stambaugh, Trans.). Albany: State University of New York Press. (Original work published 1927)

Heisenberg, W. (1930). *The physical principles of quantum theory* (M. Hirzel, Trans.). Chicago: University of Chicago Press.

Hock, D. (1999). *Birth of the chaordic age.* San Francisco: Berrett-Koehler.

Hugo, V. (1909). *Napoleon the little. The works of Victor Hugo.* New York: Little, Brown. (Original work published 1852) Retrieved from www.gutenberg.org/catalog/world/readfile?fk_files=1520924

Hurley, T. J., & Brown, J. (2009). Conversational leadership: Thinking together for a change. *The Systems Thinker, 10*(9), 2–7. Retrieved from www.theworldcafe.com/articles/Conversational-Leadership.pdf

King, A. (1993). From sage on the stage to guide on the side. *College Teaching, 41*(1), 30–35.

Kohn, A. (1993). *Punished by rewards: The trouble with gold stars, incentive plans, A's, praise, and other bribes.* Bridgewater, NJ: Replica Books.

Kronman, A. T. (2007). *Education's end: Why our colleges and universities have given up on the meaning of life.* New Haven, CT: Yale University Press.

Kuhn, T. S. (1996). *The structure of scientific revolutions* (3rd ed.). Chicago: University of Chicago Press. (Original work published 1962)

Li, C. (2010). *Open leadership: How social technology can transform the way you lead.* San Francisco: Jossey-Bass.

Liker, J. K. (2004). *The Toyota way: 14 management principles from the world's greatest manufacturer.* New York: McGraw-Hill Professional.

Luke, J. S. (1998). *Catalytic leadership: Strategies for an interconnected world.* San Francisco: Jossey-Bass.

Lyotard, J. F. (1984). The postmodern condition: A report on knowledge (Vol. 10: *Theory and history of literature*; G. Bennington & B. Massumi, Trans.). Minneapolis: University of Minnesota Press. (Original work published 1979)

Machiavelli, N. (2004). *The prince* (G. Bull, Trans.). London: Penguin. (Original work published 1961)

Martínez-Lorente, A. R., Dewhurst, F., & Dale, B. G. (1998). Total quality management: Origins and evolution of the term. *The TQM Magazine, 10,* 378–386.

Mayberry, M., Crocker, M. W., & Knoeferle, P. (2009). Learning to attend: A connectionist model of the coordinated interplay of utterance, visual context, and world knowledge. *Cognitive Science, 33,* 449–496.

National Research Council. (2000). *How people learn: Mind, brain, experience and school* (Expanded ed.). J. D. Bransford, A. L. Brown, & R. R. Cocking (Eds.). Washington, DC: National Academy Press.

National Research Council. (2001). *Knowing what students know.* J. W. Pellegrino, N. Chudowsky, & R. Glaser (Eds.). Washington, DC: National Academy Press.

Nielsen, J. S. (2004). *The myth of leadership: Creating leaderless organizations.* Palo Alto, CA: Davies-Black.

Niles, D. (2009, August 3). *Leadership: The secret of successful scenario planning.* Forbes.com. Retrieved from www.forbes.com/2009/08/03/scenario-planning-advice-leadership-managing-planning.html

Northouse, P. G. (2007). *Leadership: Theory and practice* (4th ed.). Thousand Oaks, CA: Sage.

Papert, S. (1980). *Mindstorms: Children, computers, and powerful ideas.* New York: Basic Books.

Papert, S., & Harel, I. (1991). *Constructionism.* New York: Ablex.

Participative Management. (n.d.). *Encyclopedia of management.* Retrieved from www.enotes.com/management-encyclopedia/participative-management

Peterson, G. D., Cumming, G. S., & Carpenter, S. R. (2003). Scenario planning: A tool for conservation in an uncertain world. *Conservation Biology, 17*(2), 358–366.

Piaget, J. (1970). Piaget's theory. In P. Mussen (Ed.), *Manual of child psychology* (pp. 703–732). New York: Wiley.

Piaget, J. (1999). The construction of reality in the child. *International library of psychology* (Vol. 20: Developmental psychology). Abingdon, Oxon, UK: Routledge. (Original work published 1954)

Richland, L. E., Bjork, R. A., Finley, J. R., & Linn, M. C. (2005). Linking cognitive science to education: Generation and interleaving effects. In B. G. Bara, L. Barsalou, & M. Bucciarelli (Eds.), *Proceedings of the Twenty-Seventh Annual Conference of the Cognitive Science Society.* Mahwah, NJ: Lawrence Erlbaum.

Rittel, H.W.J., & Webber, M. M. (1973). Dilemmas in a general theory of planning. *Policy Sciences, 4*(2), 155–169.

Rost, J. C. (1993). *Leadership for the twenty-first century.* Westport, CT: Greenwood Publishing.

Schwartz, P. (1996). *The art of the long view: Planning for the future in an uncertain world* (2nd ed.). New York: Currency Doubleday.

Sen, A. K. (1988). The concept of development. In H. Chenery & T. N. Srinivasan (Eds.), *Handbook of development economics* (Vol. 1, pp. 9–26). Amsterdam: Elsevier.

Sen, A. K. (1999). *Freedom as development.* New York: Knopf.

Senge, P. M. (2006). *The fifth discipline* (2nd ed.). New York: Currency Doubleday.

Shirky, C. (2008). *Here comes everybody: The power of organizing without organizations.* New York: Penguin Press.

Smith, F. (1998). *The book of learning and forgetting.* New York: Teachers College Press.

Spring, J. (1997). *The American school: 1642–1996* (4th ed.). New York: McGraw-Hill.

Sun Tzu. (2003). *The art of war* (L. Giles, Trans.; D. Galvin, Ed.). New York: Barnes & Noble Classics. (Original work published 1910)

Surowiecki, J. (2004). *The wisdom of crowds: Why the many are smarter than the few and how collective wisdom shapes business, economies, societies and nations.* New York: Little, Brown.

Tapscott, D., & Ticoll, D. (2003). *The naked corporation: How the age of openness will revolutionize business.* New York: Simon & Schuster.

Tapscott, D., & Williams, A. D. (2006). *Wikinomics: How mass collaboration changes everything.* London: Penguin Group.

Thomas, D., & Brown, J. S. (2011). *A new culture of learning: Cultivating the imagination for a world of constant change.* Charleston, SC: CreateSpace.

Tress, B., & Tress, G. (2003). Scenario visualisation for participatory landscape planning, a study from Denmark. *Landscape and Urban Planning, 64*(3), 161–178. Retrieved from www.sciencedirect.com/science/article/pii/S0169204602002190

Tytler, R., & Prain, V. (2010). A framework for re-thinking learning in science from recent cognitive science perspectives. *International Journal of Science Education, 32*(15), 2055–2078.

Waldrop, M. M. (1992). *Complexity: The emerging science at the edge of order and chaos.* New York: Simon & Schuster.

Walzer, N., & Deller, S. (1996). Rural issues and trends: The role of strategic visioning. In N. Walzer (Ed.), *Community strategic visioning programs* (pp. 1–20). Westport, CT: Greenwood Publishing.

Weick, K. E. (1995). *Sensemaking in organizations.* Thousand Oaks, CA: Sage.

Weimer, M. (2002). *Learner-centered teaching: Five key changes to practice.* San Francisco: Jossey-Bass.

Wheatley, M. (1994). *Leadership and the new science: Learning about organization from an orderly universe.* San Francisco: Berrett-Koehler.

Womack, J. P., & Jones, D. T. (2003). *Lean thinking: Banish waste and create wealth in your corporation.* New York: Simon & Schuster.

Woody, T. (1949). *Life and education in early societies.* New York: Macmillan.

World Café. (n.d.). *World Café design principles.* Retrieved from www.theworldcafe.com/principles.html

World Commission on Environment and Development. (1987). *Our common future.* Report of the World Commission on Environment and Development. New York: United Nations. Retrieved from http://upload.wikimedia.org/wikisource/en/d/d7/Our-common-future.pdf

Chapter Five

Leadership Education

The Power of Storytelling

Kimberly Nehls

Once upon a time, children's literature was used to develop leaders. My purpose in this chapter is to introduce storytelling of children's books as a powerful instructional strategy. Storytelling has long been a part of our culture, especially when describing leaders (Boje, 1999; Bullough, 2010; Collison & Mackenzie, 1999; Danzig, 1999). Because leadership is rooted in storytelling (Boje, 1999; Denning, 2005), it is natural to bring stories into the leadership classroom. From the leader perspective, Denning has written several texts on leadership and storytelling. According to Denning, storytelling is a key leadership technique because it is quick, powerful, free, natural, refreshing, energizing, collaborative, persuasive, holistic, entertaining, moving, memorable, and authentic. Storytelling is more than an essential set of tools to get things done; it is a way for leaders, wherever they may sit, to embody the change they seek (Denning, 2005). Leaders establish credibility and authenticity through telling the stories that they are living. When they believe deeply in them, their stories resonate, generating creativity, interaction, and transformation. Storytelling is often the only thing that works to inspire change (Denning, 2005). A wonderful feature about children's books is

Kim would like to thank her three children, Grant (age seven), Liberty (age five), and Reagan (age three), for being the inspiration for her chapter on the power of storytelling.

that they also can be used to inspire change, and they are available on a variety of topics, from diversity to teamwork. Children's books are usually simple, noncoercive ways to introduce or further explain complex leadership themes.

Conceptual Framework

Studies have shown that incorporating "fun" into an organizational setting increases creativity and productivity. It also encourages less absenteeism and greater loyalty (Hsieh, 2010; Matthes, 1993). Avolio, Howell, and Sosik (1999) reported that the use of humor and play in organizations was associated with improved morale, enhanced group cohesiveness, increased motivation and inventiveness, and higher levels of productivity. Workplace fun is defined as "playful social, interpersonal, recreational, or task activities intended to provide amusement, enjoyment or pleasure" (Lamm & Meeks, 2009, p. 614). Activities such as watching a comedic movie or receiving candy would fall into the category of workplace fun. In their study, Isen, Daubman, and Nowicki (1987) found "four experiments indicated that positive affect, induced by means of seeing a few minutes of a comedy film or by means of receiving a small bag of candy, improved performance on two tasks that are generally regarded as requiring creative ingenuity" (p. 1122). Overall, organizational play, "in addition to providing enjoyment, can serve the purpose of adding significant value to organizational life" (Statler, Roos, & Victor, 2009, p. 88).

Incorporating story time into leadership and organizational settings is also a construct in which workplace fun can occur. Armstrong, in his popular book *Managing by Storying Around*, wrote, "Telling stories is friendly and enjoyable. People want to hear what you have to say. They want to know how the story ends. They pay attention" (1992, p. 9). Few activities can grab the attention of developing leaders quite like a children's story. Children's books are quick and colorful. They invite familiarity and discussion. Additionally, "because stories are vivid and memorable, they help us understand in ways that are meaningful and relevant. And because storytelling is a collective act, it encourages us to share meaning and establish a cohesion that might otherwise be beyond our reach" (Kaye & Jacobson, 1999, p. 45). Storytelling can bring leaders together.

Most individuals worldwide can recall being read to as a child or at least being told stories by relatives. Individuals are eager to share their favorite story or book from childhood and the feelings that story evoked. I personally loved *Robert the Rose Horse* by Joan Heilbroner, originally published in 1962. I can still recall the words, "Roses made Robert sneeze, and not just any old sneeze but a huge KERCHOO" (Heilbroner, 1962, p. 8). Robert had severe allergies—just like me! His allergies, however, eventually became a help rather than a hindrance. I have warm feelings of the book, and of it being read to me many, many times growing up. I am now pleased to share Robert and his sneezing adventures with my children. When a book is read well, the first thing a child says is, "Read it again!" Children's books simply have a way of evoking a desire for more fun and more creativity. What was your favorite story or book as a child? What themes, lessons, or bywords do you remember from that book? What feelings do you recall from reading books as a child? Stories enrich us. In fact, Kaye and Jacobson (1999) suggest that "a good story taps into the intellect and emotions of the audience; it leaves listeners enriched in their learning and feelings. In truth, only a story can accomplish that. Lectures, question-and-answer sessions, seminars, and coaching dialogues are not as likely to be as powerful" (p. 46).

There are many ways to incorporate children's books into leadership lessons. Professional speakers typically open with a story. Consider opening your next speech with a children's book. Or think about using a children's book to help explain a unique or challenging concept in a leadership seminar. Literature can supplement nearly any topic. Children's books offer rich

opportunities for learning about a variety of topics in a fun, suc-
cinct, and easily understandable package. In formal and informal
contexts, storytelling is appropriate and encouraged (Quong,
Walker, & Bodycott, 1999).

Children's Books in Leadership Situations

One can introduce children's books in a variety of contexts. I
share two occasions when I used children's books. Recently, I was
asked to deliver a presentation to a first-year-experience class at
my university. All new students on campus are required to take
this "FYE 101" class. As part of my lecture and classroom discussion, I read the book *Grasper: A Young Crab's Discovery Out of
His Shell,* written and illustrated by Paul Owen Lewis (1999).
When Grasper the crab explores a world beyond his home, he
grows physically and intellectually. The beautiful illustrations
show Grasper visiting new parts of the ocean unbeknownst to
his other crab friends who would not dare leave the confines of
their place of origin. He meets new creatures and sees amazing
sites: "Grasper couldn't believe his new eyes. There was a whole
world out there! He set off to explore, and he found . . ." (Lewis,
1999, p. 12). After reading the story, I asked students to relate
Grasper's stories to their own stories of embarking on college and
starting anew. Many students described having trepidations at
first. Some first-generation students suggested that, like the crab
in the story, their friends discouraged them from leaving home
and going to college because, in their experiences, no one they
knew had left home to go to college and the college-bound
scholar would be "different." Other students started a discussion
about studying abroad during college to continue to explore their
own worlds. Grasper's story was a powerful metaphor, and the
book helped the students articulate concerns and excitements.

In a different setting, I was coaching a group of leaders about
diversity issues. We were having a discussion that simply strug-
gled to move forward. Some individuals seemed not to be inter-

ested in the topic. Some even lamented that they had "talked diversity to death." I needed a valuable pedagogical tool to take the discussion to a deeper level. Dr. Seuss's Sneetches helped me do just that. From the first time I uttered, "They had stars upon thars!" everyone was suddenly engaged in the topic. The Sneetches (Seuss, 1961) became the noncoercive resource that I needed to get the entire group involved. Storytelling became a powerful way to promote an understanding of the subject matter. Although it is a fun rhyming story to read, The Sneetches addresses heavier issues of prejudice and authority. When I finished reading, the group that was earlier complacent about the topic had a variety of comments and insights. It was delightful to further my educational aims through storytelling.

When an instructor or coach pulls out a bright and shiny Dr. Seuss book, barriers to learning suddenly come down. There is no pressure when children's books are introduced because they are not intimidating. Better yet, when read aloud, stories can create community and shared meaning among the participants. Ellis (1997) offers several compelling reasons for using storytelling. Storytelling is the embodiment of the whole language; stories stretch the audience's attention span and their imagination. Storytelling is interdisciplinary and the perfect thread for tying curriculum together. Stories also contain conflicts and hurdles to overcome so students can work through issues together. Storytelling is a perfect tool for meeting different learning styles. For the auditory learner, books have the spoken word and vivid descriptions. For visual learners, clear imagery and illustrations make the story come to life. For affective learners, emotional depth, conflict, and feelings are embedded in stories. Kinesthetic learners can be provided with opportunities to "act out" an issue or problem through the story, even in their own minds. Colorful stories, in words and pictures, are great for all audiences. For example, in The Chicken-Chasing Queen of Lamar County (Harrington, 2007), Miss Hen has feathers as "shiny as a rained-on roof" and is as "plump as a Sunday purse." The words are so alive!

Additionally, storytelling is a dynamic way to teach higher-level thinking skills. Students move beyond simple knowledge to more evaluation and analysis. Stories encourage critical and active listening and thinking. Is the dot just a dot in Peter Reynolds's book of the same name? Is the box just a box in Antoinette Portis's book, also of the same name? Stories like these push adults and children alike to use their imaginations. Storytelling also facilitates cooperative learning and the development of social skills. Lessons are captivating and meaningful. Through stories, the audience can open their minds and hearts to new possibilities.

Finally, storytelling builds self-esteem and motivates hard-to-reach students. Stories can inspire and deepen understanding of topics. Shel Silverstein's classic *The Giving Tree* (1964) starts out featuring a leafy playground for a little boy that develops into a lifelong companion that teaches selflessness and generosity. The tale is frequently cited and often open to interpretation. Silverstein evokes an emotional connection that is not easily generated without the timeless illustrations and careful wording in this children's book.

Armstrong (1992) offers a few more reasons to tell stories. Storytelling is simple, timeless, demographic proof, an excellent way to pass along traditions, a great form of training, a way to empower people, a wonderful form of recognition, a way to spread the word, and good fun. From my perspective, I would add that stories are memorable. When I saw a leader from my "Sneetches" group at a chamber of commerce meeting a short time ago, the first thing he said to me was "Hey, Stars upon Thars!" Long after the instructional session ended that day, the story resonated with him . . . and I hope the lessons did as well.

Swap, Leonard, Shields, and Abrams (2001) explain, "Anything that tends to make information more memorable will have a greater likelihood of assuming significance. Because stories are more vivid, engaging, entertaining, and easily related to personal experience than rules or directives, the research would predict they would be more memorable, be given more weight, and be more likely to guide behavior" (p. 103). Swap and colleagues also offered the example of Stanford MBA students who were presented with an advertisement for a new white wine. All students read advertising copy about the wine being made using procedures from the Chablis region of France. Some students read only a policy paragraph, while others also read a supportive story about how the founder of the winery would be making the wine. A third group read the policy statement and were provided with numerical data supporting the statement. A final group read the story and the data. In all cases, those who read the story were more convinced of the truthfulness of the policy statement and remembered it longer. The story made the procedures more vivid and understandable, even for these quantitatively minded MBAs. To conclude the article, the authors note that stories are always "more memorable, and hence, more effective carriers of knowledge than less vivid, purely listed information. More important, rich narratives are more likely judged as true or likely to occur. If you want people to remember information and believe it, your best strategy in almost every case is to give that information in the form of a story" (p. 107). Because stories are dramatic and stimulating, and combine visual and verbal information, they are memorable and supported.

If an instructor is working with a leadership group over a period of time and a reminder of a concept is needed, the instructor can say, "Remember how Grasper explored . . ." or simply, "Click, Clack, Moo" and the understanding is immediate. These stories become part of the class's shared subculture (Stallings, 1997). Stories are a powerful and memorable tool for leadership lessons. The ability to tell the right story at the right time is emerging as an essential leadership skill (Denning, 2005).

Selection of Children's Books for Leadership

In Table 5.1, I list twenty-five of my favorite books—all successfully used in my varied leadership settings. I would first encourage the reader, however, to reflect on childhood memories

Table 5.1. Nehls's Top Twenty-Five Children's Books for Leadership Lessons

Book Title	Author	Theme(s)
The Name Jar	Yangsook Choi	Diversity, acceptance, new activities
Grasper: A Young Crab's Discovery Out of His Shell	Owen Paul Lewis	Overcoming obstacles, personal growth
Harold and the Purple Crayon	Crockett Johnson	Dreaming big, goal setting
The Dot	Peter H. Reynolds	Encouraging visionaries, goal setting, creativity
The Sneetches	Dr. Seuss	Diversity, acceptance, groupthink
Ish	Peter H. Reynolds	Creativity, seeing something anew
It Could Always Be Worse	Margot Zemach	Acceptance, appreciation
Zoom (wordless)	Istvan Banyai	Big picture
David's Drawings	Cathryn Falwell	Teamwork and individuality, diverse perspectives
How My Parents Learned to Eat	Ina Friedman	Diversity, cultural harmony, cultural pride
Paper Bag Princess	Robert Munsch	Feminism, individual strength, and decision making
Stand Tall, Molly Lou Melon	Patty Lovell	Belief in self, determination
Spaghetti in a Hot Dog Bun	Maria Dismondy	Individuality, courage, strength, be true to yourself
Click, Clack, Moo: Cows That Type	Doreen Cronin	Activism, peaceful protest, cooperation, negotiation
The Story of Jumping Mouse	John Steptoe	Perseverance, faith, courage, compassion
Chrysanthemum	Kevin Henkes	Belief in self, importance of teacher and mentor, bullying
Doña Flor	Pat Mora	Tall tales, getting to the root of problems
I Will Make Miracles	Susie Morgenstern	Dreams: "I'll meet everyone on Earth, and ask about their dreams. Because life is more, much more than it seems" (p. 16).

Table 5.1. (Continued)

Book Title	Author	Theme(s)
The Chicken-Chasing Queen of Lamar County	Janice N. Harrington	Change, determination, colorful metaphors
Come on, Rain	Karen Hesse	Anticipation, change, power of nature, celebrating with community
The Giving Tree	Shel Silverstein	Giving, friendship, unconditional love
Anansi Goes Fishing	Eric Kimmel	Trickster, lessons learned, hard work
A Chair for My Mother	Vera B. Williams	Hard work, overcoming obstacles, goal setting
Help! A Story of Friendship	Holly Keller	Friendships, gossip, trust
Not a Box	Antoinette Portis	Celebration of creativity, imagination

or memories of reading to children, one's own or those cared for. What books were unforgettable or had a tremendous impact? One could also ask an elementary teacher or children's librarian for books that are repeatedly popular during story time or frequently checked out or on reserve. Which books are the most dog-eared? These are beloved and typically have important lessons. Kaye and Jacobson (1999) also offer seven principles to guide story selection:

- *Look for patterns.* Plots and themes that build on your leadership concepts and the group's values are important.
- *Look for consequences.* The narrative of our lives seems to be influenced by Newton's third law: to every action there is always an equal and opposite reaction. In stories, cause and effect also resonate with the listener.

- *Look for lessons.* The audience can learn from the stories; they can discover something about themselves, the group, or the future: stories that impart lessons are often the best way to advise others, especially staff or colleagues. The usual advice about patience, persistence, timing, interpersonal interaction, and other realities of organizational life can be didactic and prescriptive. But when the same advice is given in the form of an experience that demonstrates a personal lesson, it is generally easier for the other person to embrace.

- *Look for utility.* Identify what makes a story transferable to the group. Illustrate the key elements of the story to make certain it will resonate.

- *Look for vulnerability.* Everyone has imperfections, and children's books tend to highlight some. Find better approaches to problems.

- *Look for the future experience.* Be creative. Learn from example.

- *Look for recollections.* Find stories that will especially resonate based on past experience of the individual or the group.

Additionally, I recommend two excellent resources: *What to Read When* (Allyn, 2009) and *Everything I Need to Know I Learned from a Children's Book* (Silvey, 2009). Allyn offers ten reasons why parents should read to their children, provides lessons on how to read aloud, and lists children's books that fall within fifty popular themes, from adoption to making a mistake. Allyn's book is a timely and worthwhile resource, especially when one must find a story on a particular topic. In fact, two books that I recommend in Table 5.1, *Chrysanthemum* and *Doña Flor,* are listed in Allyn's section on courage. Silvey's book is a compilation of noteworthy lessons learned in children's books. It features over one hundred celebrities, for example, talk show host and comedian Jay Leno and Steve Wozniak of Apple, and the impact a book had on their lives. Silvey (2009) writes, "At times, single lines from a book have resonated for a lifetime: William DeVries, the cardiothoracic surgeon who implanted the first artificial heart, has thought about a statement from *The Wizard of Oz* all his career: "I will bear all the unhappiness without a murmur, if you will give me a heart" (p. vi). It is hard to argue with the impact of children's books when one reads testimony from a heart surgeon while perusing this book.

Final Thoughts: How to Debrief a Story

To cultivate further comprehension, it is essential to debrief the story. Debriefing the story through discussion and reflection will help the group react and reflect on the story. As a facilitator, one can ask what was noticed, experienced, heard, or felt during the story and how these points of view relate to the current leadership situation of the group. Additionally, one can encourage discussion about what lessons or applications can be gleaned from the book.

The facilitator's goals and intent of the topic should guide the application of the debriefing session. More specifically, there are several ways to approach the debriefing session. One possibility could be to have the participants offer one-word descriptions of what values they heard in the story. Then have them offer two words, and so forth. They start to describe the important aspects of the story that build on one another. Another way to approach debriefing is to have the participants "think, pair, share." With this concept, the participants think on their own about the meaning and lessons of the story, then they pair with a partner to discuss, and then the twosome shares their ideas with the entire group. Yet another way to debrief is to use Kolb's (1984) model. Conceptually, the process is designed like a funnel, that is, participants sort out what they heard and what they think is important. The facilitator keeps the discussion broad then narrows the discussion toward the issues that are key to the intent of the session.

The facilitator could also have the participants create an action plan that will enable the group to move forward using the energy created by the storytelling session (Denning, 2005). To provoke change, Denning suggests crafting a "springboard" following a story. He suggests questions that might serve as a catalyst for change, for example, "What is the specific change in the organization or community or group that the story sparked?" or "What would have happened or could have happened without a change?" Individuals or small groups can answer these questions on sheets of paper or as part of a "chalk talk" with the entire group.

If the intent is to keep the fun going following a lively children's story, one can use a beach ball for the debriefing session. Beach balls are inexpensive, colorful, and instantly provoke a sense of fun—very much like a children's book! One can simply bounce the ball around the room and as each participant catches it, ask him or her to briefly interpret the story. Another option that I have used is to write questions on each section of the ball in permanent marker and as the ball bounces around the room, the participant has to answer the question where his or her right thumb lands. Some beach ball questions might be, "What did you like best about the story? What did you like least about the story? What changes could be implemented because of the story? What does this story tell us about leadership? How did it make you feel when . . . ?" Just for fun, I like to throw in an additional question such as, "What is your favorite flavor of ice cream?" The beach ball debrief seems to encourage additional creativity and spontaneity even though it is structured and relatively controlled.

Overall, structured reflection helps participants in a multitude of ways. While debriefing a story, the deeper learning occurs. Participants contemplate ways that the story shaped their ideas on a topic, they formulate new ideas on how to use the experience in other facets of their lives, and they are encouraged to share feelings and communicate the value of the story. When the participants are leaders, the reflection encourages these leaders to make appropriate changes in future activities as well. The instructor is helping develop a better leader.

Conclusion

The purpose of this chapter is to introduce the storytelling of children's books as a powerful instructional strategy in leadership settings. Educators who develop leaders can include children's literature as an enjoyable supplement to further educational aims. Children's books are available on a variety of topics, from diversity to teamwork, from goal setting to personal growth, and they are usually simple, noncoercive ways to introduce or further explain complex leadership themes. Storytelling is a powerful example of incorporating organizational play and fun at work for the benefit of the leaders and the group. Mainstream management theory indicates that imagination, interaction, and continual learning are beneficial to organizations (Statler, Roos, & Victor, 2009). We also know that humor and organizational play are beneficial for performance and morale, as well as group cohesiveness and creativity (Avolio, Howell, & Sosik, 1999; Hsieh, 2010). The telling of children's stories certainly encourages all of these characteristics and more. When we hear a children's book that touches us profoundly, our lives are suffused with meaning. Once a connection is made between a book and a leadership lesson, a radical shift in understanding may have taken place. So I say to you, "Click, clack, moo."

The end.

References

Allyn, P. (2009). *What to read when: The books and stories to read with your child—and all the best times to read them.* New York: Penguin Group.

Armstrong, D. M. (1992). *Managing by storying around.* New York: Doubleday.

Avolio, B. J., Howell, J. M., & Sosik, J. J. (1999). A funny thing happened on the way to the bottom line: Humor as a moderator of leadership style effects. *Academy of Management Journal, 42*(2), 219–227.

Boje, D. (1999). Storytelling leaders. *Organizational Change Management, 9*(5), 5–26. Retrieved from http://cbae.nmsu.edu/~dboje/leaders .html

Bullough, R. V. (2010). Parables, storytelling, and teacher education. *Journal of Teacher Education, 61*(1–2), 153–160.

Collison, C., & Mackenzie, A. (1999). The power of story in organizations. *Journal of Workplace Learning, 11*(1), 38.

Cronin, D. (2000). *Click, clack, moo: Cows that type.* New York: Scholastic.

Danzig, A. (1999). How might leadership be taught? The use of story and narrative to teach leadership. *International Journal of Leadership in Education, 2*(2), 117–131.

Denning, S. (2005). *The leader's guide to storytelling: Mastering the art and discipline of business narrative.* San Francisco: Jossey-Bass.

Ellis, B. F. (1997). Why tell stories. *Storytelling Magazine, 9*(1), 21–23.

Harrington, J. N. (2007). *The chicken-chasing queen of Lamar County.* New York: Farrar, Straus and Giroux.

Heilbroner, J. (1962). *Robert the rose horse.* New York: Random House Books for Young Readers.

Hsieh, T. (2010). *Delivering happiness: A path to profits, passion, and purpose.* New York: Business Plus Publishing.

Isen, A. M., Daubman, K. A., & Nowicki, G. P. (1987). Positive affect facilitates creative problem solving. *Journal of Personality and Social Psychology, 52*(6), 1122–1131. doi: 10.1037/0022–3514.52.6.1122

Kaye, B., & Jacobson, B. (1999). True tales and tall tales: The power of organizational storytelling. *Training and Development, 53*(3), 44–51.

Kolb, D. A. (1984). *Experiential learning: Experience as the source of learning and development.* Upper Saddle River, NJ: Prentice Hall.

Lamm, E., & Meeks, M. D. (2009). Workplace fun: The moderating effects of generational differences. *Employee Relations, 31*(6), 613–631.

Lewis, P. O. (1999). *Grasper: A young crab's discovery out of his shell.* Berkeley, CA: Tricycle Press.

Matthes, K. (1993). Lighten up! Humor has its place at work. *HR Focus, 70*(2), 3.

Quong, T., Walker, A., & Bodycott, P. (1999). Exploring and interpreting leadership stories. *School Leadership and Management, 19*(4), 441–453.

Seuss, Dr. (1961). *The Sneetches.* New York: Random House.

Silverstein, S. (1964). *The giving tree*. New York: Harper and Row.

Silvey, A. (2009). *Everything I need to know I learned from a children's book*. New York: Roaring Book Press.

Stallings, F. (1997). Honesty, respect, compassion: Strengthening character through stories. *Storytelling Magazine, 9*(1), 24–27.

Statler, M., Roos, J., & Victor, B. (2009). Ain't misbehavin': Taking play seriously in organizations. *Journal of Change Management, 9*(1), 87–109.

Swap, W., Leonard, D., Shields, M., & Abrams, L. (2001). Using mentoring and storytelling to transfer knowledge in the workplace. *Journal of Management Information Systems, 8*(1), 95–114.

Chapter Six

Developing Leaders for a Complex World

Mapping ILA's Guiding Questions to an Undergraduate Interdisciplinary Minor in Leadership

Scott J. Allen and Beth Ann Martin

The development of an interdisciplinary curriculum is an important undertaking that affects the learning and instructional system as well as student development (Gaff & Ratcliff, 1997). A curriculum can be profiled in prescriptive terms (for example, what the students should learn) or based on outcomes (for example, what the students actually learn). The recognition that there is often a gap between what students achieve and what was intended identifies a potential problem. Well-intentioned programs often unintentionally skip over the development of the link between what students *should* learn and what they *do* learn. Recognition of this problem creates an ideal starting point for the development of a new academic program. Surprisingly, there are few publications that provide guidance for the development of academic majors and minors in higher education (for example, Gaff & Ratcliff, 1997; Lattuca, Haworth, & Conrad, 2002). Grounded in basic leadership theory, the International

The authors would like to thank Steve Ritch and Matthew Sowcik for their feedback and input on this chapter.

Leadership Association (ILA) published *Guiding Questions: Guidelines for Leadership Education Programs* (2009). The guiding questions are designed to create discussion among program architects such that the collective result is a well-developed and mature program of study. The questions focus on five specific areas: context, conceptual framework, content, teaching and learning, and outcomes and assessment. In this chapter, we share an application of ILA's guidelines. For each of the five areas we will provide a brief description of the guideline and map our program onto ILA's framework.

Our institution is a small, private, Jesuit university. Our goal was to develop an interdisciplinary leadership minor that proactively addressed the five described concerns. A group of ten faculty members from a variety of disciplines met weekly for one academic year to identify ways to formalize academic leadership learning opportunities. The group began by reviewing programs and minors at approximately seventy other schools, identifying the goals for our leadership minor, and developing the curriculum and assessment structure. The following is a summary of the way our institution used ILA's guiding questions (GQs) to develop its minor in leadership.

GQ: How Does the Context of the Leadership Education Program Affect the Program?

Starting with context, one can best situate the program based on institutional or programmatic traditions, values, and objectives. According to ILA (2009), "Context of the leadership program affects the conceptual framework, which, in turn, determines in large measure program content, teaching and learning approaches, and outcomes and assessment" (p. 12).

Our university president stated, "We strive to develop each student as a whole person—mind, body, and soul. At the same time, we challenge them to make a difference in our world through leadership and service" (Leadership development minor,

2011). Given the importance of leadership to our culture and mission, and the growing importance to prospective students of studying leadership (Greenwald, 2010), providing students with opportunities for academic inquiry in the field of leadership is a particularly relevant and valuable initiative.

First, the minor is interdisciplinary, which aligns well with the liberal arts curricular values of the institution. The interdisciplinary leadership minor introduces students to historic and current leadership theory and practice, guides students in their leadership development, and offers students opportunities to gain significant leadership experiences. Likewise, the minor uses existing resources, capitalizes on the institution's strengths, and helps the university live its mission of inspiring "individuals to excel in learning, leadership, and service in the region and in the world." The minor is rooted in an academic curriculum that fosters conceptual understanding and provides students with opportunities to build leadership acumen, gain feedback, and grow as persons in a global society.

Drawing from business, the arts and sciences, and military science, the minor has the flexibility to align with the needs and interests of individual students. Perhaps the most unique aspect of the leadership minor is that students will have the opportunity to participate in a number of one-credit "learning labs" designed to experientially reinforce leadership concepts and provide an opportunity to translate theory into action. The labs focus on topics such as creating a vision, motivating others, building a team, and implementing a strategy.

Given the university's identity and an institutional focus on interdisciplinary studies, the design committee identified four primary objectives for the minor in leadership studies:

- Provide students with the conceptual understanding of leadership theory and practice
- Assist students in their personal growth toward becoming stronger leaders

- Provide students with opportunities to step into leadership roles on and off campus
- Prepare students to intervene skillfully when serving in a formal or informal leadership role

GQ: What Is the Conceptual Framework of the Leadership Education Program?

The committee identified the primary conceptual frameworks that have guided the development and design of the minor. According to ILA (2009), "The conceptual framework contains questions that will help program developers make explicit the underlying conceptual framework, beliefs, theories, and philosophies that guide their work" (p. 15). Our program rests on three theoretical frameworks. We will explain the three frameworks starting with the most theoretical followed by those that are more applied.

Conger's Four Approaches

The first conceptual framework is based on the work of Jay Conger. After reviewing qualitative research (participant observation and field interviews of leadership development programs), Conger (1992) determined that leadership development programs (or aspects of programs) fall into four primary categories discussed in his book *Learning to Lead*: personal growth, conceptual understanding, feedback, and skill building.

Personal growth programs are "based, generally, on the assumption that leaders are individuals who are deeply in touch with their personal dreams and talents and who will act to fulfill them" (Conger, pp. 45–46). Essentially, the purpose is to increase self-awareness and emphasize self-exploration. With *conceptual understanding*, Conger primarily focuses on theories of leadership. Often, this curriculum is delivered in a classroom and focuses on a cognitive understanding of theories of leadership and the attributes of effective leaders and effective leadership. Leadership development through *feedback* is Conger's third category. Assessment instruments are a fundamental contribution to an individual's leadership development. Feedback can include assessment feedback of one's knowledge of theories as well as feedback on one's learning style, confrontation style, and communication style. Conger's final category, *skill building*, is a topic addressed by many in the leadership literature (Avolio, 1999; Conger, 1992; Hunt, 1991; London, 2002; Popper & Lipshitz, 1993; Yukl, 2010). Skill building requires students to learn the actual processes and behaviors that effective leaders practice, for example, skills such as communication and motivation, which Conger asserts can be taught.

The conceptual model on which the current leadership minor is built rests cleanly within Conger's four-category framework. In essence, we are developing students with a sound knowledge of self, a strong understanding of the academic literature, an interest in and way of being that facilitates feedback, with the opportunity to build the skills needed to lead others.

The Five Ps Conceptual Model

A second component of our framework focuses on the concept of leadership itself. A clear challenge of leadership studies and leadership development has been a lack of clarity and agreement regarding what is being developed. We have defined leadership within the context of our minor through what we call the five Ps conceptual model: personal attributes, position, purpose, practices and processes, and product. The five Ps model is the foundation for the interaction between our theory courses and our laboratory experiences.

Discourse about leadership concepts can be difficult to navigate because people enter the conversation at different points. Having the background to discern how others are thinking about the topic can affect a conversation and one's success as a leader.

Our expectation is that by exploring the five Ps, students will have a better understanding of the inherent complexity and nuances of the topic as an area of study and activity.

Personal attributes are the traits, knowledge, skills, and abilities that leaders and followers bring to a situation (Goleman, Boyatzis, & McKee, 2002; McCrae & Costa, 1997). These attributes vary from person to person but an awareness of their importance is an essential topic for any leadership learning experience.

Position is about the role of leader. When others speak about the "leader," they often do so in deference to the role the individual occupies. Most often this person is in a position of authority over others with a title such as president, executive director, or branch manager (Gardner, 1993; Heifetz & Linsky, 2002). The important point to note with position, however, is that there does not need to be a formal title; that is, if leadership is a process of influence, then the position need not be a formal one. It is important to examine the role of leader, formal or informal, and provide students with a clear understanding of the aspects that accompany the role, both positive (fulfilling a vision) and negative (stress).

Purpose answers the question, "Leadership for what?" Leaders are aligned around a cause or purpose that energizes others (Bass, 1985; Burns, 1978; Kouzes & Posner, 2007). Purpose is essential. Without purpose, a leader will have a difficult time motivating others to work hard, innovate, and affect positive outcomes.

The *practices and processes* of leadership are the behaviors and actions of the leader to make the vision a reality (Bass, 1985; Blanchard, Zigarmi, & Zigarmi, 1985; Heifetz & Linsky, 2002; Kouzes & Posner, 2007). At times, these practices and processes are simple and straightforward and other times there exists a complex maze of possibilities. Regardless, knowledge of the behaviors essential for leading others is crucial and may mean the difference between success and failure.

What is the end *product*? Some wonder if we can determine if leadership was provided prior to knowing the results (Ulrich, Zenger, & Smallwood, 1999). Thus, in retrospect, did the individual make a positive contribution that did, in fact, "lead" the organization, country, or cause to new and better places? Or is the institution worse off because of the intervention (Kellerman, 2004; Lipman-Blumen, 2005)?

In the context of the leadership minor, the learning labs focus on each of the five Ps of leadership. The labs provide not only an opportunity for students to gain a deeper understanding of the concepts, they also provide an opportunity to practice the skills associated with each.

Know, See, Plan, Do

A third and final component of our conceptual framework is the "know, see, plan, do" model, which was developed as a way to operationalize Conger's conceptual model into an undergraduate academic curriculum. The intent of the interdisciplinary minor is to avoid developing unidimensional leaders and rather develop students who can use a multilevel approach for understanding the concept of influence. This model is fairly simple and allows us to plan every aspect of the curriculum so that there is certainty that students will have a well-orchestrated curriculum that will allow them to (1) learn facts and theories about leadership (know), (2) recognize leadership in context or practice (see), (3) use their existing information to plan a course of action (plan), and (4) carry out a course of action (do). By no means a comprehensive taxonomy of educational objectives, as described by Bloom (1956) or Marzano and Kendall (2007), the know, see, plan, do model seeks to provide general guidelines for four major levels of knowledge.

The first level, *know,* ensures that a student will have basic information such as retrieval of and comprehension of a large body of knowledge related to the topic of leadership. Students will be well read and acquainted with basic theories, influence strategies, and other current information. They will have a sound conceptual academic knowledge base (Bloom, 1956; Marzano & Kendall, 2007) for historical and contemporary leadership theory.

Resulting from the second level, *see*, the student (depending on what is happening in a specific context) can diagnose or "see" the dynamics in real time. A leader needs to use data in his or her environment to evaluate and analyze a situation. Students will be led through exercises so they see the world through the lens of the content. We expect students to develop the ability to identify leadership in practice, which includes the ability to see and explain leadership styles from movie clips, from vignettes, or from actual life experiences (see "translation" in Bloom, 1956). At this point we are not concerned that students can fully use all of the information but that they are able to experience, see, or read a situation and recognize, recall, and analyze the experience using leadership theories, approaches, and practices (Marzano & Kendall, 2007).

With the third level, *plan*, students can use knowledge and understanding of situations to plan skillful interventions (Meissen, 2010). Described as "specifying" by Marzano and Kendall (2007), students should use their knowledge to plan strategies, to forecast the outcomes of various plans of action, and to critically think about and evaluate the options available for action. By engaging in these activities, individuals can become more adept at intentionally choosing appropriate courses of action.

The fourth level, *do*, requires students to apply knowledge and to examine knowledge from different perspectives (Marzano & Kendall, 2007). Just because a leader conceptually understands that she or he needs to confront a difficult individual does not mean that he or she can behaviorally accomplish this. If an individual has a default of avoiding conflict, it will be difficult for him or her to adjust and use a more confrontational approach.

Designing experiences and activities for students to practice various leadership styles will create a safe environment for them to participate in leadership.

Our expectation is that students will engage in leadership activities that will incorporate all of these levels. Students will know the basics of leadership theory, recognize theories and concepts in real time, analyze various strategies and evaluate them in light of available information, and ultimately intervene with skill (Meissen, 2010).

GQ: What Is the Content of the Leadership Education Program and How Was It Derived?

The ILA (2009) suggests programs include content such as foundations of leadership, strategic leadership, personal development, organizational leadership, and ethical leadership. These topics are woven throughout the curriculum of the leadership minor. The following section examines some of the high points of our approach.

Fundamental to leadership development is transfer of learning described by Caffarella (2002) as "the effective application by program participants of what they learned as a result of attending an education or training program" (p. 204). Ultimately, if the learning does not result in "development" or a change in behavior, one could argue that the desired "output" was not achieved. According to some research, learning does not transfer to the job in 90 percent of cases (Phillips, Jones, & Schmidt, 2000). Responding to this finding, we designed this academic minor to reinforce and consistently revisit topics to ensure retention and learning. Our intent is for students to know the information well and in such a way that they can apply it to various settings.

A list of content topics was developed and agreed on by the committee (see Table 6.1). This list includes the theories, models, and concepts that students are expected to learn in the minor as

Table 6.1. Sample Planning Template for Courses in the Leadership Minor

Course	Topics	Conger's Four Approaches	Sources of Learning	Texts and Resources	Know, See, Plan, Do	Leadership Identity Development (LID) Stage
LP 101	Leadership defined	Conceptual	Lecture	Northouse	Know	Stage 1/2/3
	Skills theory	Conceptual	Lecture	Northouse	Know	Stage 1/2/3
	Personal values	Personal growth	Reflection	Kouzes and Posner	Know	Stage 1/2/3
	Leader styles	Conceptual	Lecture	Northouse	Know	Stage 1/2/3
LP 202	LMX	Conceptual	Lecture	Nahavandi	Know	Stage 2/3
	Teams	Conceptual	Film	Glory	Know	Stage 2/3
	Ethics	Conceptual	Simulation	StarPower	Know, see	Stage 2/3
LP 302	SLPI	Feedback	Assessment	Kouzes and Posner	Know, see	Stage 4/5
	Personal vision	Growth, skill	Reflection, goal setting	Allen	Know, see	Stage 4/5
	Five practices	Conceptual, skill	Simulation, game	Common Currency	Know, see	Stage 4/5
LP 402	Legacy Project	Skill, growth	Action learning	N/A	Know, see, plan	Stage 5/6

Note: The LID Model developed by Komives and colleagues (2005) is discussed later in the chapter.

well as topics that would create learning opportunities at all four levels (know, see, plan, do). These topics are divided among four required theoretical development courses, four leadership laboratory courses, and one senior project course. The leadership minor consists of twenty-one credit hours (see Table 6.2) and is composed of the following categories: leadership theory courses (5 hours), leadership components courses (6 hours), leadership context courses (3 hours), leadership laboratories (4 hours), and the leadership legacy project (3 hours).

Students first take four, one- to two-credit leadership theory courses. Content in these courses covers the historical theories of leadership in addition to new and current literature. This knowledge provides a foundation in leadership that will support their application of topics in other classes and elevate students' understanding of leadership (or conversely, apply leadership concepts to the topics in other classes). Although these four courses (five credits) focus primarily on conceptual understanding (know), there are also planned activities to create opportunities for students to identify leadership (see) and to begin developing their own sense of leadership style (plan). Feedback and personal growth opportunities are woven into the curriculum as well.

Following the foundational courses, students participate in two components courses (Table 6.2, column B) that focus on additional foundational concepts in leadership. The first focus is on ethics. The second set of component courses (Table 6.2, column B) is a list of available classes that address fundamental practices of a leader, such as problem solving, communication, organization and reasoning, and behavioral understanding, as a topic or part of the course. There are, of course, many other practices that can be identified but the committee agreed that these categories are fundamental across most contexts. Each course in this category covers topics that are identified in the leadership development literature as elemental to leadership. Students take one course from the approved list (of about twenty

Table 6.2. The Minor in Leadership Studies

Leadership Theory—A	Leadership Components—B (A Before B)
Required: All four:	Required: Two courses (one from A and one from B):
	A
Leadership 1— Introduction to Leadership I (1 credit)	Applied Ethics
	Business Ethics
	Contemporary Ethical Problems
	Catholic Moral Theology
Leadership 2— Introduction to Leadership II (1 credit)	Ethical Theory
	Introduction to Ethics
	Justice and the Economy
Leadership 3— Introduction to Leadership III (2 credits)	Moral Decision Making
	B
	Industrial Psychology
Leadership 4— Introduction to Leadership IV (2 credits)	Interpersonal Communications
	Leadership Skills Development
	Logic
	Military Tactical Leadership
Must be taken sequentially	Nonverbal Communication
	Organizational Communication
	Persuasive Communication Theory
	Project Management
	Problem Solving
	Public Relations
	Small Group Communications
	Theater Production

Leadership Context—C (A Before C)	Leadership Labs—D (A Before D)	Leadership Legacy Project—E (A, B, C, D Before E)
Required: One course:	*Required:* All four:	*Required:* All three:
The Age of Michelangelo	Personal Attributes: The Who of You	Leadership Project Planning
Matisse		Leadership Project Implementation
Picasso and Duchamp	Finding Purpose: Vision and Voice	
Campaign Issues		Leadership Reflection and Portfolio Presentation
Integrated Communications	Position: The Good, The Bad, and The Ugly	
Presidential Communications		
Economic Development	The Process: Strategies for Change	
Human Resource Management		
Public Administration		
Social Movements		
Catholicism in the Political Development of Latin America		
American Presidency		
Life, Times, and Theology of Martin Luther King Jr.		
History of the Papacy		
Models of God		
Culture and Community in Northern Ireland: Dynamics of Conflict and Peace		
Environmental Justice Movements		
Social and Cultural Change		

courses). Because these courses will be taken after the four introductory courses, it is expected that students will gain depth of
understanding from the leadership topics covered in these components courses.

Along with the components courses, students take one
context course (Table 6.2, column C) that allows them to develop
an awareness and understanding for how leadership acts as an
agent of influence in different contexts. Specifically included are
the arts, public office, business, religion, and social and community contexts. The topic of leadership (in terms of leadership
theory) is not meant to be included as a topic for study in these
classes. These courses provide students with the opportunity to
explore various contexts where leadership occurs. To ensure that
the connections between the leadership theory courses and the
context course are being made, the first activity in the Leadership
Capstone course (described following) will require students to
identify and delineate these connections. Ultimately, the component and the context classes are intended to strengthen the
know and to develop the *see* skills in students.

Following these classes, students have the opportunity to
participate in skill building when they select four one-credit
leadership laboratories (Table 6.2, column D). The leadership
laboratories are experiential applications of specific leadership theories and concepts previously examined. The goal is
that the laboratories help students put much of the conceptual
understanding into practice (*plan* and *do*). Each lab focuses on a
different aspect of leadership (personal attributes, position,
purpose, practices and processes, and product) and is designed to
prepare students for their capstone project.

Having previously taken all required leadership classes, students learn that the capstone project experience is designed to
be a leadership legacy project, meaning the projects will be
expected to have a significant impact on participants and recipi-
ents. Typical categories of legacy projects may include leading
an immersion experience; implementing a community service

project; leading a university service project; leading a substantial project with a university department, for example, university enrollment; and leading a substantial project through an internship with a local business or community partner.

GQ: What Are the Students' Developmental Levels and What Teaching and Learning Methods Are Most Appropriate to Ensure Maximum Student Learning?

The teaching and learning section focuses heavily on the leadership identity development (LID) model (Komives, Owen, Longerbeams, Mainella, & Osteen, 2005). "The essential developmental influences that fostered the development of a leadership identity included adult influences, peer influences, meaningful involvement, and reflective learning" (Komives, Owen, Longerbeams, Mainella, & Osteen, 2005, p. 596). Each of these influences has been intentionally woven into the design of the minor to enhance and facilitate learning. Additionally, because Komives and colleagues suggest that involvement is crucial to development, students have a number of opportunities to participate in and lead projects with others. Doing so will provide students with the theory-to-practice experience and help them move from conceptual understanding to skill building and personal growth (Conger, 1992). Within the context of the minor, we see the capstone project as an opportunity for a student to lead others in an intentional manner and provide an opportunity for a student to lead with confidence.

The role of the instructor at each stage of development is to create a space for learning and development to occur. Because each student will enter and leave the program at different points, the minor is designed to provide students with developmental experiences and the resources (peer and adult influences) to develop and grow at their own pace. Likewise, the instructor is charged with identifying appropriate sources of learning for each activity and course. Allen and Hartman (2009) suggest that sources of learning are key components for delivering learning activities in leadership development programs.

Not only is it important to be intentional about the general approaches to leadership development (conceptual understanding, skill building, personal growth, feedback), but it is also important to identify the best sources of learning to facilitate growth and development for students at each developmental level. As a result, we have identified a number of sources of learning that are incorporated into the design and delivery of the leadership minor and, in a general sense, aligned these to the LID model. The LID model is a developmental stage model based on a grounded theory study conducted by the authors. Komives and colleagues (2005) suggest that several developmental influences affect the development of leadership identity: peer and adult influences, meaningful involvement, and reflective learning.

Students in stage one of developing their leadership identity (awareness) have likely not given much thought to leadership and its inner workings. Although it is expected that college students would have already worked through this developmental stage, we chose to begin the first leadership classes with several self-exploration activities focusing on values and beliefs. Similarly, we have intentionally inserted several reflection activities. These activities are followed with a focus on leadership theories. Through sources of learning such as film clips, case studies, lecture, reflection activities, and group discussions, students begin to develop a deeper understanding not only of leadership theory but also of what it means to provide leadership.

The LID model stage two (exploration and engagement) is often marked with involvement in any number of groups and a realization that there are opportunities to engage and explore. Students often take on responsibilities but are likely not yet in a formal leadership role (Komives, Owen, Longerbeams, Mainella, & Osteen, 2005). In the leadership foundation courses, sources of learning appropriate for this stage will include student leader panels, reflection and journaling, group discussions, presentations that highlight opportunities for involvement, and several assessments that will clarify interests.

Komives and colleagues (2005) discuss LID stage three (leader identified) as an awareness of leaders and followers and a sound understanding that leadership is an activity. Students become aware that leadership is indeed a process; their perspective, however, is "leader-centric," and perceptions of leadership are often decidedly position oriented. Providing students with team-building activities, case studies, film clips, personal stories, journaling and reflection opportunities, and group dialogue will help students recognize or see informal leadership around them.

Stage four in developing a leadership identity (leadership differentiated) is marked by an awareness that leadership is an activity not held for a chosen few. There is a greater understanding that leadership is positional *and* nonpositional. In the advanced courses, faculty members will incorporate sources of learning such as simulations, role-play activities, and internships, encouraging students to take on formal leadership roles, group presentations and projects, team courses, mentor and developmental relationships, small-group discussions, and organization involvement.

At stage five (generativity), students see leadership as relational. There is also an "others orientation" at this level; students have an opportunity to develop future leaders (Komives, Owen, Longerbeams, Mainella, & Osteen, 2005). Most of this development is expected to occur through the leadership laboratories and the leadership legacy project. The sources of learning at this level of development will include activities such as peer mentoring, individual goal setting and visioning, assessments, research on developing future leaders, observation and shadowing of a leader, networking activities, individual development plans, case studies, and 360 feedback.

Stage six of LID (integration and synthesis) marks an increasing level of confidence in one's knowledge, skills, and abilities

(Komives, Owen, Longerbeams, Mainella, & Osteen, 2005). In the minor, our expectation is that students will vary in the degree to which they master this stage and sources of learning are similar to stage five. It is our hope that the Leadership Legacy Project (action learning) provides students with the opportunity to continue their development.

GQ: What Are the Intended Outcomes of the Leadership Education Program and How Are They Assessed and Used to Ensure Continuous Quality Improvement?

The evaluation of a leadership academic minor is a challenging endeavor. When evaluating educational and development programs, the goal is to find a link between program objectives and behavior change or development. Objectives establish the goals, and assessments help to determine progress toward those goals.

A critical rule of evaluation is that it is planned for at the beginning of the process. Evaluating the effect of any program after the fact will be ineffective (Waagen, 1999). Depending on the program objectives, there may be a need for quantitative and qualitative evaluation of participant learning and development. As the competencies become more complex or a higher-order activity, it is generally more of a challenge to measure.

The purpose of evaluation and assessment is to investigate the relationship between the program objectives and the actual outcomes. It is important to go beyond assessment of knowledge and facts; a good assessment, consequently, should identify if program participants are making connections across a number of topics. Aper, Cuver, and Hinkle (1990) suggest that individuals who are the most knowledgeable about the students and program being assessed create the best assessment instruments. Therefore, the faculty members who are involved in developing the interdisciplinary minor and teaching the leadership courses have created this assessment process.

To assess the four levels of knowledge (*know, see, plan, do*), we designed a full evaluation plan. The plan of evaluation involves having a control group so that comparisons can be made between students in the leadership program and those not in the program. Many leadership opportunities exist on a college campus outside of the leadership minor, and it is important that we can point to value-added outcomes for students who participate in and complete the minor.

Our plan involves assessment at various times in the program, but there are three specific points of interest. The first structured assessment will be made of those students who enter the first leadership course. Because the leadership minor takes a minimum of three academic years to complete, the students will begin during their freshman or sophomore years. In addition, a group of approximately two hundred introductory psychology students (not participating in the leadership minor) will constitute the control group.

The first part of the assessment will be an online questionnaire that measures factual knowledge of leadership. This questionnaire will serve as a pretest developed from a list of approximately sixty specific topics that form the basis for the initial leadership foundation courses. This is the theoretical and factual information we believe students should know by the time they complete the minor; these topics will serve as a measure of the *know* section of our conceptual framework. In addition to the knowledge-based test, in the second section of the assessment the students will watch a short movie clip and answer specific questions about the clip. The intent of this assessment is to identify students' ability to *see* various leadership concepts. Students in the leadership minor have classroom exercises that will allow them to develop this skill, so it is essential that we ascertain if seeing leadership concepts is achieved. The third part of the evaluation will be to present students with a problem and have them go through the steps to solving the problem, indicating which leadership strategies they might consider, various ways they might solve it, and their strategy for going forward. Our intent is to assess students' skills at identifying problems and planning a course of action. Thus, the evaluation should allow assessment of the *know, see,* and *plan* parts of our conceptual model.

This evaluation will be repeated three times during the course of a student's undergraduate education. The first will occur at the beginning of students' first leadership class, the second on completion of the four introductory core leadership courses, and the third near the end of the final capstone course. For students in the leadership minor, these assessments will take place as part of the usual class experience. The corresponding control groups will be introductory psychology students who are in their first year, third year, and fourth year.

Expected Outcomes

We expect low scores in all areas at the first evaluation. At the second evaluation, we are expecting students in the minor to score higher on the knowledge portion of the assessment than the control group, and that they will improve somewhat on the identifying (seeing) portion of the assessment, but will remain fairly low on the planning portion. By the end of the third year and the completion of the capstone course, we expect students in the leadership minor to have a solid mastery of all areas of the assessment, although we expect some variation due to standard fluctuation in student learning. We expect the students in the control group to improve somewhat due to participation in various majors, groups, and clubs, but that there will be a significant difference in the mastery level in all areas between the control group and students who complete the minor.

Areas where there is limited improvement will allow us to revise and improve the minor as we move forward. We should be able to identify the specific problem areas. Combining the assessment with the topic and course grid (see Table 6.1) should provide strong and definitive feedback for continually improving the classroom and learning experience for the students.

Conclusion

The purpose of this chapter was to share our approach to developing an interdisciplinary minor in leadership. With the International Leadership Association's *Guiding Questions: Guidelines for Leadership Education Programs* as a resource, we have outlined how the minor focuses on five specific areas: context, conceptual framework, content, teaching and learning, and outcomes and assessment. To our knowledge, we are one of the first institutions to use the ILA framework as a guide to our development and design. There are innovative conceptual models embedded in the design of the minor. For instance, our approach to evaluation (*know, see, plan, do*) will shed new light on this important discussion. If we can show that students in the leadership minor are thinking and behaving in different ways from students in the control group, we will be in a better position to assert that what we are doing does develop leadership capacity in students.

Within the context of this interdisciplinary endeavor, several opportunities for faculty development emerged. The process was one filled with rich and meaningful learning on our part. For example, we found that having faculty members from multiple disciplines was extremely positive and brought depth and energy to the meetings. We were quite surprised to find the many ways that different disciplines conceptualize and teach leadership. Although most of the faculty members embraced these differences, one should have an advance plan for working with individuals who are unable to accept discipline-specific differences in approaches. We navigated these natural challenges in a couple of ways. We began the process by creating a direct link between the mission of the leadership minor and the mission of the university. When objections arose regarding some aspect of our proposal, committee members identified the link between that aspect of the minor and the university mission. Along with this direct link to the mission was the intentional involvement of key university decision makers. In addition to faculty members from several departments, the development committee had two academic deans, one associate academic dean, and a representative from the academic vice president's office involved throughout the process. Their insights and support proved advantageous for program development and for final program approval.

As one reviewer of this chapter suggested, the process of developing a new program with an institution is "loaded with political implications." We agree. As with most change, there were critics, naysayers, and those who simply did not see the purpose of our efforts. Throughout the process, we experienced this truth firsthand and were often reminded that, ultimately, the process of designing and gaining approval is an exercise in leadership itself.

References

Allen, S. J., & Hartman, N. S. (2009). Sources of learning in student leadership development programming. *Journal of Leadership Studies, 3*(3), 6–16.

Aper, J. P., Cuver, S. M., & Hinkle, D. E. (1990). Coming to terms with the accountability versus improvement debate in assessment. *Higher Education, 20*, 471–483.

Avolio, B. J. (1999). *Full range leadership: Building the vital forces in organizations.* Thousand Oaks, CA: Sage.

Bass, B. (1985). *Leadership and performance beyond expectations.* New York: The Free Press.

Blanchard, K., Zigarmi, P., & Zigarmi, D. (1985). *Leadership and the one minute manager.* New York: William Morrow.

Bloom, B. S. (1956). *Taxonomy of educational objectives. Handbook I: The cognitive domain.* New York: David McKay.

Burns, J. M. (1978). *Leadership.* New York: Harper and Row.

Caffarella, R. S. (2002). *Planning program for adult learners: A practical guide for educators, trainers, and staff developers.* San Francisco: Jossey-Bass.

Conger, J. (1992). *Learning to lead: The art of transforming managers into leaders.* San Francisco: Jossey-Bass.

Gaff, J. G., & Ratcliff, J. L. (1997). *Handbook of the undergraduate curriculum.* San Francisco: Jossey-Bass.

Gardner, J. W. (1993). *John W. Gardner on leadership.* New York: Free Press.

Goleman, D., Boyatzis, R., & McKee, A. (2002). *Primal leadership: Realizing the power of emotional intelligence.* Boston: Harvard Business School Press.

Greenwald, R. (2010). Today's students need leadership training like never before. Retrieved from http://chronicle.com/article/Todays-Students-Need/125604/

Heifetz, R. A., & Linsky, M. (2002). *Leadership on the line.* Cambridge, MA: Harvard Business Review.

Hunt, J. G. (1991). *Leadership: A new synthesis.* Newbury Park, CA: Sage.

International Leadership Association. (2009). *Guiding questions: Guidelines for leadership education programs.* Retrieved from www.ila-net.org/Communities/LC/GuidingQuestionsFinal.pdf

Kellerman, B. (2004). *Bad leadership: What it is, how it happens, why it matters.* Boston: Harvard Business School Press.

Komives, S. R., Owen, J. E., Longerbeams, S. D., Mainella, F. C., & Osteen, L. (2005). Developing a leadership identity: A grounded theory. *Journal of College Student Development, 46*(6), 593–611.

Kouzes, J., & Posner, B. (2007). *The leadership challenge: How to keep getting extraordinary things done in organizations* (4th ed.). San Francisco: Jossey-Bass.

Lattuca, L. R., Haworth, J. G., & Conrad, C. F. (Eds.). (2002). *College and university curricula: Developing and cultivating programs of study that enhance student learning.* Boston: Pearson/Simon & Schuster.

Leadership development minor. (2011). Retrieved from www.jcu.edu/leadership/minor/

Lipman-Blumen, J. (2005). *The allure of toxic leaders: Why we follow destructive bosses and corrupt politicians—and how we can survive them.* New York: Oxford University Press.

London, M. (2002). *Leadership development: Paths to self-insight and professional growth.* Mahwah, NJ: Lawrence Erlbaum.

Marzano, R. J., & Kendall, J. S. (2007). *The new taxonomy of educational objectives* (2nd ed.). Thousand Oaks, CA: Corwin Press.

McCrae, R. R., & Costa, P. T. (1997). Personality trait structure as a human universal. *American Psychologist, 52,* 509–516.

Meissen, G. (2010). Leadership lexicon. *Journal of Kansas Civic Leadership Development, 2*(1), 78–81.

Phillips, J., Jones, W., & Schmidt, C. (2000). *Level 3 application: Business results.* Alexandria, VA: ASTD.

Popper, M., & Lipshitz, R. (1993). Putting leadership theory to work: A conceptual framework for theory-based leadership development. *Leadership & Organization Development Journal, 14*(7), 23–27.

Ulrich, D., Zenger, J., & Smallwood, N. (1999). *Results-based leadership: How leaders build the business and improve the bottom line*. Boston: Harvard Business School Press.

Waagen, A. (1999). *Essentials for evaluation*. Alexandria, VA: ASTD.

Yukl, G. (2010). *Leadership in organizations* (7th ed.). Upper Saddle River, NJ: Prentice Hall.

Part Two

The Complexity of Leadership Practice

Gloria J. Burgess

Leadership visionary and pioneer Max De Pree asserts that "leadership is an act of becoming," suggesting that leaders must continually learn and develop themselves to acquire and attune their repertoire of awareness, knowledge, rituals, instincts, habits, and skills to artfully approach myriad complexities of their worlds. The evolutionary opportunities and challenges of today's organizations, communities, nations, tribes, and families require leaders to be multifocused, keenly perceptive, adaptive, and resilient.

This part explores the theme of complexity by reflecting on the multifaceted nature of leadership practice, including the multiple roles leaders play and the diverse intersectionalities they encounter as they lean into who they are becoming. The authors here shed much-needed light on realms of leadership that have been largely ignored, marginalized, misunderstood, or all of these combined.

We begin with a chapter by Dionne Rosser-Mims and Juanita Johnson-Bailey, who acknowledge the often-overlooked significance of lived experience as leadership development *and* leadership practice in "Black Women's Political Leadership Development: Recentering the Leadership Discourse." Delving into the heart of black women's leadership, they focus on women called to lead in the political arena, surfacing treasure that could enrich the practice of any leader—leaders who have experienced a cultural legacy of oppression and resistance as well as those who have experienced a cultural legacy of privilege and subjugating others.

To enhance the dominant culture's legacy, what other leadership voices might we include and learn from? In "Leadership Lessons from the Criminal World," Jeanne Martinson addresses this question, exploring what she calls an "odd" facet of leadership practice—the criminal underground of street gang leaders. Martinson opens her chapter by correctly asserting that "leadership is not an easy job in today's world." Indeed, its many complexities include the mysterious realm of the human heart and how leaders, in multiple contexts, are called to cocreate environments that cultivate a strong sense of community and belonging.

Continuing with a chapter on leadership and lessons learned from the world of competitive sports, Michael S. Lane, Kathleen Patterson, and Paul B. Carr remind us of the many nuances involved in soccer, or football, as it is called in the world beyond the United States and Canada, and the similarities in navigating the challenging and chaotic landscape of organizational expansion, overseas no less. In "Soccer Tactics and Complexity Leadership," they provide an opportunity to step back, reflect on, and better understand the strategies, skills, and subtleties required for effective engagement and success in the realm of sports and organizational transformation.

This part concludes with Patricia Carr's evocative chapter, "A Complex Landscape: Reflections on Leaders and the Places

They Create," which transcends the conventional complexities of leadership. Moving beyond the nexus of leadership and place, she reflects on leadership and leader *as* place. In this sense, leaders become positive attractors who by their ineffable presence—physical, virtual, or both—provide a place to connect and belong. Extending the metaphor, leaders can also become a haven of hospitality, a sanctuary for others. Such leaders are recognized as authentic and worthy of our confidence.

As we lean into complexity, multidimensional, multicultural, multifaceted leaders will become highly prized. For in their presence, we are augmented not diminished, and the environments evoked by such leaders are edifying and life-giving, offering fertile ground in which they and others can flourish.

Chapter Seven

Black Women's Political Leadership Development

Recentering the Leadership Discourse

Dionne Rosser-Mims and Juanita Johnson-Bailey

The study of women in politics has garnered considerable attention in the political science and leadership disciplines. However, the literature base is scant relative to examining the complexities of black women's leadership, especially in regards to understanding the process by which black women acquire the knowledge and leadership skills needed to enter the political arena. Furthermore, there is a dearth of research examining the societal forces that shape black women's decisions to select politics as a career. In fact, information about black women's experiences serving in elective political leadership roles in a long-term capacity, and their leadership and career development experiences, has been drawn largely from the few autobiographical and biographical memoirs about prominent black women political leaders in the United States. In effect, more is known from what is called figurative literary sources. For example, the commonalities that emerge from the profiles of historic black women political leaders such as Shirley Chisholm (1970), Barbara Jordan (Jordan & Hearon, 1979), Jocelyn Elders (Elders & Chanoff, 1996), Donna Brazile (2004), and Condoleezza Rice (2011) show that they share the experience of having overcome numerous racial, sexual, and even class barriers in their paths to elective office or other roles within the political sphere. Their stories also reveal that these women placed strong value on education and community solidarity.

With respect to career development, leadership, and political science literature, none adequately study black women's leadership development experiences. Hence, current research must fill this gap. In our study, we explored why so few black women consider elective office as a career option and specifically explored black women's leadership development experiences as they pursued careers for elective office in Georgia. The questions guiding this study were as follows:

- How do black women develop their political leadership skills?
- What are the paths black women take in their political careers?
- How has the intersection of race and gender affected black women's journeys to elective office as political leaders?

Background

The black women politicians in this study negotiate between competing social forces with regards to their use of power, authority, and influence to promote equality for themselves and their community. The nature of black women's circumstances uniquely exposes them to how politics operate, thus contributing to their development as political leaders. In this same vein, former congresswoman Barbara Jordan comments on black women's plight engendering a natural tendency to leadership: "I believe that black women have a very special gift of leadership, because we have been called upon to lead in very trying times. And history has recorded the fact that black women rose to the forefront in times of struggle during periods of conflict about civil rights" (Gill, 1997, p. 3).

One must then consider how a black woman's leadership development path looks if she endeavors to serve in political leadership roles in a long-term capacity. How can she prepare to meet the social, racial, and sexual barriers that historically have negatively affected black women's representation as state and national political leaders? In particular, how can lessons learned by black women politicians be shared with other black women who have political aspirations? How can an environment that provides an ongoing support system and networking opportunities be provided for black women with political aspirations? Instead of conveying to these black women the notion of sink or swim, what mechanisms should be put in place to assist them toward successful pursuit and attainment of political leadership roles?

Black Women's Leadership Reexamined

Stokes-Brown and Dolan (2010) and Kaba and Ward (2009) argue that because of their race, gender, and even class status, black women continue to be denied the access to traditional sources of power and decision making afforded to males. This lack of access has had an effect on the kinds of leadership training black women have been able to obtain. According to Allen (1997), black women's second-class status ascribed to them in society's power structure has forced them to seek "alternative means of leadership training in nontraditional ways" (p. 2). For example, black women have developed leadership skills through a variety of roles—serving in nontraditional leadership roles in the church, serving as matriarchs of families, leading their families out of poverty, and leading behind the scenes in political and civil rights activist movements for social change. Thus, the emergence of black women leaders in the United States represents a triumph over oppression (Allen, 1997) to "lift" the black community out of racial, economic, and educational subjugation.

When classical career development theories, leadership theories, and contemporary leadership models are examined, the glaring omission of an account of black women's contributions to their communities emerges. From the perspective of this study, the literature also ignores the impact of a seamless web of class, race, and gender oppression manifested in black women's quests to become political leaders in the United States. With the emergence of more black women assuming leadership roles in the public and private sectors, exploring the impact of their leadership on these institutions as well as their unique leadership experiences is critical to effectively facilitate and support their leadership development.

Education: A Conduit for Black Women's Leadership Development

Black women have contributed greatly to the black community's educational progress at the familial and community levels. Their contributions to such advances have been a result of influential leadership and the policymaking roles they assumed, including roles in administrative bodies that govern US education (Brown, 2008; DeLany & Rogers, 2004). Indeed, the greatest number of black female elected officials is to be found in the educational arena. Black women have pioneered as members of local boards of education, superintendents, and supervisors of education. Education has often offered the foundation of their political involvement. For example, Mary McLeod Bethune, a black American teacher, was one of the great educators in the United States. She was a leader of women, a distinguished advisor to several US presidents, and a powerful champion for racial equality (Alexander, 1999). Bethune gained national recognition in 1936 when President Franklin D. Roosevelt appointed her to be director of African-American Affairs in the National Youth Administration and a special advisor on minority affairs (Alexander, 1999). Bethune's leadership helped black Americans throughout the United States gain greater education and employment opportunities. Also of particular note is Shirley Chisholm, the first black woman to make a serious bid for the United States presidency in 1970, who compelled America to recognize black women's experiences and to acknowledge their plight as one of having to triumph over racism, sexism, and economic exploitation (Brownmiller, 1970). Bethune, Chisholm, and other black female leaders have demonstrated that in the face of great obstacles black women strengthen their communities through their leadership in churches, women's groups, charitable organizations, and political groups and their contributions to the larger community as writers, activists, educators, and political leaders (Hine & Thompson, 1998).

The work of these black women attests to the intellectual and political contributions black women in general have made toward attaining equality, especially educational equity and political rights, for black Americans. Although black women's voices had been silenced for centuries, they did not sit idly by, waiting for the dominant culture to relax its grip on their intellectual and political rights. Instead they took on leadership roles at various levels of society (familial, community, and institutional) to ensure community survival. We can recognize the legacy of black women developing their leadership skills through promoting familial, educational, and political activism.

Black women's lives are inherently saturated with "politics" through their daily encounters with sexism and racism. Consequently, paramount to black women's survival has been their ability to gain knowledge and wisdom about the dynamics of race, gender, and class oppression. Such wisdom helps guide them to become political leaders and to remain in office. Cooper (2000) writes, "The black woman, then, should not be ignored because her bark is resting in the silent waters of the sheltered cove . . . watching the movements of the contestants nonetheless and is all the better qualified, perhaps, to weigh and judge and advise because [she is] not herself in the excitement of the race" (p. 93).

Despite the progress that has been made and although black women's voices continue to be marginalized in the context of political leadership discourse, black women are observing, learning, and taking action based on the information they have collected. Progress takes place sometimes through black women serving in informal leadership roles, often working behind the scenes to help facilitate community change. Countless numbers of black women have developed their leadership skills by serving as educators, organizers of women's groups, and leaders of community organizations. Many have been the strong forces behind political and social movements through organizing rallies or voter registration drives, or leading in recruitment efforts. Hence, an important dimension of black women's leadership experience is to understand "how they lead," which is the focus of the section that follows.

Black Women's Way of Leading

Since about 2000, greater attention has been focused on black women's unique leadership experiences and the complex process through which they have arrived at political leadership (Allen, 1997; Brown, 2008; Gostnell, 1997; Hardy-Fanta, Pie-te, Pinderhughes, & Sierra, 2006; McCluskey, 1994; Philpot & Walton, 2007; Rogers, 1998, 2003, 2005; Smooth, 2001, 2008, 2010; Stokes-Brown & Dolan, 2010). Historically, black women have held positions of leadership in organizations "whose mission is institutional change," such as the National Association for the Advancement of Colored People (NAACP) and the Southern Christian Leadership Conference (SLCC) (Collins, 1997). Additional evidence shows that black women activists hold decidedly different viewpoints from traditional and contemporary concepts of "leadership"; their ideas about using power and of the purpose and role of leaders differ from traditional conceptions. Collins (2000) asserts that "Black women's organizational style within predominantly Black organizations reveals much of how many U.S. Black women exercise power. Understandings of empowerment gained as community othermothers and cultural workers shape Black women's political activities. Drawing on the models of education as empowerment, many Black women routinely reject models of authority based on unjust hierarchies" (p. 218). For example, the leadership style of renowned civil rights activist Fannie Lou Hamer exemplified unique ideas about leadership and empowerment in the black community. Hamer believed that a leader is responsible for cultivating and developing more leaders and promoting group solidarity (Allen, 1997). Although she did not hold a formal position of authority with the Mississippi Democratic Freedom Party (MDFP), the model of leadership she exercised reveals the considerable power she held, which was a result of her viewpoint on social change. In other words, Hamer effectively challenged and held the Democratic Party of Mississippi accountable for taking the necessary steps to ensure that *all* the people of Mississippi were fairly represented. In so doing, she challenged the white and black male leadership, which held the general belief that women, and certainly black women, could work behind the scenes but that they should not try to come forward and lead.

During Hamer's involvement in the formation of MDFP in 1964, and in preceding years, black women had to contend with overt sexism by black men and with racial, sexual, and class oppression by white men and women (Marble, 1990). These forces compelled them to create safe havens from a hostile environment, and often these shelters prohibited personal growth, although they ensured community survival (Allen, 1997). For black women these circumstances created a "culture of political resistance" that required them to "expand their roles as homemakers and laborers to incorporate that of 'caretakers' of the race" (Allen, 1997, p. 65). Black female leadership was therefore cultivated and operationalized within roles in the family and the community (that is, churches, schools, political organizations). In effect, black female leadership developed from and continues to be shaped by external and internal forces that affect black women's everyday life experience.

Do these myriad ways of leading suggest that there exists a universal definition of black women's leadership? A search through black leadership literature for a definition of black female leadership reveals that no single universal definition exists. However, the following three themes focusing on black female leadership surface in black leadership literature (Allen, 1997, p. 2):

- Black female leadership exemplifies survival techniques in family, church, and community organizations that show creativity and commitment to group well-being.
- Black female networks, formal and informal, are dynamic, interrelated entities that constitute a matrix of reinforcement holding the black community together, while developing leadership for a better future.
- Black female leadership represents collective experiences and actions toward community empowerment.

These themes indicate that black women tend to formulate ideas and models that express the reality of their own experiences while opposing an ideology of domination.

The underlying message of the literature on black women's leadership is that they hold what they believe to be the tenable responsibility of ensuring community survival and "uplifting" the race. Black community survival implies that black female leaders must continue to play a vital role in improving the black community. Moreover, black female networks have offered a structure or matrix from which black women's leadership historically has emerged (Allen, 1997). It was important to such black female networks to ensure that cultural traditions were transferred to future generations. A web of networks enabled black women to work together to combat the institutional and social barriers holding back disadvantaged groups.

Overall, analyzing historical accounts of how black women's leadership emerged and their career development experiences, viewed from a black feminist perspective, creates an entirely different picture from the one produced by the dominant culture, which is a picture of inferiority and powerlessness. The picture presented through a black feminist lens is a poignant reminder of how oppressive forces have become institutionalized and thus invisible to the uncritical eye. The black feminist perspective shows that, through education, political activism, and engagement at all levels, black women continue to succeed in the fight for social, educational, and economic parity.

Methodology

To gain a deeper understanding of black women's experiences in seeking political leadership positions, a qualitative methodological approach with an emphasis on the use of narrative inquiry was used for this study. This method allowed the researchers to explore further black women's paths to their goals, how their career trajectories are affected by race and gender, and to gain insights into who these women are and how they see themselves in the context of elective office. Additionally, narrative inquiry was used for this study because it is a research tool conducive to exploring how black women negotiate issues of race and gender. It is also useful in gathering information central to understanding the life and viewpoints of black women (Collins, 2000). In particular, "narrative analysis can be used for systematic interpretations of others' interpretations of events. This can be an especially powerful research tool if the narratives are accounts of . . . epiphanic moments, crises, or significant incidents in people's lives, relationships or careers" (Cortazzi, 2001, p. 384). Narratives enable participants to organize their life experiences and derive meaning from them. In this study the focus of participants' stories is a segment of their lives revealing how they see themselves in relation to their career and leadership development paths to elective office.

Participants

Nine black women who have served or currently serve in elected positions at the local, state, or federal levels in Georgia were purposefully selected to participate in this study. The participants ranged in age from fifty to eighty and were geographically diverse, representing southeast, southwest, middle, and north Georgia as well as the Atlanta metro area. Table 7.1 presents demographic information based on participants' status in 2005 to include name, age, profession, age elected to first office, elected office held, and years served in office.

Data Collection and Analysis

Primary data collection was based on in-depth semistructured interviews. Interviews, which ranged from one hour to two and a half hours in length, were conducted with the nine study participants. Pseudonyms were not assigned in this study because most of the study participants were the first black women to serve in their respective positions and some remain the only black women in their positions to date. We determined that due to the nature of the positions in which most participants have served, ensuring anonymity would be virtually impossible. Therefore, in addition to seeking permission from the participants to audiotape their interviews, we also requested permission of each participant to use her name. All nine participants consented. Secondary and tertiary data sources included the collection and analysis of documents supplied by participants (that is, résumés, newspaper articles, bios) and documents collected from an Internet search for background information on each study participant.

Each audiotaped interview was transcribed for the purposes of constructing narratives, coding, and analyzing the data. We returned transcripts to participants to ensure that they approved of them and to give them an opportunity to make any desired changes. Only one participant requested changes.

Table 7.1. Demographic Profile of Study Participants

Name	Age	Profession	Age Elected to First Office	Elected Office	Years Served in Office
Jackie Barrett	55	Criminal justice	38	Sheriff	11
Emma Gresham	80	Retired educator	63	Mayor	17
Sonja Mallory	51	Cosmetologist	46	Mayor	5
Glenda Battle	50	Nurse	30	County commissioner	20
Evelyn Turner-Pugh	55	Finance manager	39	City council	16
Myrtle Figueras	62	Retired educator	54	Council member	8
Georganna Sinkfield	62	Real estate sales agent	38	State representative	24

(Continued)

Table 7.1. (Continued)

Name	Age	Profession	Age Elected to First Office	Elected Office	Years Served in Office
Nadine Thomas	53	Nurse	39	State senator	13
Denise Majette	50	Judge/attorney	38	US Congressional representative	11

Note: Demographic information is based on status in the year 2005. Jackie Barrett, the first black female elected sheriff of Fulton County, Ga. and in the US, retired in 2005. Emma Gresham, the first black and female mayor of Keysville, Ga., did not seek reelection in 2006. Sonya Mallory, the first black and female mayor of Jeffersonville, Ga. Glenda Battle, the first black female county commissioner of Decatur County, Ga. and the first black female president of the Georgia Association of County Commissioners. Evelyn Turner-Pugh, city council member of the City of Columbus, Ga. Myrtle Figueras, city council member of the City of Gainesville, Ga., and she served one term as mayor, making her the first black female mayor of the city. Georganna Sinkfield, the longest serving black female in the Georgia General Assembly. Nadine Thomas, the first black female elected to the Georgia State Senate, did not seek reelection after her 2004 unsuccessful bid for a US House of Representatives seat. Denise Majette, US congressional representative of Georgia's 4th congressional district, did not seek reelection after her 2004 unsuccessful bid for a US Senate seat.

During each interview, a series of open-ended questions, facilitated by an interview guide, was employed to get each participant to tell the story of how she acquired her political leadership skills and to learn her perceptions of the role racism, sexism, and classism played in her path to elective office. Interview guides, according to Patton (2002), help researchers ensure that "the same basic lines of inquiry are pursued with each person interviewed . . . [and] provide topics or subject areas within which the interviewer is free to explore, probe, and ask questions that will elucidate and illuminate that particular subject" (p. 343). Field notes were also taken during each interview as yet another source of data. We recorded key areas that needed further discussion and captured an environmental scan of the interviewees' nuances such as body language, facial expressions, and intonations to help us formulate additional interview questions as the interviews moved along and to help facilitate the data analysis process.

Data analysis involves making sense of what people have said. More specifically, it is a process in which the researcher "moves[s] back and forth between concrete bits of data and abstract concepts, between inductive and deductive reasoning, between description and interpretation" (Merriam, 1998, p. 178). It is a continual process. Data analysis in this study began with the construction of a narrative summary of each interview transcript. We summarized the interview transcripts to orient us to the participants' narratives of their political leadership development. Next, each interview transcript was analyzed from Alexander's (1988) psychobiological perspective, which offers a nine-part framework in analyzing narratives. To allow the data to be analyzed in manageable units, Alexander recommends using nine indicators of salience: primacy, frequency, omission, uniqueness, isolation, negation, emphasis, error, and incompleteness. For example, when one participant failed to mention the conflict that ensued after she had been asked to step down from her position, this represented an omission, one of Alexander's

(1988) nine indicators of salience. Frequency was another indicator of salience. When all participants repeatedly mentioned spirituality and faith as an influencing factor in their lives, this began to emerge as a theme. Next, each transcript was analyzed according to Denzin's (1989) approach. These analytic methods helped to draw attention to what participants considered important, which subsequently helped focus themes that appeared to be important. Initial coding revealed general categories such as "nonlinear leadership development path," "grounded in spirituality and faith," "learned by doing; no model," and "intraracial challenges." Next, we analyzed each narrative separately by fragmenting the data (Polkinghorne, 1995). Finally, from the summary, preliminary factors of these women's leadership development experiences emerged across data sets. These components were strong family support, challenges in personal life, and the discovery that sexism and racism still exist.

Coding is a systematic method of "naming and locating data bits" (Glesne, 1999, p. 133). As we began to sort, define, and re-sort data bits, as well as to analyze the interview transcripts, researcher notes, and notes from relevant literature, we searched for emergent themes and concepts that appeared important. These themes were assigned a preliminary code. Initial coding revealed general categories such as "nonlinear leadership development path," "grounded in spirituality/faith," "learned by doing/ no model," and "intra-racial challenges."

To counteract threats to validity and to increase the credibility of and confidence in the study's findings, three data-gathering techniques were employed. This triangulation approach (Glesne, 1999) consisted of face-to-face audiotaped interviews, document analysis (using key insights from the literature and other relevant material), as well as artifacts such as résumés and newspaper articles, researcher notes, and member checks (informant feedback to validate study findings). Additional measures were taken to clarify and validate our interpretation of data. We recognized and monitored how the subjectivities we brought to the study

(Glesne, 1999; Peshkin, 1988) would influence study findings by recording personal reflections about the interview process in a researcher journal immediately after each interview. In addition, we employed a peer-review process to examine the data collected and the plausibility of emergent findings. Accuracy and consistency in coding methods were peer reviewed, too. Finally, as a way of engaging study participants in the construction of meaning, and to check our own interpretations of their stories, each study participant checked her transcript to "identify sections that, if published, could be problematic for either personal or political reasons" (Glesne, 1999, p. 152).

Findings

Women are neither a homogeneous group in society, nor do they form a standardized group of leaders. The same is to be noted of black women leaders. This study's findings reveal, nonetheless, that black women do share common features in their leadership, features stemming from their culture that remain rooted in the roles in which black women have historically served, a legacy of leadership that is evident in contemporary society. Although we are not suggesting that black women exhibit one style of leadership, we discovered the women in this study show seven common features in their leadership styles that converge to reveal the following:

- Self-determination cultivated by mentors and black female role models
- Intrinsic motivation to serve and improve the black community
- Reliance on faith and spirituality in decision making
- Strong values of learning and education
- Informal learning as a primary source of their learning and leadership development

- Balancing role expectations associated with biculturality
- Familial and community-based support systems

In addition to the seven leadership style features common to the participants, in the following sections we discuss four themes that emerged from the analysis of data: cultural legacy, developing a political consciousness, the personal is political, and black women's conceptions of politics.

Cultural Legacy

Numerous examples exist in black history of the leadership roles black women often assumed, out of necessity, to ensure that the family and community survived. From slavery to emancipation, from the civil rights movement to the present, black women have served in numerous leadership capacities as mothers, wives, grandmothers, church leaders, community leaders, and civic leaders, their principal motivation being to uplift the black race. Historically, black women have demonstrated leadership characteristics inconsistent with traditional leadership models; and the ways in which they learn to and become leaders differ from the experiences of middle-class white males on whom leadership theory is based (Smooth, 2008, 2010). Black women's leadership is characterized by cultural values of uplifting their race, and of communality and collectivism shaped by their lived experiences as black American women.

The women in this study provided exemplary illustrations of how race and gender affected the ways in which they learned to become and to operate as leaders. For example, Myrtle Figueras, city council member, states that a major reason she ran for office was to ensure that the black community was represented among the elected leadership. She felt that it was her responsibility to ensure that the needs of her black constituency were addressed and would not be overlooked. Former congressional representative Denise Majette describes how she would remind herself of the historic black female leadership from which she had come, women who overcame adversity against seemingly insurmountable odds. In particular, she describes the leadership of Harriet Tubman and how others like her left a valuable legacy of leadership for black women to follow. She observes: "[Harriet Tubman] couldn't read, and write. . . . She managed to move 300 people from slavery to freedom across the country with a bounty over her head. . . . That is the kind of inspiration and creativity that we as black women need to have now, to hold on to that kind of history and the legacy that was created for us."

Other examples of common features of black women's leadership are evident in the history of black women who served in leadership roles in black American history. For example, Dr. Anna Julia Cooper, a former slave and black female political leader, educator, and advocate for human rights, declared herself "the voice of the South," and accurately predicted that the twentieth century would require the recognition of women's growing status in society, and that women had and would continue to play a significant leadership role in guiding the country to "greater plains." More specifically, it would be black women's leadership that would be a guiding force in "lifting" the black community to greater self-empowerment. Historically, one way of uplifting the race was through pursuit of an education. Cooper and other black women leaders such as Mary Church Terrell, Ida B. Wells Barnett, Fannie Lou Hamer, and Shirley Chisholm all represent a legacy of black female leaders whose work was guided by a political agenda of attaining racial and gender equality. These women demonstrated a leadership style grounded in their lived experiences as black women who confronted racial, sexual, and class oppression and resisted. As a result, they led with compassion and community solidarity, inspired by a fundamental belief that education is the means to gain freedom, achieve economic success, and obtain the social and political mobility to improve their own lives and the quality of life of the black community. These women and others emerged as leaders often not as a result of personal choice but as a way of surviving individually and as a community.

Developing a Political Consciousness

The identities of study participants (that is, black women who came of age between the late 1960s and early 1970s, and were born in the South, exposed to the civil rights movement, of lower middle-class origins) and their experience with race and gender opposition and resistance from birth through adulthood culti-vated and sharpened their political consciousness. The women in this study and the women in a study by Rogers (1998) learned through their lived experiences, which inculcated and sharpened their awareness, that the "personal is political." Their experi-ences, their feelings, and their personal possibilities were not just a matter of personal preferences and choices but were limited, molded, and defined by the broader political and social setting in which they lived. From birth to adulthood, black women's lives are shaped by racism, sexism, and class prejudice (Collins, 2000). At an early age, black females become aware of the mar-ginalized status to which they are relegated by their race and gender. In effect, they operate in a system in which they are systematically marginalized throughout their lives; this margin-alization is a form of oppression that breeds resistance; as a result of it, they begin to understand and process their life experiences from a political perspective, using a lens that forms the basis of their worldview.

The Personal Is Political

The concept of the "personal is political" has implications for black women's place in the political arena. Scholars of black politics typically assume that the experiences of all black elected officials are similar, whereas scholars who study women in politics typically assume women's experiences in politics do not differ. A major oversight resulting from these assumptions is the glossing over of the impact of gender and race in shaping the leadership experiences of black women in politics. Although a few studies have focused on analyzing the intersection of race and gender in politics (Barrett, 1995, 1997, 2001; Button & Hedge, 1996; Rogers, 1998; Ruderman & Hughes-James, 1998; Smooth, 2001, 2008, 2010), it was the seminal work of Githens and Prestage (1977) on the thirty-five black women who served in state legislatures from 1971 to 1973 that underscored the unifying thread of their lived experience. These were black women grappling with the vestiges of Jim Crow and segregation, opposition, and racism. These social challenges effectively influenced these black women to enter the political arena; there were challenges the women in this study experienced in varying degrees.

It is important to view this study in the sociopolitical context of the 1960s and 1970s, when all of the participants came of age. With the exception of one participant who was twelve to thirty years older than the other participants, the women credited the civil rights movement, either implicitly or explicitly, as exerting a major influence on them. It shaped their growing sense of politics and the relationship of politics to the interlocking system of racism and other sources of marginalization. This study's findings also reveal that these women's lived experiences of encountering resistance and opposition, due not only to race but also to gender, laid the foundation of much of their understanding of politics. It was the very experience of asserting their identities in the face of racism, sexism, and oppression that showed them how politics work in the political arena. One participant comments that most of what she learned about politics in college was exactly the kind of politics that operate in the electoral context. As a black student she had to learn how to build alliances with people and find ways to overcome resistance in order to be successful.

Black Women's Conception of Politics

The women in this study reject contemporary definitions of politicians as those who "wheel and deal," in the words of one participant, and "who are corrupt." Instead they embrace the term *public servant* because their core conviction is that true leadership stems from serving those whom one leads rather than striving to gain power and control over them. This is consistent with the notion of "Afritics" derived from a 1998 ethnographic case study of twenty-three Chicago black female political leaders in which the researcher's participants learned about politics from their own lived experience as black women and their interactions with family, church, and community. Likewise, McCluskey (1994) represents another illustration of black female leadership and the relationship existing between such leadership and black women's political consciousness. The multiple levels of consciousness shown in Mary McLeod's leadership are explored by McCluskey. In equal parts educator, politician, and social visionary, Mary McLeod Bethune was one of the most prominent black women of the first half of the twentieth century—and one of the most powerful (Hine & Thompson, 1998). Known as the "First Lady of the Struggle," she devoted her career to improving the lives of black Americans through education and political and economic empowerment, first through the school she founded, Bethune-Cookman College, later as president of the National Council of Negro Women, and then as a top black administrator in the Roosevelt administration (Hine & Thompson, 1998). McCluskey described the overwhelming drive required of Bethune to fulfill multiple expectations in the workplace, family, and community. "In terms of community, black women have a bicultural (or at times polycultural) need to fulfill expectations within the black community and the larger society," observe King and Ferguson (2001, p. 127). Hence, it is the multiple lenses through which black women view the world that not only prepare them for a political life but also influence the way they lead.

In summary, the leadership experiences of the women described in this study show that black women share common features in their leadership. An element consistently identified in existing studies of black women's leadership is their sense of "connectedness." Gostnell defines this sense of connectedness in three ways: (1) "black women's leadership [is] built upon connectedness and responsibility for others"; (2) "their leadership cannot be separated from the private self [and] public/leadership self"; and (3) "[their] leadership [is] embedded and interwoven in [their] daily acts of life" (Gostnell, 1997, p. 202). Finally, black women's experiences of oppression and resistance on the basis of race and gender, from birth to adulthood, indeed shape the way they view the world around them and how they understand their life experiences, experiences that are inherently and systemically political.

Conclusion

Two major conclusions were derived from the findings of this study. First, these women's leadership experiences were grounded in their culture as black American women. It was their informal learning experiences, self-determination, and interactions with family and community, along with their spirituality, that proved the most important in shaping their leadership. Moreover, because of their cultural experiences as black women and their experiences of racism and sexism, common features surfaced in the leadership of the women studied, such as their understanding and awareness of politics being shaped by their Southern heritage and coming of age in the Jim Crow era, and negotiating through the prism of positionality best characterized by the race and gender challenges the participants faced as black women political leaders in Georgia.

The second conclusion drawn is that the black women in this study have a conception of politics that is grounded in their experience of opposition and resistance from birth through adulthood (Brown, 2008; Rosser-Mims, 2005; Stokes-Brown & Dolan, 2010). As a result of such experiences, the study participants developed a political consciousness that uniquely prepared them for political life. In effect, their lived experience of leading lives in opposition and resistance prepared them to apply political analysis as the basis of their worldview.

We conclude that black women initially learn about politics through experience in dealing with oppressive systems that force them to live with unwritten customs and practices that discriminate and compel them to learn how to navigate inequitable power structures. They have found ways of surviving and overcoming barriers based on a dual handicap of race and gender in their everyday experience. Confronting and overcoming such barriers uniquely cultivates and shapes their political consciousness from birth through adulthood, preparing them for political life. This study fills a gap in the literature on black women's leadership development experiences in pursuit of careers in elective office or other roles within the political sphere; it is an effort to help break a cycle of subjugation. The findings of this study will assist researchers and adult educators who offer leadership training by facilitating their endeavors to conduct research and to develop leadership programs that will better prepare black women and, perhaps, other women of color for leadership roles, not only in elective politics but also in other leadership contexts they aspire to enter and in which they have heretofore been underrepresented.

References

Alexander, A. (1999). *Fifty black women who changed America*. New York: Citadel Press.

Alexander, I. E. (1988). Personality, psychological assessment, and psychobiography. In D. P. McAdams & R. L. Ochbert (Eds.), *Psychobiography and life narratives* (pp. 265–294). London: Duke University Press.

Allen, B. (1997). Re-articulation of black female leadership processes, networks and a culture of resistance. *African American Research Perspectives, 7*, 61–67.

Barrett, E. J. (1995). The policy priorities of African American women in state legislatures. *Legislative Studies Quarterly, 20*, 223–247.

Barrett, E. J. (1997). Gender and race in the state house: The legislative experience. *Social Science Journal, 34*(2), 131–146.

Barrett, E. J. (2001). Black women in state legislatures: The relationships of race and gender to the legislative experience. In S. J. Carroll (Ed.), *The impact of women in public office* (pp. 185–204). Bloomington: Indiana University Press.

Brazile, D. (2004). *Stirring the pots in American politics: Cooking with grease.* New York: Simon & Schuster.

Brown, T. L. (2008). "A new era in American politics: Shirley Chisholm and the discourse of identity." *Callaloo, 31*(4), 1013–1025.

Brownmiller, S. (1970). *Shirley Chisholm: A bibliography.* New York: Doubleday.

Button, J., & Hedge, D. (1996). Legislative life in the 1990s: A comparison of black and white state legislators. *Legislative Studies Quarterly, 21*, 199–218.

Chisholm, S. (1970). *Unbought and unbossed.* New York: Avon.

Collins, P. H. (1997). Towards an Afrocentric feminist epistemology. In S. Keys & J. Squires (Eds.), *Feminisms* (pp. 198–206). Oxford: Oxford University Press.

Collins, P. H. (2000). *Black feminist thought: Knowledge, consciousness, and the politics of empowerment.* New York: Routledge.

Cooper, A. J. (2000). *A voice from the south. By a black woman of the south* (Rev. ed.). New York: Negro Universities Press.

Cortazzi, M. (2001). Narrative analysis in ethnography. In P. Atkinson, A. Coffey, S. Delamont, J. Lofland, & L. Lofland (Eds.), *Handbook of ethnography* (pp. 384–394). London: Sage.

DeLany, J., & Rogers, E. (2004). Black women's leadership and learning: From politics to Afritics in the context of community. *Convergence, 36*(2), 91–106.

Denzin, N. K. (1989). *Interpretive biography.* London: Sage.

Elders, J., & Chanoff, D. (1996). *Joycelyn Elders, M.D.: From sharecropper's daughter to Surgeon General of the United States of America.* New York: Wilson Morrison & Company.

Gill, L. M. (1997). *African-American women in Congress: Forming and transforming history.* New Brunswick, NJ: Rutgers University Press.

Githens, M., & Prestage, J. L. (Eds.). (1977). *A portrait of marginality: The political behavior of the American woman.* New York: David McKay.

Glesne, C. (1999). *Becoming qualitative researchers: An introduction.* New York: Longman.

Gostnell, G. M. (1997). The leadership of African-American women: Constructing realities, shifting paradigms. *Dissertation Abstracts International, 57*(08), 235A. (UMI No. AAT 9701103)

Hardy-Fanta, C., Pie-te, L., Pinderhughes, D. M., & Sierra, C. (2006). Gender, race, and descriptive representation in the United States: Findings from the gender and multicultural leadership project. *Journal of Women, Politics & Policy, 28*(3/4), 7–41. doi:10.1300/J501v28n03_02

Hine, D. C., & Thompson, K. (1998). *A shining thread of hope: The history of black women in America.* New York: Broadway Books.

Jordan, B., & Hearon, S. (1979). *Barbara Jordan: A self-portrait.* New York: Doubleday.

Kaba, A. J., & Ward, D. E. (2009). African Americans and U.S. politics: The gradual progress of black women in political representation. *Review of Black Political Economy, 36*(1), 29–50.

King, T. C., & Ferguson, S. A. (2001). Charting ourselves: Leadership development with black professional women. *NWSA, 13*(2), 123–141.

Marble, M. (1990). Groundings with my sisters: Patriarchy and the exploitation of black women. In D. C. Hine (Ed.), *Black women in United States history. Black women's history: Theory and practice* (Vol. 2, pp. 407–439). Brooklyn: Carlson Publishing.

McCluskey, A. T. (1994). Multiple consciousnesses in the leadership of Mary McLeod Bethune. *NWSA Journal, 6*(1), 69–81.

Merriam, S. B. (1998). *Qualitative research and case study applications in education.* San Francisco: Jossey-Bass.

Patton, M. G. (2002). *Qualitative research and evaluation methods.* Thousand Oaks, CA: Sage.

Peshkin, A. (1988). In search of subjectivity: One's own. *Educational Researcher, 7*(17), 17–22.

Philpot, T. S., & Walton, H., Jr. (2007). One of our own: Black female candidates and the voters who support them. *American Journal of Political Science, 51*(1), 49–62. doi:10.1111/j.1540–5907.2007.00236.x

Polkinghorne, D. E. (1995). Narrative configuration in qualitative analysis. In J. A. Hatch & R. Wisniewski (Eds.), *Life history and narrative* (pp. 5–24). London: Falmer Press.

Rice, C. (2011). *No higher honor: A memoir of my years in Washington.* New York: Crown Publishers.

Rogers, E. (1998). An ethnographic case study of Chicago African-American female political leaders: Implications for adult continuing education (Doctoral dissertation, Northern Illinois University, 1998). *Dissertation Abstracts International, 58,* 185.

Rogers, E. (2003). A critical review of the women who served the Congressional Black Caucus: Implications for adult education. *AERC Conference Proceedings. 44th Annual Adult Education Research Conference.* San Francisco State University, June 6–8, 2003.

Rogers, E. E. (2005). Afritics from margin to center: Theorizing the politics of African-American women as political leaders. *Journal of Black Studies, 35*(6), 701–714.

Rosser-Mims, D. (2005). *An exploration of black women's political leadership development* Unpublished doctoral dissertation, University of Georgia, 2005.

Ruderman, M. N., & Hughes-James, M. W. (1998). Leadership development across race and gender. In C. McCauley, R. S. Moxley, & E. Van Velsor (Eds.), *The Center for Creative Leadership handbook for leadership development* (pp. 291–335). San Francisco: Jossey-Bass.

Smooth, W. (2001). Perceptions of influence in state legislatures: A focus on the experiences of African-American women legislators. *Dissertation Abstracts International, 62*(12), 325A. (UMI No. AAT 3035826)

Smooth, W. (2008). Gender, race, and the exercise of power and influence. In B. Reingold (Ed.), *Legislative women: Getting elected, getting ahead.* Boulder, CO: Lynne Rienner.

Smooth, W. (2010). Intersectionalities of race and gender and leadership. In K. P. O'Connor (Ed.), *Gender and women's leadership: A reference handbook* (pp. 31–40). Thousand Oaks, CA: Sage.

Stokes-Brown, A., & Dolan, K. (2010). Race, gender, and symbolic representation: African American female candidates as mobilizing agents. *Journal of Elections, Public Opinion & Parties, 20*(4), 473–494. doi: 10.1080/17457289.2010.511806

Chapter Eight

Leadership Lessons from the Criminal World

Jeanne Martinson

Leadership is not an easy job in today's world. The complexity of organizations and the diversity of employees compel leaders to look to the oddest quarters to gain new and enlightening leadership wisdom. Certainly looking to criminal leaders for wisdom to manage corporate environments would be considered odd. It would be equally odd to consider criminal leaders as chief executive officers, but criminal leaders do, in fact, lead organizations, albeit illegitimate or illegal ones. Like their counterparts in legitimate organizations, criminal leaders seek to attract, retain, and engage their workforce.

The dictionary defines *organization* as "the state of being organized, an organized body, systemic arrangement" and *organized crime* as "widespread criminal activity organized under powerful leadership" (*Canadian Oxford Dictionary*, 1998, p. 1024). Criminal leaders are leaders of organizations in which illegal behavior is the primary source of activity, and all personnel involved in the organization are fully aware that their activities are primarily illegal. North American examples of such organizations would be street gangs, outlaw motorcycle gangs, and Italian crime organizations (Nathanson Centre on Transnational Human Rights, Crime and Security, 2006, ¶81).

This chapter is based on existing literature and research conducted with corrections workers and social service workers who have firsthand experience observing gang leaders. The criminal leaders who were observed by the research participants for this project were street gang leaders in the Province of Saskatchewan in Canada. My purpose with this research was to address the question, "How do criminal leaders behave that allows them to attract, retain, and engage an effective workforce?" In this chapter I will discuss the leadership traits of effective corporate and gang leaders found in current literature, the findings of the study, and the comparison of the leadership traits of effective criminal and corporate leaders.

Corporate Leadership Traits That Attract and Retain

Historically, researchers are beginning "to define an integrative conceptual framework that encompass[es] all of the relevant [leadership] traits" (Yukl, 2006, p. 69). Leadership trait analysis, such as the work done by Kouzes and Posner (2007) and the GLOBE study discussed in Grove's (2005) report, attest to the fact that leadership characteristics, traits, and behaviors can be studied and evaluated. According to Kotter (1990), leaders have three responsibilities: to set direction, align people, and ultimately to motivate and inspire others toward the fulfillment of the leader's vision or direction. Setting direction means determining vision and the overarching strategies to achieve that vision. Aligning people is about finding the best match between people and the vision, not just managing the best match between positions and staff. Motivating and inspiring is about change, and leaders must connect with others at a fundamental level where they instill a sense of belonging and enthusiasm for the big dream.

To achieve this leadership formula espoused by Kotter, a person must be an "authentic leader" who possesses character and competence. An effective framework for an authentic leader, therefore, would include the essential character elements of self-discipline, courage, and ethical behavior as well as the competence elements of insight and influence (Martinson, 2001).

Character

Self-discipline is essential for leaders to continue learning and growing as people and leaders. Eventually leaders confront difficult tasks and problems, and it takes self-discipline to push through the wall of procrastination and frustration to the other side. "Excellence in anything—whether it's leadership, music, sports, or engineering—requires disciplined practice" (Kouzes & Posner, 2007, p. xiii). Leadership can be learned and steps toward mastery taken. Leaders can be made and developed.

Another area of self-discipline that connects to influence and ethics is self-discipline in the ethical use of the trappings of power that often accompany leadership and management roles. An authentic leader must be able to explain how she uses organizational resources for the betterment of others and not solely for the benefit of herself.

The second element to character is courage and is required in three areas: accountability, self-knowledge, and power sharing. "The only one who is able to hold the organization accountable is the leader" (De Pree, 1997, p. 5). A leader cannot delegate the role of final oversight. The leader is the one who is ultimately responsible. To take responsibility in positive situations is easy to do, but to take responsibility in negative situations often requires courage.

It also takes courage to be willing to look clearly and deeply into who we are and why we respond to others and interpret the world in the fashion that we do. Challenging our mental models is essential for effective leadership (Senge, 2006). If a leader is unwilling to "look inward" (p. 8), as Senge suggested, the response is limited to that of defensiveness. Self-knowledge should help with the willingness to share power and information within the system. If "the primary purpose of power is not to use it, but to share it" (De Pree, 1997, p. 8), then one's courage welcomes a vulnerability to talents and decisions of others.

Ethical behavior, the third element of character, involves living our values and taking the needs and rights of others into consideration. Ethical behavior is about "struggling to develop a well-informed conscience, being true to ourselves and what we stand for, having the courage to explore challenging questions and accepting the consequences" (Ross, 2000, p. 2). The challenge occurs when our ethics collide with the behavior of those around us or pressure is exerted from above or below to conform to behavior that is not in alignment with our own values. Then ethical behavior requires courage as well if we wish to stand up for what we profess.

Leaders set the tone for an organization and its employees and, therefore, must ensure that they consistently demonstrate the espoused ethics of their organization. All employees should be held to the same standard; however, leaders must ensure they are seen as role models in this area (Kouzes & Posner, 2007). If employees experience a dichotomy between the professed ethics of their leader and their experience of them, they may then develop mistrust and eventually the forward movement of the leader is lost. This results in a lack of employee retention and engagement.

Competence

Insight, an element of competence, is more than vision; it is an ability for leaders to see 360 degrees around themselves. An effective leader with vision focuses on three questions: What happened in the past? What is happening right now? What might happen in the future? Insight involves understanding the combination of oneself, plus one's employees, organization, industry, relevant global and political forces, and possible change. Insight is required to envision change and the rethinking of an organization by asking good questions and being open to answers from everywhere and anyone.

A second element of competence is influence over others. "Leadership has been defined in many different ways, but most definitions share the assumption that it involves an influence process concerned with facilitating the performance of a collective task" (Yukl, 2006, p. 20). Influencing behaviors include building a shared vision, welcoming and accepting challenge from subordinates, supporting new ideas, encouraging others in their learning and growing, and giving appropriate positive and negative feedback. These are all skills that can be developed to a high level of competency if leaders are willing to identify their personal skill gaps and hone their abilities.

Last, leaders with exceptional influence can manage conflict, not only in homogeneous groups but also across diversity barriers (Gerzon, 2006). In our complex world, Gerzon suggests that leaders must understand that ever-present conflict is an outcome of different needs, cultures, and agendas.

Effective leadership is not simple. A leadership behavior framework is complex and must contain these essential elements such that if any one of these elements were missing the loss would endanger the leader's success. Insight is not enough. It only adds to a person's intelligence. Courage alone may send one enthusiastically in the wrong direction. Influence alone may mean one is taking others collectively down the wrong path. Self-discipline or ethics alone will not provide the momentum to move forward. All five of the elements that combine for competence and character are vital to authentic leadership, which compels success.

Gang Leader Traits That Attract and Retain

The traits gang leaders possess that assist them in attracting and retaining members are their ability to exploit marginalized potential recruits, to recruit in fruitful locations, to create a structured and parallel society, and to encourage hope for a successful future.

Ability to Exploit Marginalized Potential Recruits

The environment in which most potential gang members live creates a lack of hope for a successful future in the mainstream world. The presence, for example, of racial stereotypes that Aboriginal gang members internalize affect whether gang members can see that "experiences of poverty and abuse are an outcome of impersonal forces and policies rather than personal actions by oneself, one's parents or one's community" (Deane, Bracken, & Morrissette, 2007, p. 136). For potential gang members from a marginalized group not to join a gang would involve a "cognitive change of seeing oneself as not conforming to a negative stereotype . . . moving from a position of being excluded from social opportunities to seeing oneself as deserving to be included" (Deane, Bracken, & Morrissette, p. 136).

In an environment that creates a belief that success in mainstream society is unattainable, gang activity is a means to a livelihood for the gang member who does not recognize other economic opportunities (Hagedorn, 2002). Potential Aboriginal gang members already live lives characterized by social isolation, so building trust with mainstream society that would lead to employment opportunities is challenging (Deane, Bracken, & Morrissette, 2007).

Ability to Recruit in Fruitful Locations

The community where potential gang members live affects their potential of becoming involved in gangs. Key recruiting characteristics (Meares & Kahan, 1998) are "the level of supervision of teenage peer groups, the prevalence of friendship networks and the level of neighbourhood participation in formal and voluntary organizations" (p. 809). Meares and Kahan noted that without these characteristics of a healthy neighborhood, potential gang members look to each other for the support that should be coming from adults in their environment. The gang members then place their loyalty and support in the hands of their peers and create their own codes of behavior. Levitt and Venkatesh (2000), who studied gangs in the United States, state that communities with high gang membership had the socioeconomic factors of higher numbers of single-parent families, higher unemployment, lower income levels, lower education achievement, and less home ownership.

Ability to Create a Structured, Parallel Society

Gang leaders create a parallel culture to mainstream society. "The culture of the gang is composed of a set of attitudes that portrays the gang in a positive light and paints a hostile picture of outsiders" (Liu, 2004, p. 52). This creates a vision of a safe place, a bastion against the enemy that has already discarded the marginalized citizen. Liu also describes the gang as a place where members can freely be themselves, where a male can be a "man" (p. 52), not affected by the gender equity of mainstream society and, therefore, free to exhibit extreme masculine characteristics such as aggression and violence without censure.

Gang leaders create organizations that parallel mainstream society to address the individual's unconscious desire for structure. Many gangs are similar to legal organizations of similar size (Baker, Gibbs, & Holmstrom, 1994) with central leadership; there are local gang leaders with specific territories, officers, foot soldiers, and gang members on the fringe.

Ability to Create Hope for Success in the Future

Gang leaders maintain the hope of possible higher income. There are more foot soldiers or regular gang members to officers and more officers to leaders, yet the hope of rising to the top is encouraged. Weisfeld and Feldman (1982) interviewed a former gang leader who stated that employment opportunities in "many urban areas are insufficiently appealing to compete effectively with the attractions of street crime and its associated value system" (p. 581). Young people adopt the criminal lifestyle because the quick money is appealing and because they see available jobs to be "boring, dangerous, low paying, humiliating and dead-end" (p. 581).

Methodology

The purpose of this research was to identify behaviors of gang leaders. My intent was to address the question, "How do criminal leaders behave that allows them to attract, retain, and engage an effective workforce?" The "collaborative approach to inquiry or investigation" (Stringer, 2007, p. 8), known as *action research*, was the methodology used in this study. Action research engaged the research participants from the studied system as part of the research team, not merely subjects being analyzed. Qualitative data was gained from the two data collection methods of anecdote circles and interview matrices.

Research Participants

The two groups selected to participate as research participants were corrections officers working in reduced custody facilities and probation officers in the community. Reduced custody facilities are more commonly known as halfway houses, where the convicted person lives between full incarceration in a jail or prison and full release or release with probation. Probation officers work with the gang leaders in the community once they have been released from custody. To arrive at a more complete picture of gang leader behavior, the distinction between these two separate but related research participant groups is important. Gang leaders may behave quite differently when they are being closely observed versus when they are not incarcerated or in reduced custody situations. The individual research participants were selected on the criteria of having close or regular contact with gang leaders, not merely gang members.

If I were to address a research question regarding employee retention and engagement in a noncriminal organizational setting, the research participants would include that organization's leaders and the leaders' subordinates. The benefits to the leaders and their organization in understanding leadership behavior are fairly easily determined and explained. However, in a criminal organization, interviewing leaders and those who report to them is a much more challenging endeavor. There is limited benefit for a gang leader to engage in research that could lead to incarceration, censorship from his organizational members, or a possible loss of power. Data gained directly from past gang leaders is challenging as well because of the difficulty in identifying participants, connecting with them for research purposes, and minimizing any physical risk for them as participants or for the primary researcher. Probation and corrections officers were identified as the most appropriate research participants because they are accessible and spend a great deal of their workday time observing and interacting with gang members and gang leaders.

Data Collection

Two research methods for data collection were used. I developed and used interview matrices with the probation officer research participants. I also used an anecdote circle with the corrections officers in the reduced custody facility research participant group.

Interview Matrices. An interview matrix is a data collection tool in which a large amount of data can be systematically collected from a large group of people. This process allows input from all the participants regardless of status in the group. An interview matrix also allows for systematic data collection, analysis from the research participants themselves, immediate label affixing, and simultaneous recording of the process and findings (Chartier, 2002). Due to the immediacy of the process, by the end of the exercise everyone in the room had an understanding of the knowledge every other person in the room had on the specific questions addressed.

An interview matrix was used with the probation officers and included the following four questions:

- What behaviors do gang leaders display—what have you observed (seen, heard) from gang leaders that you would consider positively or negatively influences their ability to attract, retain, and engage their workforce?
- How do other gang members respond to these behaviors of gang leaders?
- What beliefs have gang leaders communicated to you regarding their leadership?
- What are your beliefs about gang leaders as to their leadership abilities?

Four interview matrices were facilitated in four different communities with four, six, seven, and twelve research participants respectively, for a total of twenty-nine participants. Citations throughout this document identify the community location and the participant number. For example, *NB1* identifies the first research participant who registered and the community from which he comes. The research participants in the anecdote circle were identified alphabetically according to the order they registered as participants, with the first participant coded as A, the second as B, and so on.

Anecdote Circle.   An anecdote circle was the second method used for data collection. Anecdote circles are a guided method to gain data through storytelling. An anecdote circle is similar to a focus group in that it is a small-group process led by a facilitator (Callahan, Schenk, & Rixon, 2006), but an anecdote circle is less "concerned with the group's opinions and judgments. Rather it seeks to elicit experiences, anecdotes and stories"

(Callahan, Schenk, & Rixon, 2006, p. 6). One anecdote circle was facilitated in one location and included five reduced-custody workers. The research participants responded to the following prompts: "Tell me a story about an interaction you had with a gang leader. Focus on where he affected others in his desire to attract, retain, or engage others as a leader. Were other gang members or possible gang members present? How did they respond?"

Data Analysis

The data collected from the interview matrix were in the form of the flip chart sheets of summarized and themed data completed by the research participants, memos taken by me during the process, and the original interview forms where notes were taken by each interviewer of the responses to their questions from those they interviewed in the matrix. Data collected during the anecdote circle were in the form of audiorecordings and memos. I took the memos, or short notes of reflection, during the data collection.

The first step of analysis was the cross-referencing of the memos and audiorecording transcription from the anecdote circle. This was also to create the most complete record of the process. The second step of analysis was the cross-referencing of the flip chart sheets, individual interview sheets, and my researcher notes from the interview matrices. In the third step in the analysis, I looked at the findings first from the interview matrices and then from the anecdote circles, identifying themes, repetitions, and outlying ideas.

The complete data from both methods were cross-referenced using the constant comparative method as described by Glaser and Strauss (1967). With the constant comparative method, I sorted the data as to what is the same and what is different among the information. Then the data were sorted and sifted for themes, and labels were affixed. Two questions, for example, that were asked to guide my decision-making process were, "How do the themes relate?" and "Is one behavior causal for another?" The final step in analysis was to see the data through the lens of spiral dynamics (Beck & Cowan, 1996) and to identify any further relationships and patterns before drawing on all of the findings to determine the conclusions. Beck and Cowan describe a concept of differing value systems that could be present in an organization. Leaders who understand where their organization's value system currently is can manage at that level or move up or down the rainbow, or spiral, if they have the skill to do so.

Research Findings

The findings of my research are grouped under two segments: gang attraction and retention and engagement of gang members. Direct and indirect quotes from research participants are included.

Gang Attraction

Occasionally gang members are born into gang life; their parents or older siblings are leaders in the gang and it is a given that they will embrace the gang life. To not be involved in gang life in this situation would often require people to emotionally and geographically distance themselves from their gang family. To resist gang involvement and stay in the community would "often attract threats and violence to themselves" (NB1). Generally, gang members are enticed or threatened into the gang. I discovered that possible gang members are enticed mainly for the opportunity to work with a powerful leader, for belonging, and for financial success.

A Golden Opportunity. Gang leaders offer benefits that the potential gang member believes he could not realize otherwise. These benefits include "access to women, drugs and alcohol, firearms and other weapons, money, a kind of family and protection" (R4). The most important of these benefits in the recruiting stage are "protection, a kind of family, and money" (R3).

Many potential gang members are attracted to the gang simply because of the promise of safety, protection, and the food and shelter necessary for survival (NB5, PA2, R3, R6, R11). The research participants shared several examples wherein youth were pulled into gangs simply because they "perceive no other option to staying safe" (PA3). The opposite behaviors of gang leaders may create the same result. If a gang leader wishes to recruit a specific person into his gang and that specific person is resisting joining the gang, the gang leader will use negative behaviors to achieve the goal of recruitment. Through threats or violence against the potential member or the potential member's family, the gang leader creates no option for potential recruits, so they join to keep themselves and their family members safe (PA1, PA2).

Gang leaders are intelligent in identifying vulnerabilities in potential recruits: "They create a sense of family for young people who are alienated from their own families. They create an environment of fun and partying for people who struggle with boundaries. The gang leader's charismatic personality creates a sense of confidence in those [who] lack confidence" (R1).

Recruits see senior gang members and the gang leader as being financially successful. In the recruiting stage, a gang leader will be more generous with a recruit financially, encouraging the recruit to spend the money quickly and promising increases in the future once he has been in the gang longer (NB6).

Mystique and Reputation of the Gang Leader. Research participants described a successful gang leader as one who has a "good reputation for protection, good connections to supplies of women and drugs, is good at crime and doesn't get caught, can deliver good gang supports to his members including physical protection" (R3). Research participants agreed on leadership traits of gang leaders such as "charismatic, convincing, intelligent, and organized" (LR1, LR4). However, the gang leader is also seen as one who is ruthless, who will follow through on his threats and would use intimidation to bring in new members (NB2).

A successful gang leader separates himself from mainstream society, portraying himself as an "anarchist" (LR6), above and separate from a society that may have been unsupportive of the gang member. Part of the attraction to the gang is to be "outside the system, part of a tight-knit group . . . where it is all for one and one for all" (LR3).

Gang leaders believe that "laws do not affect them" (R6). They believe that if justice needs to be carried out it is within their power and within their purview. "They take their leadership personally and think it is their responsibility to right the wrongs in the gangs" (LR6). A gang leader believes it is his role to "protect himself and others from harm" (PA4) and "care for his gang members" (PA3). He believes he has the "best interest of his members at heart" (NB3) and sees himself as "the father figure or alpha figure keeping the pack together" (LR1).

Rituals of Belonging. A gang leader creates "rituals and ceremonies" (LR4) to address the unconscious needs for belonging and identity. The leader creates a culture outside of the mainstream culture, which is supported with identifying marks and symbols. This is seen in tattoos, art, tagging (graffiti), and colors (NB4). Additionally, an adult gang member cannot get into the juvenile detention system, so gang leaders depend on underage gang members to recruit within its walls. Being in a juvenile detention facility exposes a potential gang member to other youth who may already be in the gang. "A kid goes in and the next thing they know they are sitting with a kid who is working their magic. They ask, 'Do you have a place to live when you get out? Do you have money when you get out? We can help you out'" (B).

Retention and Engagement of Gang Members

It is as essential to retain members and encourage them to take on more serious illegal activities as it is to first recruit them into the organization. To retain and engage gang members in the difficult and dangerous work of the gang, leaders establish organization from chaos, lead with fear and enticement, manage their emotions, and create strong negative consequence to poor performance.

Establish Organization from Chaos. The gang is an organized, hierarchal system in which the gang leader delegates to the lieutenants or middle managers of the organization. The lieutenants are the ones who ensure the work of the gang is done and that everyone pulls his weight. The lieutenants have "soldiers, recruiters, runners, and enforcers" (NB2) to assist in achieving the goals of the gang leader. The research participants saw gang leaders as organized. "They have to be able to organize, delegate and supervise their members. Leaders have to have good problem-solving skills and possess exceptional cognitive abilities" (PA2).

A gang leader believes that he runs his organization well, his leadership is deserved, and "he is the best one to be in control" (NB7). He also believes that the extensive control used is "necessary" (NB7). As the leader, it is important that the gang leader is protected. Gang leaders believe that their members desire to and will protect them, even "taking the rap for them or taking the fall for them" (PA2). Gang leaders see themselves as being feared, but at the same time "well liked" (R4).

Balance the Carrot and the Stick. Gang leaders use enticement and punishment interchangeably to guarantee that gang members remain in the gang and do what is necessary for the good of the gang and the gang leader. Alternating between promises of monetary opportunities and "fear tactics to intimidate anyone thinking of leaving" (R8) is a successful strategy. This leadership style is seen as a positive one and the gang's middle managers see this intimidation by their leader as "powerful and something to emulate if they want to eventually achieve the same power" (R7) as the leader. As an encouraging carrot strategy, gang leaders have "taught people to earn quick money with little skill" (NB4) and continue to promote the possibility of further income, which has a positive effect on retention.

Communicate According to the Audience and Manage Their Emotions. Gang leaders are intelligent and know when to behave in a docile, conciliatory, aggressive, or ruthless manner. Depending on the person with whom a gang leader is communicating and the goal of the interaction, his behavior may be radically different. A gang leader must be able to switch communication and leadership styles as their needs of the moment demand. This skill is very important, and without it, or without the self-discipline to develop it, a gang member will not rise to the top of the organization.

Gang leaders have the skills to manage their emotions and maintain respectful relationships with those in the jail system, unlike gang members who might not have the emotional control or maturity to do so. A research participant commented on gang leaders' ability to maintain their emotional balance: "You would have to really push a gang leader to get [him] to snap" (C). Another research participant described the unlikelihood of a particular lower-level gang member rising to a top leadership spot in the gang: "I can see that he would be a worker that you would want to be on your side as an intimidator or enforcer. But he couldn't control himself at the top" (B).

The flexibility of behavior of gang leaders is evident when they are incarcerated. Their acquiescent, positive behavior is partly to ensure their safety, partly to maintain the gang leader persona, and partly to ensure their privileges are maintained so they can continue their business from inside (A, C, D). To keep a clean record inside and still access drugs and control their system, gang leaders use other incarcerated gang members.

Create Consequences to Poor Performance. Several research participants described the instant and extreme conse- quences of nonperformance of gang members (A, B, C, E). "If you don't do it, your family is going to get beat. You are going to get beat. You are going to lose your position if you don't get the job done" (C). Often the lieutenants have flexibility on how the work gets done, but sometimes they do not. "Sometimes, there are specific orders, like break his kneecaps or cut off his fingers. If you don't there are repercussions" (C).

Lieutenants are not outside of having to perform against their best judgment or conscience. "It is not unusual for you to have a good friend and if the boss says you have to whack her, you just do it. You don't like it but you do it. Your life and the lives of your family depend on it" (B).

Conclusion

After analyzing my findings, I made several conclusions that I will discuss in the following sections. Gang leaders exploit the perceived lack of choice of potential and current gang members. Gang leaders and corporate leaders can both be mentored and developed as leaders. Gang leaders enter and exit leadership roles earlier than their corporate equivalents, but both corporate and gang leaders engage in entrepreneurial leadership early. Finally, effective gang and corporate leaders understand and adapt to multiple value systems and worldviews.

Gang Leaders Exploit Others' Lack of Choice

Gang leaders exploit the perceived lack of choice of potential and current gang members. Gang leaders succeed because many potential gang members have little, or perceive they have little, choice but to be part of gang life, so the gang leaders capitalize on the marginalization that potential gang members' experience. Gang leaders use appealing promises as well as violence and intimidation to attract and retain their workforce. Because potential gang members may feel that there is no place but the gang to ensure their safety, survival, and financial well-being, gang leaders are at an advantage in attracting and retaining new members as well as increasing the criminality of existing gang members.

Only in a few situations in corporate recruitment and retention does the perception of lack of choice exist. If there is only one industry in a community and employees wish to stay in that community, they may feel they have no choice but to join that organization. Second, if an employee has limited skills and education but works his way up through an organization, he may feel he has no option but to stay in the organization because there are no other well-paying choices outside of his current employment. In both these cases, this perceived or real lack of choice allows leaders the opportunity to lead in ways that are dominating and autocratic, with little regard for employees.

Gang and Corporate Leaders: Born and Made

As in legitimate corporate life, a leader often has an advantage being born into the family business. However, even if a gang leader is raised in a gang environment, that fact alone is not enough to guarantee a leadership role (A, D, E). Gang leaders have a powerful belief in their own authority, entitlement, and abilities and do not believe that society is able or willing to protect or provide meaningful, profitable employment for their members. Yet, as in corporate leadership, gang leaders must be able to learn and grow, honing their communication and leadership skills. The literature supports this idea. To excel in any field, disciplined practice is required (Kouzes & Posner, 2007). Therefore, leaders, criminal or not, are born and can be made and developed.

Gang Leaders Enter and Exit Leadership Roles Earlier

Gang leaders join the workforce in their teens and rise up to leadership roles. By the time the gang member becomes the leader, he is usually an adult (A, B, C, D, E). To be successful in this role, he has learned leadership skills from watching others and leveraging his natural abilities and intelligence. Most corporate leaders, however, enter senior management roles after several years of formal education and a decade or more of working in lower positions. By the time a gang leader is thinking about getting out of the gang, disappearing "into the background" (C), or becoming less visible, a corporate leader is barely hitting his stride and becoming a visible, powerful leader.

Corporate and Gang Leaders Enter Entrepreneurship Early

Entrepreneurship is often a young person's game for both gang and corporate leaders. New gang leaders emerge when a gang member finds himself unhappy with the direction or leadership of the gang or his own slow progress to the top (C, D, E). In the corporate world, where a younger person finds his creativity stifled or career path stalled, one too might stretch out and start his own venture. Whereas in the corporate arena, the new entrepreneur might be more creative than the organization he left, the gang entrepreneur is often "more violent" (B) than his previous gang and impatient with advice or warnings from leaders older than himself (B).

This research has implications to society in its goal to reduce gang leader influence and implications to corporate leaders in their goal to increase influence with employees. The community where potential gang members live affects their potential of becoming gang involved; to alleviate this situation, supervision by adults of teenagers plus neighborhood involvement in formal and voluntary organizations were identified as key characteristics in minimizing gang involvement (Meares & Kahan, 1998). Without this kind of support, youth are more likely to place their loyalty in the hands of their peers and create their own code of behavior.

The challenges of creating community activities, structured and run by parents and other involved adults, is a challenge in every neighborhood. There are additional barriers for parents of children at risk of being involved in gangs. Parents might be less likely to have available financial resources to put their children into formal sports or activities. Parents of children at risk may also lack the contacts or resources to put a plan for organized activities into action.

Three key strategies that gang leaders employ to attract and retain their workforce that corporate leaders could adopt or adapt are to create an organization that has its own identity through rituals of belonging, to create reasonable consequences to poor performance, and to communicate according to the audience and manage their emotions effectively. Certainly some corporate leaders embrace these strategies already, but the importance of all three combined are effective strategies among gang leaders that would be effective in corporate settings.

Leadership lessons can be gained from any milieu—even the criminal underworld. Leaders who look beyond their familiar academic, corporate, government, or nonprofit system may find value in embracing the lessons of leaders of crime.

References

Baker, G., Gibbs, M., & Holmstrom, B. (1994). The wage policy of a firm. *Quarterly Journal of Economics, 109*(4), 921–955.

Beck, D., & Cowan, C. (1996). *Spiral dynamics: Mastering values, leadership and change.* Malden, MA: Blackwell.

Callahan, S., Schenk, M., & Rixon, A. (2006). *The ultimate guide to anecdote circles.* [White paper] Retrieved from www.anecdote.com.au/papers/Ultimate_Guide_to_ACs_v1.0.pdf

Canadian Oxford Dictionary. (1998). Don Mills, ON, Canada: Oxford University Press.

Chartier, B. (2002). *Blueprints: Field guide for learning organization practitioners.* Retrieved from www.managers-gestionnaires.gc.ca/documents/chartier/blueprint_e.pdf

De Pree, M. (1997). The leader's legacy: A conversation with Max De Pree. *Leader to Leader, 5,* 8.

Deane, L., Bracken, D. C., & Morrissette, L. (2007). Desistance within an urban Aboriginal gang. *Probation Journal, 54*(2), 125–141.

Gerzon, M. (2006). *Leading through conflict: How successful leaders transform differences into opportunities.* New York: Harvard Business School Press.

Glaser, B., & Strauss, A. (1967). *The discovery of grounded theory: Strategies for qualitative research.* Chicago: Aldine.

Grove, C. N. (2005). *Introduction to the GLOBE research project on leadership worldwide.* Retrieved from www.grovewell.com/pub-GLOBE-intro.html

Hagedorn, J. M. (2002). Gangs and the informal economy. In C. R. Huff (Ed.), *Gangs in America III* (pp. 101–120). Thousand Oaks, CA: Sage.

Kotter, J. (1990). What leaders really do. *Harvard Business Review, 69*(5), 103–111.

Kouzes, J., & Posner, B. (2007). *A leadership challenge.* San Francisco: Jossey-Bass.

Levitt, S. D., & Venkatesh, S. A. (2000). An economic analysis of a drug-selling gang's finances. *The Quarterly Journal of Economics, 115*(3), 766–789.

Liu, J. (2004). Subcultural values, crime, and negative social capital for Chinese offenders. *International Criminal Justice Review, 14,* 49–68.

Martinson, J. (2001). *Escape from Oz—Leadership for the 21st century.* Regina, SK, Canada: Martrain.

Meares, T. L., & Kahan, D. M. (1998). Law and (norms of) order in the inner city. *Law and Society Review, 32*(4), 805–838.

Nathanson Centre on Transnational Human Rights, Crime and Security. (2006). *Organized crime in Canada, A quarterly summary.* Retrieved from www.osgoode.yorku.ca/NathansonBackUp/Current Events/2006_Q3.htm#OMGS

Ross, S. (2000). *What is the value of ethics?* Retrieved from www.ethics.org.au/ethics-articles/what-value-ethics

Senge, P. (2006). *The fifth discipline: The art & practice of the learning organization.* Toronto, ON, Canada: Currency/Doubleday.

Stringer, E. (2007). *Action research* (3rd ed.). Thousand Oaks, CA: Sage.

Weisfeld, G. E., & Feldman, R. (1982). A former street gang leader reinterviewed eight years later. *Crime and Delinquency, 28*(4), 567–581.

Yukl, G. (2006). *Leadership in organizations* (Custom 6th ed.). Upper Saddle River, NJ: Pearson Custom Publishing.

Chapter Nine

Soccer Tactics and Complexity Leadership

Michael S. Lane, Kathleen Patterson, and Paul B. Carr

The game of soccer is of great fascination to many people around the world. The rather fast-paced flurry of strategy, design, and interactions provide great entertainment yet are quite purposeful toward a literal goal. The interesting observation here is that this mystery of engagement follows many of the same themes that we see in the complexities of leadership. This chapter tells the story of a leader who must negotiate a complicated overseas venture and how the world of soccer sheds light on his success.

Today, the learning that many international companies are being asked to engage in is not proactive, discretionary, or generative. It is not initiated by a great learning organization (LO) seminar or an inspirational CEO. Often, dynamic global markets are driving businesses to learn on the run as they relocate overseas in search of lower production costs. As the CEO in this chapter explained, the company is "facing extinction, we're looking at getting over there [to China] now with all possible speed" and "we don't have a two-year plan. We're reacting." His VP in charge of manufacturing added, "A big company has perhaps the muscle and financial ability to move into China in a brute force way. . . . We're not like that. . . . We've got to go in and do it right the first time."

Case Study: An Electric Component Company

Over a five-year period, between 1999 and 2004, a small electronic component factory in the United States had experienced a very volatile business environment. This company's products were distributed worldwide and it had assembly contract relationships with companies in Taiwan and China. Sales and market indicators were usually positive, at least until the Asian economic downturn in 1999. This collapse, the expiration of patent rights, and the subsequent rise of competitors in Asia supported by extremely cheap labor pressured the family business owners to launch a wholly owned subsidiary in Asia. The move was complex. Critical learning arenas included safeguarding expertise, interdepartmental cooperation, downsizing the stateside operation, coordinating transcontinental shipping, global communication, and cross-cultural leadership. Because of this complex set of challenges, I was invited into the organization to provide assistance as a cross-cultural business consultant.

During initial interviews, the CEO described the organization as a family business. This leader's informal, face-to-face style underscored the warm, relational qualities of the family. His father, the founder, had been an engineer, and in the early years engineering technology specialists led the organization. Over time, however, the engineering emphasis reached a plateau and extreme market pressures caused manufacturing and customer-driven strategies to take center stage in the organization. The son of the founding CEO had a background in sales, and he gave direction to the company by leading a team of VP-level manufacturing experts and engineers.

Initially, interviews revealed a faltering business, a business that should not have survived the complexity of a move overseas. Risky attempts to keep the operation stateside had failed and left the company with limited resources for an overseas venture. Paradoxically, over a three-year period the organization handled uncertainty and learning well enough to turn the company around and declare a success; that is, the critical trajectory of the company's development was moving in a positive direction, production was leveraged to compete long term in the market, and the leadership had a hopeful, workable strategy. As the story unfolded, analysis revealed unresolved gaps in the organization's learning profile, at least in terms of the conventional principles of the learning organization movement. I began to wonder what mitigated these weaknesses. Were more tacit aspects of leading organizational learning responsible for buoying up this company and neutralizing the effects of some of its poor learning postures? I wanted to know and understand.

As a cross-cultural consultant, I decided to launch an exploratory qualitative investigation that I hoped would explain this organization's surprising success. Opportunities arose to pursue qualitative inquiry through taped, open-ended interviews, e-mail records, and additional conversations that were transcribed into notes. Observations spanned a three-year period.

The Company Should Have Failed

In light of several key success indicators—commitment to learning, a vision for change, low appreciation or rewards for innovation, and so on—the company should have failed. It should no longer be in business.

Poor Commitment to Learning. Organizational learning calls for top leadership to have a strong and purposeful vision for change (Senge, 1990). Though early interviews with the CEO revealed a leader with a sense of urgency about the move overseas, his learning organization and complexity leadership appeared hesitant and weak. Initially, I measured the personal ambiguity tolerance of the company's managers using the AT-20 (MacDonald, 1970). Comparatively speaking, the CEO's tolerance for ambiguity was low, indicating a robust distaste for uncertainty and change. His aversion for moving into unknown territory was compounded by a very limited commitment to learning. The CFO explained, "We have always reacted . . . and this is due to the fact that if we can make three million and keep production in the States and have the possibility of making five million in

China, we would choose the former—family values and low aggressiveness of stockholders [is the cause]. . . . We've not been good at thinking forward and being big-picture people. We're a small family-owned business that has gotten into the international world because everybody else around us is gone." Adding to this low commitment to learning was the fact that the initial vision from the top was questionable. In fact, at first the CEO revealed in interviews that his dream for the executive team was not to create a long-term sustainable business but to raise levels of productivity high enough to "sell the company and make money . . . [so that] everybody, all the top guys who worked . . . would share in that, for their loyalty and their hard work." The CEO was involved emotionally; he felt a personal commitment to executive staff and family stockholders; however, he seemed uncommitted to the risk taking and learning required to create a viable business in a new dynamic, global environment.

Lack of Appreciation and Rewards for Innovators. Inertia and fear of the unknown often hinder change within an organization, but successful leaders of innovation will reward and appreciate those who are spearheading the new business initiative (Bandura, 1997; Kline & Saunders, 1998). Yet, by his own admission, the CEO was not personally ready to lead a learning organization into the new venture; however, he felt compelled to move forward and by the end of the first year, crises emerged that reflected a lack of appreciation and rewards for those shouldering the entrepreneurial start-up. An emotional e-mail response from the China-side chief engineer to a home office manager reflected this lack of appreciative support for the innovative move overseas. He said, "I WOULD APPRECIATE IT IF YOU WOULD ADDRESS ME IN YOUR RESPONSES TO MY EMAILS. IT IS A COMMON DECENCY." [Capital letters in original e-mail.] This kind of exchange is probably often found in communications between people in stressful situations and, by itself, the text has little meaning, but it was part of a larger cluster of comments. The stateside staff admitted that he himself had "no idea" about the Chinese managerial situation he spoke about everyday through e-mail. This lack of understanding was perhaps why the China-side Western managers would send the following e-mail back to the home office. It seemed the staff in China felt the stateside manager did not appreciate the cross-cultural risks and pressures that an innovative move entails. "If these . . . reports are useless to you then I will STOP copying you. . . . Please remember that we are starting up a new factory and there are many things to do, people to train, and things to get set up. There are TWO of us [the GM and the chief engineer] trying to do all of this and we are doing the best we can. You will get your reports soon enough. Be happy that we actually got our shipment out ON TIME. Thanks for your praise, encouragement, and support!" What came through in this sarcastic e-mail was that the stateside manager did not understand or appreciate the pressures and the level of innovation challenges in the China plant. A culture that supported innovation would have created better conditions for supporting the company's cross-cultural innovators and would have educated stateside leaders regarding the overseas staff's valued expertise in meeting such a complex cross-cultural challenge.

Though it was difficult, the CEO found an in-company chief engineer and an Australian general manager for the China plant. The CEO admitted they were unique because of their high qualifications and willingness to accept the overseas assignment. Their special expertise and courage were a cause for praise and a cause for anxiety because the company had no backup plan if the two decided to leave China. Ironically, although their cross-cultural entrepreneurial competency was highly valued in the company, compensation did not sometimes match up with these assessments. The CEO revealed in conversation that the China-side GM was not paid like other staff. In fact, the Australian GM was not as highly paid as the China-side American chief engineer, and yet the GM was supposed to be the senior entrepreneur and innovator for the start-up. When interviewed, the China-side GM jokingly said that his wife made more money than he did, and she ran a textile exporting business out of their home. So, a feeling of unfairness may have precipitated the GM's resignation about eighteen months into the project. This discrepancy in rewards underscored the lack of support for cross-cultural risk takers, innovators, and change makers in the organization.

Poor Systems Thinking. According to Senge (1990), systems thinking is crucial to organizational learning, and although systems thinking is seeing not only the functional connections, it also is about intuiting the tacit and symbolic linkages inside and outside the organization that were critical to company viability. In part, the CEO's poor systems thinking was a root cause of the company's initial predicament. First, when a very valuable international product patent expired, the company leaders failed to recognize how a change in that system would affect business during the emerging recession. Second, once the downturn was unavoidable, downsizing and envisioning a move overseas began to be discussed; however, as the CEO and CFO indicated in their interviews, it was difficult for the company leaders to see how this change would influence their management system— previously they were a business with an American, family climate, but they failed to realize how being more global required changes in management style and communication technology.

Low Priority on Training and Technology Upgrades. An organization facing a learning challenge needs to invest in the skills and technologies required by the new complex environment (Farago & Skyrme, 1995). However, in spite of multiple complications and difficulties caused by the new global dimensions of the company business, the CEO was not willing to upgrade technologies and to help staff acquire the training they needed. At one meeting, I suggested cross-cultural training and this was ignored. One executive at the company said, "A lot of stuff that ought to be automated is done by hand. . . . There is not a premium put on information for managing. Some of the way we do things . . . makes it hard to manage the business sometimes to keep track of things. . . . There has never been any interest in spending money to change that." During consulting sessions, we discussed the advisability of purchasing videoconferencing technology to improve long-distance communication, but this was dismissed as too expensive. Later, the CEO revealed that in his overseas plant, one of their new Chinese engineers had to be transferred because he did not like the "archaic" production technology. Again, a low-learning organization report card was reflected in this lack of commitment to keeping up with new technological advances appropriate for an international venture.

Search for Reasons Behind the Success in Year Three

Time seems to reveal the essence of how things work, and in the second year the CEO was wondering if the company would survive. Resources were never abundant, and slowness in setup and the embarrassing turnover of the GM seemed to put profitability even farther away. Within twelve months, however, company financials indicated a win might be on the way. To uncover the tacit leadership and organizational factors that contributed to this turnaround and the company's successful launch overseas, I decided to look across disciplines for analogous organizational success in complex, uncertain environments. Prange (1999) says that "in organizational learning research, metaphors play a significant role, and if applied in a critical way, yield substantive potential for theory development" (p. 37). The insightfulness of interpretation of data and social situations can be enhanced when considered through the lens of analogy and metaphor (Morgan, 1986; Tsoukas, 1993). The value of metaphor for understanding complexity has been demonstrated as multiple analogies have been mapped from physics (for example, billiard balls interacting), biology (for example, slime mold emerging), and human activities (such as putting garbage in a can) to the target discipline of collective social learning (Cohen, March, & Olsen, 1972; Johnson, 2002).

Sports might seem to be an unusual place to look for insights regarding organizational learning; yet, soccer (also known as *football* or *futbol* in various countries)—perhaps because of its continuous action, proneness to iteration and learning, dynamic situations, and complexity of decision making—seemed an ideal metaphor for complexity in business. In fact, soccer is currently a fertile research arena and simulator for complexity and multiagent learning theorists (Ramos, Junco, & Espinosa, 2003; Salustowicz, Wiering, & Schmidhuber, 1997, 1998). I found that, metaphorically speaking, some of the attributes and relationships within the system, tactics, and strategies of soccer were useful in highlighting the organizational learning within the electronic company under study.

Soccer Codes

According to Ramos, Junco, and Espinosa (2003), "Models belonging to the cooperation within a soccer match and the domains of interaction between players, ball, and goals are typically dynamic and full of conflicting situations. . . . A soccer domain is well suited as a complex environment that allows the research community to develop" (p. 288). After reviewing soccer strategy literature, it was rather fascinating how the following codes based on soccer tactics enhanced my qualitative inquiry.

Soccer Code One: Nondirective Possession and "Moment of Play." Latin style of soccer play is considered the most aesthetically pleasing of strategies (Bangsbo & Peitersen, 2000). In *beautiful soccer*, as it is called, the pattern of touches and direction of the ball are comparatively complex and artful. Such a tactic seemed promising because aesthetics have been identified as a possible moderating factor in creative leadership under uncertainty (Lane & Klenke, 2004). To some, such ball handling may seem wasteful and undirected. Critics of beautiful soccer prefer northern European strategies that are more direct; they are called *kick-and-rush* football. The axiom is aggressive: direct play will result in more goals. However, statistical analysis of the 1986 World Cup semifinalists and finalists revealed that the most successful scorers had 5.59 touches per possession; whereas, the others had 5.22 (Bangsbo & Peitersen, 2000). The positive correlation between beautiful soccer and goals scored has been replicated in later studies (McHale & Scarf, 2007). This positive correlation reflects the power of indirect, seemingly random possession styles of play that hold the ball longer while waiting for opportunities to emerge. Wesson (2002) illustrated some of the movement of the ball between goals in the 1996 European Championship match between England and Holland and showed how the tactic can look chaotic and purposeless, but the main aim is to embrace surprises and create conditions for an attack. Unlike American football, passing the ball back toward one's own goal is as positive and strategic to goal making as passing it forward. In terms of organizational learning, this tactic fosters conditions for emergence of unspecified future productive surprises, a mainstay of complexity leadership (Marion & Uhl-Bien, 2001).

As the CEO's handling of the move overseas developed, his style was distinctively nondirective. Critics could have said he was too laissez-faire. He was self-deprecating and humble about loosely leading the charge: "I haven't provided a vision for what we're doing; everybody here kind of has a vision, for better or for worse."

He humbly admitted that technology and overseas issues were not his strength and that their only hope was the group of VPs on his executive team. Using his family-style management, however, he communicated trust and empowered his VP team to embrace the overseas venture. His style parallels Marion and Uhl-Bien's (2001) assertion that complexity leadership must facilitate emergence rather than control followers. Embracing the opportunities in uncertainty requires that ends sometimes be unspecified (Clampitt & Williams, 2005). The leadership dynamic for making the most of surprises under uncertainty is not top down but emerges from the bottom, "nondeliberatively." This nondirective organizational climate made a deep impression on me throughout my three years observing the company.

Even though the CEO was not inclined to enjoy the risky venture, the CFO proved otherwise, and he turned out to be the most talented company asset in the move. During my initial assessments of the leadership team, I discovered that, unlike the CEO, the CFO scored the highest in tolerance for ambiguity, meaning he had potential to positively embrace the opportunities in the uncertain overseas venture. Predictably, he was the one empowered by the CEO to pull the trigger on the launch. By the end of the three-year period, the CFO had become the chief strategist for the move. In many ways, he was like the soccer team striker who had the ability to sense a "moment of play" and then execute it.

What is "moment of play"? When many learners are on the soccer field, the environment is changing in unpredictable ways (Salustowicz, Wiering, & Schmidhuber, 1998), and the best players have tacit ability to maximize their opportunities under this uncertainty. An invaluable player competency on such a field is the ability to intuit alignments of multiple factors (even the learning of opponents and teammates), actions that take time, the time created by beautiful soccer. After some new space opens, those who can embrace the confusion and intuit the emerging opportunities in the uncertainty can also trigger infusion of more resources and more risky attempts at goal. This ability is called "recognizing the moment of play" (Harrison, 2002).

Such intuitive players delay the excitement of aggressive, early, and direct movement toward goal. Some inferior shot opportunities are resisted. Then, patience pays off when a richer range of options emerges. Play then gives way to the identification of the sought-for opportunity and the straight shot that aims the ball toward the net. According to learning theorists, such a delaying of gratification is a key factor in learner resourcefulness (Carr, 1999; Ponton & Carr, 2000). It was interesting to see how this kind of delay was used by the leaders to engineer the company's recovery.

Soccer Code Two: Ironic Delay and Turnabout. In the world of soccer, a basic principle is that if a player wants to receive a ball in a particular place on the pitch, that player needs to "create the space." Paradoxically, on the soccer field this involves not running toward the target space but away from it. Defenders follow, and when they are out of position, then a swift turn and dash back to the open area provides the opportunity. Figure 9.1 shows how lateral movement to the corners of the field

Figure 9.1. Widening the Field of Play and Creating the Greatest Number of Options

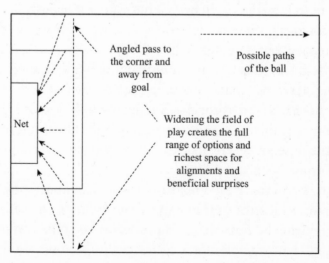

Angled pass to the corner and away from goal

Possible paths of the ball

Net

Widening the field of play creates the full range of options and richest space for alignments and beneficial surprises

creates more space and options for the ball's path toward the goal. Players wanting the ball in this situation do not run toward the ball; ironically, they move in the opposite direction. In fact, they may even reject an exciting run toward the goal in the center of the field and kick the ball to the corner in hopes of a subsequent, better opportunity.

Another paradoxical tactic is for strikers to give up control of the ball and to allow the other team to possess the ball for a long time in the high-risk, last third of the field. Ironically, this lures many opponents to give up alignment with their usual defensive positions, thus creating open space as well as alignment of knowledge and resources for a favorable attack back toward their opponent's goal. This sort of feigning vulnerability and weakness is an old tactic going back to Sun Tzu's advice in *The Art of War* (Gordon, 2002).

Organizational theorists have recognized a similar paradox in complex environments and a corresponding irony in the innovative responses to that complexity. For example, organizations are built on the premise of working toward predictable and quantifiable goals; however, innovation requires creative exploration without attempting to control matters by demanding specified goals (Clampitt & Williams, 2005). There is an emotional clash inherent in innovative environments—simultaneously new ideas are encouraged, yet unrealistic ones are constantly being opposed and weeded out (Kanter, 2006; Mumford, Scott, Gaddis, & Strange, 2002). This is an emotionally difficult type of organizational learning that sometimes looks like chaos; that is, often those who sort through ideas appear to be kicking the ball in the wrong direction, but, ironically, only ideas that are new and useful serve as the backbone of productive change and innovation.

In this manner of creating space, sometimes the CEO appeared to kick the ball in the wrong direction; however, this tactic bought the time that was needed to keep the company in the game. For example, the CEO decided that one of the company's greatest assets was its US customer network. In interviews, the CEO said that these relationships were invaluable and virtually impossible to get back once they were lost. So, over the three years the company sold products, sometimes at a loss, in order to keep their customers coming to them. With overall profits dropping even more, such a practice may have seemed foolhardy to some stockholders. Yet, in fact, it was an effective indirect advance toward the goal of recovering profitability.

Another way in which ironic turnabout occurred in the organization was in the long-term use of Asian assembly contractors. These contracts not only displayed the US company's weakness in terms of inability to produce competitive products, they also gave Asian contractors assistance in developing their own technologies and production capabilities that were increasingly competing and taking away business from the US company. Yet the CFO insisted that, because the company had been in this vulnerable position, they experientially learned a lot from the process: "We have learned a lot from dealing with our contract assembly factories. . . . I think we can change to meet the challenge. . . ." Ironically, the company turnabout was impossible without the space that was created by the apparent weakness and vulnerability that preceded it.

Soccer Code Three: Nonchalance. Beautiful soccer injects an aesthetic quality that facilitates emergence of new opportunities on the field. The player's fancy footwork insists on pleasure in spite of the intensity, uncertainty, and tension of competition. This form is intentional and strategic yet may appear to be a very easygoing, almost lazy style of nonchalant play (Bangsbo & Peitersen, 2000). The CEO was observed to be "nonchalant" in a number of difficult and uncertain situations. In observations, other words that could be used to describe him would be casual, warm, down-to-earth, unassuming, friendly, and humorous. His foibles were often on display by his own design, especially his lack of engineering expertise. He spoke openly of a failed new product development project that he masterminded early in the crisis. It was his last-ditch effort to keep production in the states, and the idea cost the company over two million dollars. Some might call the actions of the CEO incompetence revealed; however, freedom from self-protectiveness created an openness and an intimate atmosphere with the other executive leaders. Viewing the CEO's model, they could see that risk taking and a possible failure would not be a career ender. Perhaps his vulnerability reflected the humility that Collins (2001) believed to be essential to the highest level-five leadership. The CFO revealed in interviews that the CEO did not sleep well when he had to let go of so many of his line workers during the down-sizing; however, this stress did not surface, and the CEO's casual demeanor while handling the multifaceted move to China showed much grace. In some ways, like a Brazilian soccer player moving adroitly, almost dancelike, past defenders, the CEO's leadership had an aesthetic quality of casualness, humor, and calm that encouraged those around him to enjoy the process even when it was nested in urgency and turbulence.

Another side of the CEO's casual nonchalance was displayed in his ability to see how some loosely linked relationships affected the future of their organization. Nurturing these relational links in casual ways indirectly advanced the company's efforts toward profitability. One such loosely linked relationship related to family members of overseas staff. The CEO commented that he was alarmed to hear that the chief engineer's wife recently said she wanted to relocate back in the states. The CFO jokingly said that the way to gauge the future stability of the Asia venture would be to find out how the wife was doing, but this was no joke. So, when the chief engineer in China needed to come back to the home office for some meetings, the CEO insisted that the company pay for his wife to accompany him to the states as a cure for homesickness. In addition, one of the final advances that led to the company's comprehensive success was overcoming competition from their former contract assembly partners. Victory became apparent when the company successfully developed a new customer base in China's domestic market. The new American China-side GM did not develop this new market, but rather it was developed by his resourceful Chinese wife. The CEO good naturedly and coolly learned from her and welcomed the unexpected but needed bump in sales.

Conclusion

The answer to my initial question—"Were more tacit aspects of leading organizational learning responsible for buoying up this company and neutralizing the effects of some of its poor learning postures?"—surprised me. In terms of typical LO theory, almost everyone seemed ill-prepared to handle the crisis, especially the CEO. Companies undergoing change and downsizing usually become more rigid and therefore less creative and less able to handle change (Amabile & Conti, 1999); however, the CEO's nonchalance mitigated this tendency and pushed the company toward productive risk taking. Also, companies well established in their market usually demand planning that highlights predictable and specifiable goals even though this may hamper innovation. This CEO, however, had the wisdom to identify ambiguity tolerance in his CFO and to empower the CFO to act on his "moment of play" intuition when leading the overseas venture.

I watched them keep the ball in play until the time was right for a big win. Some aspects of effective complexity leadership turned out to be tacit and indirect, not straightforward, and not easily available for quantification; yet these powerful attitudes and behaviors surfaced when soccer tactics were used to analyze my experience at the company.

No doubt, what the CEO casually referred to as "luck" also helped the company along the way. However, the CEO's patient engineering of several ironic turnabouts and his humble preservation of loosely linked leverage points, such as customer networks and sensitivity to family concerns, all contributed to the successful effort. These tactics are not just good business; they also demonstrate good complexity leadership. The CEO and his leadership team were faced with many surprises within a chaotic, uncertain environment, but sound complexity leadership attitudes and behaviors created conditions for profitable surprises—the space for the learning and the timing for advantageous alignments to occur.

References

Amabile, T. M., & Conti, R. (1999). Changes in the work environment for creativity during downsizing. *Academy of Management Journal, 42*, 630–640.

Bandura, A. (1997). *Self-efficacy: The exercise of control.* New York: W. H. Freeman.

Bangsbo, J., & Peitersen, B. (2000). *Soccer systems & strategies.* Champaign, IL: Human Kinetics.

Carr, P. B. (1999). *The measurement of resourcefulness intentions in the adult autonomous learner.* Unpublished doctoral dissertation, George Washington University, Washington, DC.

Clampitt, P. G., & Williams, M. L. (2005). Conceptualizing and measuring how employees and organizations manage uncertainty. *Communication Research Reports, 22*, 315–324.

Cohen, M. D., March, J. G., & Olsen, J. P. (1972). A garbage can model of organizational choice. *Administrative Science Quarterly, 17*, 1–25.

Collins, J. (2001). Level 5 leadership: The triumph of humility and fierce resolve. *Harvard Business Review, 79*(1), 66–76.

Farago, J., & Skyrme, D. (1995). *The learning organization.* Retrieved from www.skyrme.com/insights/3lrnorg.htm

Gordon, A. S. (2002). Enabling and recognizing strategic play in strategy games: Lessons from Sun Tzu. *American Association for Artificial Intelligence,* pp. 29–33.

Harrison, W. (2002). *Recognizing the moment to play.* Indianapolis: Cardinal Publisher Group.

Johnson, S. (2002). *Emergence: The connected lives of ants, brains, cities, and software.* New York: Simon & Schuster.

Kanter, R. M. (2006, November). Innovation: The classic traps. *Harvard Business Review,* pp. 73–83.

Kline, P., & Saunders, B. (1998). *Ten steps to a learning organization* (2nd ed.). Arlington, VA: Great Ocean Publishers.

Lane, M., & Klenke, K. (2004). The ambiguity tolerance interface: A modified social cognitive model for leading under uncertainty. *Journal of Leadership & Organizational Studies, 10,* 69–81.

MacDonald, A. P. (1970). Revised scale for ambiguity tolerance: Reliability and validity. *Psychological Reports, 26,* 791–798.

Marion, R., & Uhl-Bien, M. (2001). Leadership in complex organizations. *Leadership Quarterly, 12,* 389–418.

McHale, I., & Scarf, P. (2007). Modelling soccer matches using bivariate discrete distribution with general dependence structure. *Statistica Neerlandica, 61,* 432–445.

Morgan, G. (1986). *Images of organizations.* Newbury Park, CA: Sage.

Mumford, M. D., Scott, G. M., Gaddis, B., & Strange, J. M. (2002). Leading creative people: Orchestrating expertise and relationships. *Leadership Quarterly, 13,* 705–750.

Ponton, M. K., & Carr, P. B. (2000). Understanding and promoting autonomy in self-directed learning. *Current Research in Social Psychology, 5,* 271–284.

Prange, C. (1999). Organizational learning: Desperately seeking theory. In M. Easterby-Smith, J. Burgoyne, & L. Araujo (Eds.), *Organizational learning and the learning organization: Developments in theory and practice* (pp. 23–43). London: Sage.

Ramos, F., Junco, M. A., & Espinosa, E. (2003). Soccer strategies that live in the B2B world of negotiation and decision-making. *Decision Support Systems, 35,* 287–310.

Salustowicz, R., Wiering, M., & Schmidhuber, J. (1997). Evolving soccer strategies. In N. Kasabov, R. Kozma, K. Ko, R. O'Shea, G. Coghill, & T. Gedeon (Eds.), *Progress in connectionist-based information systems: Proceedings of the Fourth International Conference on Neural Information Processing IOCNIP '97, 1,* 501–505.

Salustowicz, R., Wiering, M., & Schmidhuber, J. (1998). Learning team strategies: Soccer case studies. *Machine Learning, 33*(2–3), 263–282.

Senge, P. M. (1990). *The fifth discipline.* New York: Doubleday.

Tsoukas, H. (1993). Analogical reasoning and knowledge generation in organization theory. *Organization Studies, 14,* 323–346.

Wesson, J. (2002). *The science of soccer.* Philadelphia: Institute of Physics Publishers.

Chapter Ten

A Complex Landscape

Reflections on Leaders and the Places They Create

Patricia Carr

In her recent book, *Tweet If You [Heart] Jesus*, Elizabeth Drescher (2011) titles one of her chapters, "Leadership Is a Place: Practicing Church in the Digital Village." She begins by quoting technology entrepreneur Joi Ito, who was active in Howard Dean's 2004 presidential run: "You're not a leader; you're a place. You're like a park or a garden. If it's comfortable and cool, people are attracted" (p. 137). Although she addresses church leaders, her comments are also relevant to leaders in business, nonprofit organizations, education, and government.

Drescher proposes that one challenge for leaders today is to create places where people can interact, and the leader's role in those interactions is not necessarily directive, instructive, or, as Wergin (2004) describes in the conventional view, manipulative. Drescher clarifies that the notion of leadership as a place can easily resonate with religious leaders who can identify with the idea of creating a garden, drawing on the image of the Garden of Eden, which is, according to Christian tradition, a "place" created by God where people could flourish. Even the Creator set ego aside, relinquishing to people the task of naming all that had been created (E. Drescher, personal communication, April 2011). Drescher talks about the power of leaders who offer a word here or there, a comment on someone's Facebook page, a tweet to acknowledge an event, an occasion, or an experience. The leader, according to Drescher, leads by being present, by noticing and attending to others (Drescher, 2011).

The mode of leadership that Drescher discusses is carried out in a variety of ways and a variety of places. In this chapter, I introduce through story the way in which conductor and composer Eric Whitacre created the Virtual Choir, first in 2010 and then again in 2011, to discuss leaders and the places they create. It is important to note, however, that I do not focus on extending the analogy of leadership and symphony conductors. This theme has been explored by many, including Henry Mintzberg (1998), who offered insights on managing knowledge workers through his observations and study of Winnipeg symphony conductor Bramwell Tovey. In this chapter, I invite an exploration of the places leaders create and how they create them. I reflect on the impact these places have on followers and the ways in which these places not only make work possible but also enrich the lives of followers. I will begin with the story of the Virtual Choir and then discuss some thoughts on leadership and place.

The Virtual Choir

Consider this: there are a vast number of people with musical talent all over the world, from different countries with different cultures. They have never met each other. They have never spoken to each other. Could you make it possible for them to work together to produce something that would cause more than a million people to stop and listen, then listen again and again, that would bring people attending the March 2011 TED (Technology, Entertainment and Design) conference to their feet in enthusiastic applause?

It happened.

In spring 2011, the voices of more than two thousand individuals were blended in the Virtual Choir directed by composer and conductor Eric Whitacre; they sang in Sri Lanka, in Portugal, in Norway, and the UK. They sang in China, in Australia, in Thailand, in the United States, and in the Czech Republic. In fifty-eight countries, sopranos, altos, tenors, and basses each sang alone into a computer microphone from his or her kitchen, living room, garage, or dorm room (Whitacre, 2011). Then Whitacre, with the help of Scott Haines, a self-described warehouse worker and "average Joe" who learned some of his technical capabilities via an online software training community, combined these individual voices into the Virtual Choir (Read, 2010). The video of the performance of Virtual Choir 2.0, like its predecessor, Virtual Choir 1.0, went viral on YouTube.

Whitacre's Virtual Choir could be viewed as just another interesting Internet social experiment or, more cynically, a clever marketing gimmick. But it was more than either of those. The resulting music was stunning and moving in a way that clever Internet fads like singing hamsters and cute talking babies are not. Watching the video, I was struck by the ordinariness of the choir members, apparently average people from just about anywhere one could imagine, all engaged in an experience that was to them, and to members of the audience, deeply meaningful.

The story of Whitacre and the Virtual Choir gives us a glimpse into new possibilities for leaders and provides an opportunity to explore old questions in new ways. The magic in the story is not the charismatic leadership of the talented composer and conductor; it is not even in the "gee whiz" qualities of the finished product. The magic is in how the Virtual Choir happened and the glimpse into the future this occurrence provides.

As Eric Whitacre explains, the idea for the Virtual Choir (Virtual Choir 1.0) began when a friend e-mailed a link to a YouTube video of sixteen-year-old Britlin Losee from Long Island, New York, singing the soprano part to his composition "Sleep." The composer-conductor watched and listened to one person singing on this one video and imagined a choir. "If we could get one hundred people to do this from different parts of the world, we could cut each of their videos together, start them all at the same time and it would sound like a choir" (Seckerson, 2010).

Whitacre's first step in creating the Virtual Choir was not simply to invite people to send in their videos. He created a structure—a conductor video, technical instructions for setting up equipment and recording individual performances, and music for different voices, soprano, alto, tenor, and bass. Whitacre describes the process of preparing for Virtual Choir 1.0, in which 185 singers from twenty-five countries sang his composition "Lux Arumque" ("Light and Gold"): "I conducted Lux on camera but in complete silence. I was hearing the music only in my head. Once I had that I went back and played the piano part underneath it so the singers would have some reference. I uploaded that to YouTube, and then people downloaded their parts [and] uploaded their videos" (Seckerson, 2010). The next challenge: how does one blend 185 different videos to produce one performance?

When Scott Haines, a fan of Whitacre's music, heard about the project, he wrote to Whitacre: "Could we do this together?" In an interview for software training website lynda.com, Haines describes himself as an "average Joe who worked in a warehouse." He had used lynda.com to teach himself how to use the Adobe After Effects software that would enable him to edit and produce the video. Haines estimated he devoted seven hundred to a thousand hours over a three- to four-month period to create the final video of "Lux Arumque" for the first Virtual Choir (Read, 2010). As Whitacre explains, "Scott Haines . . . cut it all together and made this beautiful, beautiful sort of virtual space. Like a concert hall that exists only in cyberspace" (Seckerson, 2010). He continues, highlighting the individuality of each participant as they contribute to the common performance, "You can see that we're all in the position of a choir and you can see me conducting but you can also look at each little video and see each person sitting in their garage or in their kitchen" (Seckerson, 2010). Whitacre went on to create Virtual Choir 2.0, which premiered in spring 2011. More than two thousand singers from fifty-eight countries participated.

Leadership from Somewhere off to the Side

At first, one might think that the lesson from the Virtual Choir is that it takes a charismatic and inspirational leader; Whitacre, moreover, whose early ambition in life was to be a pop star, can certainly entertain. But the power of his idea—seeing a choir where there was none and creating a place where it could come to be—is what brought the Virtual Choir into being. Part of creating a place is having the willingness to open the door and invite people in to participate. It is also the reaction of acceptance when people "come as they are" and are assured that their contribution is valued.

Whitacre's approach to the Virtual Choir reflects a view of leadership that moves away from what Wergin (2004) describes as "the conventional view, a sort of leadership-as-manipulation view, which assumes that leadership is a matter of getting followers to do what you want them to do" (p. 2). Wergin, discussing the challenges of academic leadership, refers to the notion of "leadership in place"—leaders lead from where they stand "without the trappings of hierarchy and privilege, indeed any sort of authority at all. Instead, it's a type of lateral leadership" (p. 1). Whitacre himself favors a nonhierarchical form of leadership espoused by prominent conductor Sir Colin Davis (Service, 2011), who urges leaders to set aside their own egos in order to empower people to accomplish their work to the best of their ability: "The less ego you have, the more influence you have as a conductor. And the result is that you can concentrate on the only things that really matter: the music and the people who are playing it. You are of no account whatever. But if you can help people to feel free to play as well as they can, that's as good as it gets" (Service, 2011).

The message here is that leaders—even conductors who traditionally stand in front of those they lead—at times need to lead from the side, from the back, from the middle, or in the case of Whitacre from a small room where he is conducting music on camera in silence for followers whom he may never see, who are from all over the world. Even before Scott Haines produced his virtual concert hall, Whitacre, in a sense, had already created a place where people who were motivated and impassioned by an idea could work together to create something of high quality through a structured work experience that was personally and emotionally satisfying. The "place" where leadership occurs is not just a physical place or even a virtual cyberplace; *place* can also refer to the creation of a structure that enables people to work well together.

Leading with Compassionate Welcome

In an interview with Wired.com about Howard Dean's presidential campaign, Joi Ito commented about the "ownership" of place when he talked about *Deanspace,* a conceptual environment that included Howard Dean's website in relation to online and local Meetup communities. "*Deanspace* is not really about Dean," he said. "It's about us" (Wolf, 2004). Ito proposes followers at least cocreate the space where leadership happens, which puts them in a position that is not secondary to that of the leader. Is it necessary that these followers be carefully selected so as to weed out weaknesses? Can average people contribute? In an interview with the BBC in which he discussed Virtual Choir 1.0, Whitacre was asked how many entries were sent in that were not acceptable, not included in the final product. Whitacre responded, "One of the great things about choral music . . . is that the massive voices tend to blend out those that aren't so beautiful. So far we have yet to turn a single person away" (Whitacre, 2010).

One of the fears of letting lesser talents participate in any project is that they will diminish the quality of the end result. As Drescher notes, "It seems that by giving so many an opportunity to sing, perfection was amplified" (E. Drescher, personal communication, April 2011). The singers in the Virtual Choir appreciated the opportunity; many reported recording their parts over and over again to get them just right. On a Facebook page where participants wrote about the experience of singing in the Virtual Choir, many commented on feelings of being valued. Maria Petrova wrote, "I'm so moved by the fact that my contribution was *wanted*, and welcome. My voice? Really? . . . What I couldn't offer in clarity, a skilled sound engineer made up for by scrubbing my video. It's an experience of resplendent unity and acceptance, despite weaknesses, above competition, where everyone came as they were, and we sound and look glorious for it" (Petrova, 2011).

Although this was a *virtual* choir, Whitacre was struck by the sense of connection and the emotional power of the experience for those who participated. He was surprised to find that although people sang, as he referred to it, each "on their own desert islands, sending out electronic messages in bottles to each other," they seemed to be experiencing an actual sense of community, a powerful connection (Whitacre, 2011). "Something happened that I wasn't expecting," Whitacre says. "The video has a life unto itself . . . it illuminated for me the idea that human beings will go to any length to connect with others. . . . All these people singing alone together is a metaphor for the human condition" (Seckerson, 2010). Drescher concurs not only on the need for connection but on how leaders can use social media such as Facebook and Twitter to create places where connection can occur. She points out that just as ancient pilgrims stood outside the cells of wise men and women in search of connection, "[people today] are standing outside our digital cells, waiting to be invited in just as they are. They're not interested in a 'leader' in the modern sense—someone who will influence them, however benevolently, to think or do one thing or another. They're interested in someone who leads with compassionate welcome, someone who provides space to experience something of the divine in themselves, and who offers a word or two to encourage that search and the life practices it prompts" (Drescher, 2011, pp. 145–146).

Places Leaders Create: Do They Sustain or Diminish Us?

If leadership is a place, one of the challenges for leaders today is to ask, "What kinds of places have we created?" Are they the "gardens" described by Ito, noted in the beginning of the chapter? Are they places where people can accomplish work that matters in environments that sustain them physically, emotionally, mentally, and spiritually? Or have we created places that neither restore nor sustain people, but instead diminish them?

In March and April 2011, *Sixty Minutes* presented stories of two very different places: DOCX, a mortgage servicing company (Anderson & Ruetenik, 2011) and Gospel for Teens, an organization that helps young people learn the traditions and art of gospel music (Finkelstein, 2011). One diminishes and the other sustains and restores.

DOCX was a place where hourly workers with little or no skill in banking, mortgages, or law signed fake names to reconstructed mortgage documents that had been lost, misplaced, or that had never existed. Several people interviewed in the program talked about how they spent their workdays signing the name "Linda Green," a fictitious bank vice president (whose name was short and easy to spell), to documents to be used in mortgage foreclosure lawsuits. Chris Pendley, one of the "Linda Greens" interviewed for the program, said, "It seemed a little strange. But they told us and they repeatedly told us that everything was above board and it was legal" (Anderson & Ruetenik, 2011). According to the story, "Some of the bank vice presidents at DOCX were high school kids." In DOCX we have the story of a place where people were called to set aside their own identities and whatever talents they possessed to do the work of signing the name (four thousand times in a day) of a fictitious bank vice president. "Their signatures were entered into evidence in untold thousands of foreclosure suits that sent families packing" (Anderson & Ruetenik, 2011).

Gospel for Teens is the story of a leader who created a very different place. Vy Higginsen's dream was to save and preserve the tradition of gospel music. "Each week, the place she created draws teens from New York and New Jersey to Harlem to learn about and perform gospel music" (Finkelstein, 2011). Higginsen had no intention of dealing with the emotional and life "baggage" of the teens who came to her program. During the interview she says, "Any worry, any pain, any problem with your mother, your father, your sister, your brother, the dog, the boyfriend. . . . That's your baggage. Leave the bags outside, because this time is for you" (Finkelstein, 2011). In the course of the program, though, one sees evidence of unintended transformations. A young girl who has difficulty even saying her name learns to sing. Teens who struggle with home life and family issues return again and again. The young people speak movingly of the joy they find in the place Higginsen created.

Although she had no intention of addressing the life struggles of the teens who came to her program, Vy Higginsen herself began to realize the importance of the place she created beyond its intended purpose of "saving the music." In the interview, she began to reflect, almost with a sense of wonder, on how the place that was intended to save music has taken on an additional importance in the lives of teens. "They are struggling. We live in a violent society. So now what do you do with all that? . . . You have to go somewhere where there's sacred ground, where there's hope, where there's possibility, where there's a better life" (Finkelstein, 2011).

These two stories offer contrasting views of leadership and place, and they are commentaries on one of the themes that emerge from the story of the Virtual Choir, a theme of the importance of allowing individual potential to emerge and shine and to enable the people who did the work to see their own contribution in the results. "I wanted people to actually be able to see themselves perfectly clear" says Virtual Choir video producer Scott Haines, commenting on the extra time he took to edit the video so that each singer could be seen very clearly (Read, 2010). At DOCX, people's talent and identity are hidden; they cannot even sign their true name. In Gospel for Teens, the leader places such a high value on individual identity that she coaches the teens on saying their names loudly and clearly so they can be heard.

The Organization as Garden and the Leader as Gardener

Drescher talked about the garden as the archetypal place where people can flourish (E. Drescher, personal communication, April 2011). Can such places be created in corporations? Or are they limited to virtual (and actual) choirs, nonprofits, and educational settings? There is evidence, indeed, that flourishing places are happening in for-profit organizations as well. Author and consultant Tony Schwartz has worked with many types of organizations, including such prominent corporations as Google, Ford, Ernst and Young, and Sony Pictures (Schwartz, 2011). His message: "The way most of us work isn't working" (Schwartz, 2010, p. 65). Schwartz and his organization, The Energy Project, help people learn to work in ways that enable them to achieve more balance in their physical, mental, emotional, and spiritual energy. In "The Productivity Paradox," however, he notes that in much of his work to help people balance their energy in their lives, he found that people were not able to apply what they learned when they returned to their workplaces. "What we failed to fully appreciate in our early work," he explains, "was that once we finished our sessions with employees and sent them back into the workplace, they often ran into powerful organizational resistance to the very principles and practices we'd taught them" (Schwartz,

2010, p. 65). In other words, the places their leaders had created would not support and sustain people in their new ways of working. As an example, Schwartz notes that he worked with Sony Pictures to transform the way leaders work, with the hope of transforming the workplace as well (Schwartz, 2010).

More evidence of the "organizations as gardens" metaphor is found in Garvin and Tahilyani's (2010) case study of MindTree Ltd., an Indian IT firm that has given a great deal of thought as to how it will develop leaders to carry the organization into the future. A key part of the plan is called the gardening process, a way of developing people. In 2008, Subroto Bagchi, one of the MindTree founders and vice chairman of the firm, took on a new role in the organization: gardener. As Bagchi explains, "A gardener has an organic relationship with each plant in the garden. He is an extremely humble person and sees his task as never ending. In the organizations of tomorrow, I see the role of leadership akin to that of a gardener tending a garden" (Garvin & Tahilyani, 2010, p. 5).

The Call to Create Places Where People Can Flourish

In 2004, when Joi Ito made the startling statement, "Leadership is a place," it announced the reality and the power of virtual places created via social media. When Drescher reintroduced that quote in 2011, she called attention to our deep hunger for connection and the extraordinary value of being able to create places (physical and virtual) where that can happen. When Eric Whitacre introduced his Virtual Choir 2.0 at the March 2011 TED Conference, the auditorium filled with the sound of more than two thousand people from fifty-eight countries singing the ironically titled composition, "Sleep." Audience members rose to their feet. They recognized that they were hearing a wake-up call, reminding them of how uplifting a place can be and offering hope that leaders can create such places—choirs, gardens, churches, and corporations—where people can flourish.

References

Anderson, R., & Ruetenik, D. (Producers). (2011, April 1). Mortgage paper-work mess: Next housing shock? [Television series episode] *Sixty Minutes*. New York: CBS News. Retrieved from www.cbsnews.com/video/watch/?id=7361572n&tag=mncol;lst;1

Drescher, E. (2011). *Tweet if you (heart) Jesus: Practicing church in the digital reformation*. New York: Morehouse Publishing.

Finkelstein, S. (Producer). (2011, March 31). How "Gospel for Teens" is saving the music. [Television series episode] *Sixty Minutes*. New York: CBS News. Retrieved from www.cbsnews.com/stories/2011/03/31/60minutes/main20049243.shtml?tag=contentMain;contentBody

Garvin, D., & Tahilyani, R. (2010). *MindTree: A community of communities*. HBS No. 9–311–049. Boston: Harvard Business School Publishing.

Mintzberg, H. (1998). Covert leadership: Notes on managing professionals. *Harvard Business Review, 76*(6), 140–147.

Petrova, M. (2011, April 3). Eric Whitacre's music—to me—is healing in sound form. [Msg.] Message posted to www.ted.com/conversations/1710/if_you_were_a_member_of_virtua.html

Read, M. (2010, May 4). lynda.com member story: Scott Haines and the Virtual Choir project. [lynda.com blog interview] Retrieved from http://blog.lynda.com/2010/05/04/lynda-com-member-story-scott-haines/

Schwartz, T. (2010). The productivity paradox. *Harvard Business Review, 88*(6), 64–69.

Schwartz, T. (2011). The Energy Project. [Website] Retrieved from www.theenergyproject.com

Seckerson, E. (Interviewer). (2010, October 27). *Independent classical podcast: Eric Whitacre*. [Audio podcast] Retrieved from www.independent.co.uk/arts-entertainment/classical/features/independent-classical-podcast-eric-whitacre-2116778.html

Service, T. (2011, May 12). Sir Colin Davis: "You are of no account whatso-ever." *The Guardian*. Retrieved from www.guardian.co.uk/music/2011/may/12/sir-colin-davis

Wergin, J. (2004). Leadership in place. *The Department Chair, 14*(4), 1–3.

Whitacre, E. (2010, September). Virtual Choir 2.0 on BBC's flagship morning show. [Video file] Retrieved from http://ericwhitacre.com/blog/virtual-choir-2–0-on-bbcs-flagship-morning-show

Whitacre, E. (2011, March). Eric Whitacre: A virtual choir 2,000 voices strong. [Video file] Retrieved from www.ted.com/talks/lang/eng/eric_whitacre_a_virtual_choir_2_000_voices_strong.html

Wolf, G. (2004, January). *How the internet invented Howard Dean*. Wired.com. Retrieved from www.wired.com/wired/archive/12.01/dean_pr.html

Part Three

The Complexity of Leading in a Globalized World

Lena Lid Falkman

We live on the same sphere as we always have; yet it is changed. Distances around the globe shrink thanks to technology. People, ideas, products, services fly physically or digitally fast or even instantaneously. This speed influences how organizations and companies function and how leadership is constituted and performed, which in turn affects how leadership needs to be understood. This globalized world has made leadership easier in some ways; it is possible to meet and communicate often and easier with stakeholders. Globalization, however, also has made leadership more complex. The complex world of today, therefore, needs to be understood within a global context; accordingly, global leadership needs to be understood within a context of complexity. In the Introduction to this anthology, Barbour noted how the complex world needs to be understood and led, through focusing on the concept of *multi*, as in multiperspectives, multiframed, multidisciplinary, and multidimensional. To this list, the third part includes multicultural.

Due to the phenomenon of globalization, the scholarship on "global leadership" is also a growing phenomenon, but with few formal definitions. What does global leadership mean? This part begins with Jeri Darling mapping global leadership and elaborating on how the concept can be developed. In her chapter titled "Global Leadership: How an Emerging Construct Is Informed by Complex Systems Theory," Darling argues that global leadership competencies will expand. In the expansion, leadership will become increasingly holistic with the goal of aiming for consensus. The only way to accomplish consensus, Darling contends, is by transcending differences.

Leadership is a global phenomenon, but the scholarly area of leadership is dominated by the Western world. What happens when these theories meet dissimilar leadership? This concept is investigated by Deanne de Vries in "The Role of Culture and History in the Applicability of Western Leadership Theories in Africa." De Vries demonstrates how differently African leaders lead, for example, in setting community above individualism. De Vries argues that to bridge gaps, Westerners have to realize that their framing of leadership is not universal and Africans need to create their own understanding of and belief in leadership.

Theories of leadership are heavily dominated by Western thinking, often based on traditional "commonsense" approaches, but there are exceptions. In "A Tao Complexity Tool: Leading from Being," Caroline Fu and Richard Bergeon translate ancient Eastern philosophy into leadership understandings. They share a tool they created that will help leaders invoke valuable insights for decision making in complex situations and provide examples demonstrating how to employ the tool as a practical "uncommon sense" approach for anyone engaged in implementing change.

Not only leadership needs to be understood and dealt with globally. Many current problems also go beyond national or cultural or "leadership" borders. One primatologist known for living and being her leadership is Jane Goodall, who made a global impact on animal and nature ethics. In "The Leadership of Dr. Jane Goodall: A Four-Quadrant Perspective," Georgia Pappas uses a multiperspective approach and explicates an example of global leadership through spirituality and compassion combined with intellectual capacity.

The poem "If You Would Lead Me—Reflections on Leadership" by Nigel Linacre ends this anthology of chapters devoted to leading in complex worlds, symbolically, with questions urging reflection rather than giving solutions about complexity of leading. The finale encourages one to formulate one's own possible answers to questions such as, "If you're going east / And I'm heading west / Who will lead?"

Chapter Eleven

Global Leadership

How an Emerging Construct Is Informed by Complex Systems Theory

Jeri Darling

With this chapter, I seek to expand the leadership discourse and to explore how the construct of global leadership is further informed by the perspective of complex systems theory. I begin from the premise that the ability to lead effectively in a global context is becoming increasingly urgent, given growing levels of uncertainty, rapid change, and extreme conditions. In the context of complexity and related notions of discontinuous change, I would argue that the term *global leadership* does not even adequately capture the quantum leap that must be made to accurately describe the type of leadership that will be required to address emerging conditions. As we live in a globalized world, perhaps all leadership is now global leadership. It may be that a completely new construct is needed to describe leadership in the twenty-first century—however, an understanding of the contours of global leadership provides a useful starting point.

Global Leadership as an Emerging Construct

To understand and explain the impact of globalization processes on leadership, scholars have begun to expand research to more fully delineate the characteristics associated with global leadership (Mendenhall, 2006). Although the term is very much in popular use, a literature search reveals few formal definitions, mostly describing an individual who is able to effectively lead global operations for large multinational firms, or government or political leaders able to operate within an international context. There is also a view that global management competencies are different in important ways from general management competencies and distinctive competencies are identified in various global leadership models.

Concurrently, the concept of globalization is one of the most powerful recent contextual aspects of leadership. Globalization can be defined as a process by which economies, societies, and cultures have become integrated, driven by a combination of economic, technological, sociocultural, political, and biological factors (Croucher, 2004). An understanding of globalization includes the transnational circulation of ideas, languages, and popular culture.

Systems Theory and Leadership Theory

Parallel to the emerging constructs of globalization and leadership, there has been a concurrent development in systems-related theories, including complex systems theory. Schwandt and Szabla (2007) observe that systems theory and leadership theory have coevolved. In light of this evolution, it is appropriate to seek to understand how recent systems and leadership constructs inform one another.

A number of theories have emerged in recent years that address systems-level requirements and contextual variables, such as integrated views of leadership (Avolio, 2007), flexible leadership (Yukl, 1999), distributed leadership (Gronn, 2002), and complexity leadership theory (Uhl-Bien, Marion, & McKelvey, 2007). Hazy (2004) describes leadership in terms of a "meta-capability" that "realizes its effect by creating, reinforcing, and extrapolating an organizational culture that matches the needs of the environment" (p. 71)—emphasizing the critical importance of context on effective global leadership.

Although global leadership includes some of these theoretical concepts, it is distinct to the extent that global leadership is more focused on the effect of changing global conditions on leadership capacity and requirements. The construct of global leadership is also described in distinctive ways by those who research and describe it. My focus in this chapter is to examine the individual leader and those characteristics that are of particular importance within a global context rather than to examine leadership as a broader organizational process or as a collective capability. In particular, I explore how complex systems theory might inform and enhance the construct of global leadership.

Complexity and Globalization

As noted, global leadership exists within the context of, and indeed because of, the phenomenon of globalization. At the same time, many aspects of globalization exhibit characteristics of complexity. Globalization is holistic, integrative, interdependent, based on social interaction, and socially constructed. Have the concepts of globalization and complex systems emerged concurrently—that is, are they similar but separate systems-level constructs? Or is globalization simply an example of a complex system? I would propose that globalization is the most compelling current manifestation of a complex social system and that complex systems theory is particularly relevant to, and illuminating of, leadership in the context of globalization. Given that globalization is socially constructed, its effect is manifested primarily within the human sphere of activity. Thus, the relevance of globalization to leadership will be primarily enacted by the leader at the level of human interactions, decisions, and collective actions— as opposed to the level of natural or technological systems.

The Increasingly Complex Context of Leadership

Rhinesmith asserted in 1996 that the biggest challenges to leaders in the future would be the complexity of the emerging social and economic environment, managing diversity, and managing chaos and uncertainty. Bennis (2007) identifies four primary threats to world stability: nuclear or biological catastrophe, worldwide pandemic, tribalism, and the leadership of human institutions, and states that we "must think more and more about leadership in the context of globalization and instant communication" (p. 5).

Many suggest that global leaders will need a new and different set of skills to be effective. Among the skills in this set are capabilities such as leading organizational learning, the ability to manage unexpected events (Farazmand, 2007), an adaptive capacity and personal resilience (Bennis, 2007; Wise, 2006), and an ability to collaborate and foster collaboration (Jenkins, 2006). Others suggest that global leaders will need powerful relational skills in the face of an increasingly complex and uncertain environment, and the ability to "forge consensus in a divided world" (Bonnstetter, 2000, p. 142). All of these characteristics—organizational learning, unpredictability, adaptation, collaboration, and interdependency—are also features of complex systems.

Leadership Is Contextual and Situational

Leadership is embedded in organizations and is contextual (Hunt, Osborn, & Boal, 2009). Beginning with situational and contingency views of leadership, context has been shown to be a particularly important variable in leadership theory (Hersey & Blanchard, 1977), and has received an increasing focus in more recent leadership constructs such as culture (Schein, 1986), sensemaking (Weick, 1995), integrated leadership (Avolio, 2007), flexible leadership (Yukl, 1999), and complexity leadership theory (Uhl-Bien, Marion, & McKelvey, 2007).

Leadership competencies are also situational. A traditional understanding of leadership competencies is that they are "specific descriptions of the behaviors and personal characteristics that are required to be effective on the job" (Brownell, 2006, p. 311). Another view, however, is that a competency may refer to a person's ability to respond to environmental demands (Bueno & Tubbs, 2004). Aldag and Kuzuhara (2002) suggest that no single leadership style is always effective; rather, the situation dictates the most relevant leadership style.

A number of theorists view leadership behavior as unpredictable and uncertain and argue that a list of competencies is irrelevant and impractical. They posit that skills must be viewed as holistic and integrated and cannot be separated into parts (Bonnstetter, 2000; Brownell, 2006; Bueno & Tubbs, 2004)—which sounds strikingly like a complexity approach to leadership. Effective global leaders balance frameworks of perception, depending on the cultural context, and therefore require the ability to identify and to solve unfamiliar problems in unfamiliar situations.

Complexity and Social Construction in Leadership

Complexity and chaos theories have emerged strongly in recent years and have offered a way to understand the current environment, evolving beyond an open systems model to elaborate a broader systems view that includes a more holistic and subjective way of interpreting reality. Simultaneously, leadership theories have progressed from a focus on exploitation theory to include exploitation and exploration. In part, this progression began to occur to support innovation and the generation of new knowledge so that organizations could address complex challenges (March, 1991).

Researchers thus began to use the complexity sciences as a lens through which to explore leadership (Griffin, 2002; Stacey et al., 2000, as cited in Schwandt & Szabla, 2007). "Systems study moved from efficiency and effectively chemical relationships to information flow, multiple causation, and self-generation" (Schwandt & Szabla, 2007, p. 57). Information control, knowledge use, organizational learning, generative social interaction, and "emergence" have become areas of focus in leadership (Uhl-Bien, Marion, & McKelvey, 2007). In addition, the concept of complex adaptive systems (CAS)—naturally emergent networks of interacting, interdependent agents that are connected in a cooperative dynamic—has become a basic unit of analysis in complexity science and has been linked to leadership. In complex adaptive systems, context is "the ambiance that spawns a given system's dynamic persona . . . [which] refers to the nature of interactions and interdependencies among agents (people, ideas, etc.), hierarchical divisions, organizations and environments. CAS and leadership are socially constructed in and from this context" (Uhl-Bien, Marion, & McKelvey, 2007, p. 299).

Global Leadership Competencies: Different and Complex

Complexity theory has also informed an exploration of global leadership competencies. There seems to be broad consensus among researchers of global competencies that they are different than domestic or common competencies. Brownell (2006) describes global leader competencies as distinctive and suggests that global leaders require "more complex competencies dependent upon individual characteristics" (p. 310). Kets de Vries and Florent-Treacy (2002) maintain that excellent domestic leaders often have the same qualities as global leaders, but that excellent global leaders are able to retain these capabilities even in completely unfamiliar situations (Kets de Vries & Florent-Treacy, 2002).

Cognitive complexity is viewed as a core competence of global leaders (Wills & Barham, 1994). Relevant knowledge and representations from previous experiences are able to be re-formed to generate new creative solutions. This important capacity reflects the need to deal with complexity on an ongoing basis. In a dynamic global environment, leaders must be able to switch their focus of concentration quickly and have the capacity of pattern recognition to identify key facts and anomalous observations. Jokinen (2005) notes, "First, one may assume that global leaders have competencies different from those needed in the domestic context. The other assumption is that global leaders have just developed their (general) competencies into a higher (global) level" (p. 200).

Given this shared view that global competencies are "higher-order" competencies, they are referred to variously as *distinctive, multilevel, mature, meta-, situational, contextual, holistic, integrated,* and by other descriptors that separate them from common or domestic leadership competencies (Bueno & Tubbs, 2004; Jokinen, 2005; Kets de Vries, Vrignaud, & Florent-Treacy, 2004; Lobel, 1991). Researchers have generated a number of global leadership competency profiles and frameworks, which include hard and soft, general and mature, common and distinct, "basic" and "meta" competencies, as well as multilevel pyramid models of competencies (Mendenhall, 2006; Sanchez, Spector, & Cooper, 2000), and a number of personal characteristics and abilities such as synergistic learning, global perspective or mindset, and cross-cultural sensitivity, which are distinct from common competencies (Brownell, 2006).

Global Leadership Informed by Complexity Theories

Despite having defined global leadership as distinct and different from "common" approaches to leadership, the increasing complexity of the global situation is pushing leadership requirements even beyond these distinctive characteristics. Based on emerging global conditions, leaders will need to be prepared to address chaotic or unexpected situations, bring order to people when it is not otherwise provided by a structure or environment, support the ability of people to innovate and develop solutions quickly, help to create common purpose and identity, and support sense-making. Although a range of behaviors and skills useful to a leader operating within an international context have been identified, the global leadership models in use do not seem adequate to address the emerging requirements of current and future reality.

Leading at the Edge of Chaos and Beyond

The context within which leaders need to be effective is changing rapidly and becoming exponentially more complex and unpredictable, as described in complexity theories. Hunt, Osborn, and Boal see leadership as becoming "co-evolutionary" and operating at the "edge of chaos" (2009, p. 514). Pascale, Millemann, and Gioja (1990) outline the characteristics associated with managing at the edge of chaos. Hazy (2006) notes that "edge of chaos leadership moves the analysis from studying the combined impact of context and leadership on performance to *examining the co-evolutionary dynamics among the organization's environment, its viability in the setting and its leadership at multiple levels*" (p. 60, emphasis added).

Farazmand (2007) adds an additional distinction by proposing a theory of "surprise management" that is adaptive, collaborative, and "citizen-engaging" and draws on chaos and complexity theories to cope with hyper-uncertainties and unknowns (p. 157). "In this age of rapid globalization and nonlinear changes, 'surprise' may be the most commanding dimension of uncertainty" (Hermann, 1969, p. 29). Surprise management draws on chaos and complexity theories in a global context (Kiel, 1994; Pascale, Millemann, & Gioja, 1990; Prigogine & Stengers, 1984; Weick & Sutcliffe, 2001). As a social and political construction, the theory of surprise management is based on at least four principles: it rejects anything that is routine and expected; it is fluid and constantly changes in its nature, degree of flexibility, and adaptability; it demands certain preconditions to qualify as surprising and chaotic, nonlinear and unexplainable; and it demands cutting-edge knowledge, skills, and attitudes beyond the comprehension of most people in routine environments. "The theory of surprise management *integrates all features of the authoritative, collaborative, participative, and adaptive models with a quality of self-organizing fluidity and hyper-flexibility*" (Farazmand, 2007, p. 158; emphasis added).

Hunt, Osborn, and Boal (2009) assert that leaders should use the complexity theory notion of "order for free" to tread the narrow path between order and disorder (that is, help stimulate bottom-up activities and combine these activities into viable adaptations). They suggest that channeling emergence is enabled by linking the past (who we are), present (what we do), and future (where we want to go).

Fostering Relationships, Networks, and Sensemaking

Karp and Helgø (2009) suggest that because most organizations are experiencing increased complexity and change, management practices must take better account of unpredictability, uncertainty, self-governance, emergence, and other premises describing chaotic circumstances in organizations. They suggest that leaders develop practices that take these circumstances into account by focusing on people, identity, and relationships and by influencing the patterns of human interactions and communication. "Managing people amid chaos, uncertainty and complexity has become the main challenge for organizations of every kind owing to the very nature of today's economy" (p. 81).

The leader's ability to involve the right people in different stages of a change process becomes critical. Leaders need to induce others to focus their attention on specific and simple ideas, frequently enough and for a sufficient time (Rock & Schwartz, 2006). Leaders can influence relationships and the building of networks in organizations without micromanaging the discussion about organizational reality and without limiting people's involvement.

Because leading is a cultural, or sensemaking, endeavor (Paparone, 2004), the leader needs to communicate the core purpose of the organization and act as a role model to influence the direction of change. He or she will need to contribute to the making of common meaning and will need to believe in the purpose and understand the wider implications of individual tasks. "Whoever first tells stories of the 'new' that make sense to a critical mass in the organizations will also be the 'owner' of the new reality and will be looked to for leadership and guidance" (Karp & Helgø, p. 88). In a sea of turbulence, leaders need to provide meaning in a conventional way by interpreting the past, which articulates the values, beliefs, and identity of the subunit. They need to lead directly via interpersonal influence and indirectly via alterations of particular systemic components, such as formal programs, management systems, or aspects of formal structure (Hunt, Osborn, & Boal, 2009).

Focusing Attention and Fostering Emergence

A leader's experience in different cultures can help to foster the capacity to support creativity and emergence. Multicultural experiences have been demonstrated to be positively related to creative performance and to creativity-supported cognitive processes, including retrieval of unconventional knowledge for idea generation and expansion. Leaders with significant multicultural exposure are more likely to create novel combinations, see the same form as having multiple possible meanings, have access to alternative forms of knowledge, and seek ideas from diverse sources. In particular, a leader who has been exposed to different cultures is more able to take discrepant ideas from two cultures and integrate those ideas in a novel—or "third"—way (Leung, Maddux, Galinsky, & Chiu, 2008).

Most managers make the mistake of trying to solve organizational problems through linear thinking. Weick and Sutcliffe (2001) suggest that they must get out of this mind-set and think strategically and in nonlinear ways to manage the unexpected. Individuals or agents (for example, leaders) in an organization need to have the capability to monitor and influence nonlinear causes and results at the systems level. Leadership within a complex system can be described as nonlinear dynamic systems that can be observed to exhibit self-organizing and emergent phenomena. "As human systems self-organize, they often rest uneasily on the line between being merely complex and being true complex adaptive systems. Leadership, it has been posited, often makes the difference" (Hazy, 2006, p. 60). In other words, the key distinction is whether the system is constructively adaptive or simply chaotic.

For example, effective leaders can create "strategic inflection points" (Grove, 1996), that is, opportunities for others to develop new visions, create new strategies, and move the organization in new directions. In complexity literature, these strategic inflection points are sometimes referred to as related to "adaptive tensions" (Uhl-Bien & Marion, 2009, p. 643). Leaders need to "promote experimentation, change, innovation and invention without specifying what is to be altered and precisely how it will be evaluated" (Hunt, Osborn, & Boal, 2009, p. 504).

Two key approaches to creating strategic inflection points are patterning of attention and network development. Patterning of attention is an influence attempt to identify general questions, issues, and information for subordinates, which include questions of why, whom, and how. Network development involves altering the connections among individuals, both inside and outside the system. The development of networks changes the basis for schema development as well as participants' patterns of interaction, and thus influences knowledge development.

Managing Information and Attention Without Control

Leaders will need to isolate and communicate particular information that is important and is thus given attention from a potentially endless stream of other events, actions, and outcomes. The intent is to affect the degree of homogeneity and heterogeneity in the schemata held by members through information, questions, and challenges to what members believe is important (in other words, sensemaking). The leader can also change the effective size or number of those engaged in dialogue and the frequency and intensity of the interactions between individuals and groups.

Innovation requires a different ensemble of leadership signals that are received by the organization's members as action and decision cues, such as "leadership-of-variety" activities, that is, activities that increase exploration and experimentation to increase the diversity of alternatives available to the system (Hazy, 2006, p. 59). Leadership-of-variety activities are seen to enable the system to adapt and sustain itself as the environment changes. The organizing activities that occur in the complex interactions that enable transformations within a system are interpreted by the organization's members as leadership. These activities operate as signals to organizational members, who cue them in ways that bias or influence location interaction rules among agents, and between agents and resources, to catalyze the self-organization of the agents into a complex adaptive system (Hazy, 2006).

Leaders must also live with the paradox of being in control and not in control, successfully using both "at the same time constructively" (Karp & Helgø, 2009, p. 89). They will need to have the competency to allow leadership to emerge from within the organization to solve what seem to be intractable problems and to seize existing opportunities.

Using Cues, Memes, and Tags

A number of concepts to describe the method by which leaders influence interaction and knowledge development have emerged in recent years. Among these concepts are cues, memes, and tags. Cues help organizational members identify, clarify, prioritize, and communicate actions and relationships with others and support their ability to distribute and use resources, assign tasks, and determine relevant contingencies. Leaders can also spark ideas via the use of memes, which are strategic ideas a leader "plants" or "spreads" in the organization, the social equivalent to biological DNA (Karp & Helgø, 2009).

A tag is defined as a mechanism that facilitates the creation of aggregates and allows organizational members or agents to distinguish among each other, signaling when interactions are possible, as the seeds of change (Hazy, 2006). Holland notes that leaders can stimulate emergence through the use of tags that serve to coordinate activities and act as mediators between differentiated agents (Holland, 1995). Tags can be ideological (for example, *duty, honor, country*), structural (to delayer or flatten the organization), informational (who can talk to whom on what issues), or representational (how, where, and why the system will interact with another system). Leaders channel emergence through subtle changes in these four tag types or with the four types in combination.

Transcending Differences and Building Consensus

"Adaptive leaders are adept at recognizing (i.e., 'reading') and engaging with the complex interactive dynamic in which they operate" (Uhl-Bien & Marion, 2009, p. 639). A high level of attention and fluidity is required for leaders to seize opportunities to guide and influence the organization as circumstances change. One of the main priorities of global leaders is to establish and maintain an organizational culture that transcends cultural differences and establishes "beacons," values and attitudes that are comprehensible and compelling for employees with diverse backgrounds and cultural differences. "Only when leaders establish a state of complementarity with the universal motivational needs system of their followers (whatever the national culture may be) can a global corporation come into full bloom" (Kets de Vries & Florent-Treacy, 2002, p. 9). To be able to create this type of complementary relationship with organizational members, the most effective global leaders need to understand and connect with the universal basics of human functioning.

Leadership can be viewed as a dynamic that emerges between the leader and his or her followers, leading to the view that effective leadership can be defined as the result of a relationship. Leadership effectiveness is, in essence, achieved through building community. Sheridan (2005) notes that "in an intercultural environment, readiness is the extent to which followers have the ability and willingness to reach a common goal" (p. 20). Leaders will need to be able to "forge consensus in a divided world" and build relationships among those with dissimilar backgrounds and perspectives (Brownell, 2006, p. 319).

Harris, Moran, and Moran (2004) determined that a global mindset remains a requirement for leaders in guiding institutions, organizations, and nations. A global mindset prevails when a leader from one part of the world is able to be comfortable in another because of knowledge and skills that are based on understanding and awareness, and capable of leading and motivating diverse followers (Kedia & Mukherji, 1999). Ferraro (2001) also suggested that leaders need to develop a new mindset, which he called *global brains*. Leaders need to be able to assess the particular group and context and respond accordingly.

Conclusion

The global context within which leaders operate is increasingly complex. As an emerging construct, global leadership has evolved alongside complexity theories. To understand the theoretical and practical aspects of global leadership, a consideration of the characteristics of complex adaptive systems can shed significant light on the characteristics required for effective leadership in a global context.

Increasingly, therefore, leaders will need to understand what complex systems theory has to teach them. The leader and the system are profoundly interdependent. Within a globalized system, societies, cultures, and economies have become integrated; the effective leadership of global institutions is a critical component of the viability of this integrated system. In response to the emerging social and economic environment, how a leader consciously moves from interacting with and influencing a system that is "merely" complex to one that is a true complex adaptive system is the challenge of the modern global leader.

In this chapter, I have proposed a number of characteristics that will be increasingly important for leaders to be effective under emerging conditions in the context of a global system. In the following, I summarize four key points and offer three conclusions for further consideration.

First, global leadership competencies will continue to expand and to become increasingly holistic and nonlinear in nature. A broader systems view of leadership requires a more holistic and subjective way of interpreting reality. Leaders will need to be able to function in a more dynamic, unpredictable, in-the-moment manner—in a dance with the context and environment. The notion of "frameworks of perception" (Brownell, 2006) suggests a capacity to frame or reframe reality depending on the situation. Cognitive complexity (Wills & Barham, 1994) includes a capacity to re-form relevant knowledge and representations from previous experiences to generate new and creative solutions, and an ability to deal with complexity on an ongoing basis, that is, an ability to switch the focus of concentration quickly and have the capacity of pattern recognition to identify key facts and anomalous observations. It includes a parallel ability to think strategically and in nonlinear ways to manage the unexpected. Leaders will need to be highly awake, attuned, and have a keen sense of timing.

Additionally, operating in the context of complex adaptive systems, global leaders will need to influence action and support the ability of people to innovate and develop solutions. The function of leadership increasingly will become a process of discovering and promoting experimentation, innovation, and invention. Leaders will need to focus attention on specific and simple ideas and to influence patterns of attention and isolate what information is important. They will need to create linkages and alter the connections and interactions among individuals via information, questions, and challenges, including a capacity to plant and spread strategic ideas. They will also need to increase the diversity of alternatives available to the system through the introduction and oversight of activities that enable the system to adapt and sustain itself as the environment changes and operate in a manner that is dynamic and coevolutionary.

Third, successful global leaders will need to be prepared to maintain stability under unpredictable and chaotic conditions, helping followers to focus attention and maintain order when it is not present. They will need to be able to read situations quickly and help to create and foster a state of self-organizing fluidity and hyperflexibility within the organization.

Finally, global leaders will need to create supportive learning environments and foster sensemaking built on connection, coherence, mutually created meaning, dynamic relationships, and an integrated systems perspective. Organizational members are motivated to commit to engaging in complex adaptive behaviors to the extent they feel interdependent with the system (Uhl-Bien & Marion, 2009). Leaders will need to help connect the past, present, and future through dialogue and storytelling. They will provide consultation on changing paradigms, work in collaborative networks, and help people to envision and discover new possibilities. They will support shared learning, foster inter-relationships and networks, and build consensus.

A conclusion that can be drawn is that we may need to create a new model of leadership based on an environment that is more complex and dynamic than we have heretofore experienced. Perhaps we do not yet have the right term for the type of leader needed to address the conditions that are emerging. Karakas (2007) describes the twenty-first century leader as a social artist, spiritual visionary, and cultural innovator, and adds, "As we stand [several] years into the twenty-first century, one thing is abundantly clear: We aren't in the twentieth century anymore. Postmodern terror, global warming, the rapid proliferation of technology, globalization, hyper-competition for resources and markets and the labor force, the widening gap between developed and underdeveloped regions—are just a few signposts of the new age. The trends that will characterize the next several decades are . . . disrupting the old order and posing unprecedented challenges, *particularly for societies and organizations whose leaders are ill-equipped to deal with the new order*" (p. 44, emphasis added). One of the key characteristics of leaders who *are* equipped to deal with the new order will be the "ability to manage chaos and complexity and to draw on chaos and complexity sciences to understand organizations as complex adaptive systems" (Karakas, 2007, p. 45).

Another conclusion presents itself as a critically normative question: are there values and principles that can be ascribed to "good" global leadership in a complex world? Effective leadership of human institutions implies a response to global conditions and threats that leads to a more stable order and that supports and strengthens the health, well-being, and development of people and the planet rather than responses that sustain a type of complexity based on instability and the conditions that create it. One can only hope for a generation of global leaders with a willingness to read the trends of complexity and act decisively in service to a better world instead of merely "adapting" to changing conditions. We cannot be value-neutral about outcomes; the stakes are too high.

Finally, a detailed comprehension of the nature of leadership required to meet emerging global conditions is urgently needed. We can enhance our understanding of the nature of global leadership now and in the future by continuing to explore linkages between leadership theory and complexity theory. As we actively seek to define these connections, understand the related behaviors, and clarify how leaders are to be developed, we will enhance leaders' ability to respond to emerging global challenges.

References

Aldag, R. J., & Kuzuhara, L. W. (2002). *Organizational behavior and management: An integrated skills approach.* Cincinnati, OH: South-Western College Publishing.

Avolio, B. (2007). Promoting more integrative strategies for leadership theory-building. *American Psychologist, 62*(1), 25–33.

Bennis, W. (2007). The challenges of leadership in the modern world: Introduction to the special issue. *American Psychologist, 62*(1), 2–5.

Bonnstetter, B. J. (2000). The DNA of global leadership competencies. *Thunderbird International Business Review, 42*(2), 131–144.

Brownell, J. (2006). Meeting the competency needs of global leaders: A partnership approach. *Human Resource Management, 45*(3), 309–336.

Bueno, C., & Tubbs, S. (2004). Identifying global leadership competencies. *Journal of American Academy of Business, 5*(1/2), 80–87.

Croucher, S. L. (2004). *Globalization and belonging: The politics of identity in a changing world.* Lanham, MD: Rowman and Littlefield.

Farazmand, A. (2007). Learning from the Katrina crisis: A global and international perspective with implications for future crisis management. *Public Administration Review, 67,* 149–159.

Ferraro, G. P. (2001). *Global brains.* Charlotte, NC: Intercultural Associates.

Griffin, D. (2002). *The emergence of leadership: Linking self-organization and ethics.* London: Routledge.

Gronn, P. (2002). Distributed leadership as a unit of analysis. *Leadership Quarterly, 13*(4), 423–451.

Grove, A. S. (1996). *Only the paranoid survive.* New York: Doubleday.

Harris, P., Moran, R., & Moran, S. (2004). *Managing cultural differences: Global leadership strategies for the 21st century.* Burlington, MA: Elsevier Butterworth Heinemann.

Hazy, J. K. (2004). Leadership in complex systems: A meta-level information processing capabilities that bias exploration and exploitation. In K. Carley (Ed.), *Proceedings of the 2004 NAACSOS Conference.* Pittsburgh: Carnegie Mellon University.

Hazy, J. K. (2006). Measuring leadership effectiveness in complex sociotechnical systems. *Emergence: Complexity and Organization, 8*(3), 58–77.

Hermann, C. F. (1969). *Crises in foreign policy: A simulation analysis.* Indianapolis: Bobbs-Merrill.

Hersey, P., & Blanchard, K. H. (1977). *Management of organizational behavior: Utilizing human resources* (3rd ed.). Upper Saddle River, NJ: Prentice Hall.

Holland, J. H. (1995). *Hidden order: How adaptation builds complexity.* Reading, MA: Perseus Books.

Hunt, J., Osborn, R., & Boal, K. (2009). The architecture of managerial leadership: Stimulation and channeling of organizational emergence. *Leadership Quarterly, 20*(4), 503–516.

Jenkins, W. (2006). Collaboration over adaptation: The case for interoperable communications in Homeland Security. *Public Administration Review, 66*(3), 319–331.

Jokinen, T. (2005). Global leadership competencies: A review and discussion. *Journal of European Industrial Training, 29*(3), 199–216.

Karakas, F. (2007). The twenty-first century leader: Social artist, spiritual visionary, and cultural innovator. *Global Business & Organizational Excellence, 26*(3), 44–50.

Karp, T., & Helgø, T. (2009). Reality revisited: Leading people in chaotic change. *Journal of Management Development, 28*(2), 81–93.

Kedia, B. L., & Mukherji, A. (1999). Global managers: Developing a mindset for global competitiveness. *Journal of World Business, 34*, 230–252.

Kets de Vries, M., & Florent-Treacy, E. (2002). Global leadership from A to Z: Creating high commitment organizations. *Organizational Dynamics, 295*(309), 1–16.

Kets de Vries, M., Vrignaud, P., & Florent-Treacy, E. (2004). The Global Leadership Life Inventory: Development and psychometric properties of a 360-degree feedback instrument. *International Journal of Human Resource Management, 15*(3), 475–492.

Kiel, L. D. (1994). *Managing chaos and complexity in government: A new paradigm for managing change, innovation, and organizational renewal.* San Francisco: Jossey-Bass.

Leung, A., Maddux, W., Galinsky, A., & Chiu, C. (2008, April). Multicultural experience enhances creativity: The when and how. *American Psychologist, 63*, 169–181.

Lobel, S. (1991). Global leadership competencies: Managing to a different drumbeat. *Human Resource Management, 29*(1), 39–47.

March, J. G. (1991). Exploration and exploitation in organizational learning. *Organization Science, 2*(1), 71–87.

Mendenhall, M. E. (2006). The elusive, yet critical challenge of developing global leaders. *European Management Journal, 24*(6), 422–429.

Paparone, C. (2004). Deconstructing army leadership. *Military Review, 84*(1), 2–10.

Pascale, R., Millemann, N., & Gioja, L. (1990). *Surfing the edge of chaos: The laws of nature and the new laws of business.* New York: Three Rivers Press.

Prigogine, I., & Stengers, I. (1984). *Order out of chaos: Man's new dialogue with nature*. New York: Bantam Books.

Rhinesmith, S. (1996). *Managers guide to globalization: Six skills for success in a changing world*. New York: McGraw-Hill.

Rock, D., & Schwartz, J. (2006). The neuroscience of leadership, *Strategy+Business, 43*, 76–82.

Sanchez, J., Spector, P., & Cooper, C. (2000). Adapting to a boundaryless world: A developmental expatriate model. *Academy of Management Executive, 14*(2), 96–106.

Schein, E. (1986). Epilogue: International human resource management: New directions, perpetual issues, and missing themes. *Human Resource Management, 86*(25), Issue 1, 169–176.

Schwandt, D. R., & Szabla, D. B. (2007). Systems and leadership: Co-evolution or mutual evolution towards complexity. In J. K. Hazy, J. A. Goldstein, & B. B. Lichtenstein (Eds.), *Complex systems leadership theory* (pp. 35–60). Mansfield, MA: ISCE Publishing.

Sheridan, E. (2005). *Intercultural leadership competencies for US business leaders in the new millennium*. PhD dissertation, University of Phoenix.

Stacey, R., Griffin, D., & Shaw, P. (2000). *Complexity and management: Fad or radical challenge to systems thinking?* New York, NY: Routledge.

Uhl-Bien, M., & Marion, R. (2009). Complexity leadership in bureaucratic forms of organizing: A meso model. *Leadership Quarterly, 20*(4), 631–650.

Uhl-Bien, M., Marion, R., & McKelvey, B. (2007). Complexity leadership theory: Shifting leadership from the industrial age to the knowledge age. *Leadership Quarterly, 18*(4), 298–318.

Weick, K. E. (1995). *Sensemaking in organizations*. Thousand Oaks, CA: Sage.

Weick, K. E., & Sutcliffe, K. M. (2001). *Managing the unexpected: Assuring high performance in an age of complexity*. San Francisco: Jossey-Bass.

Wills, S., & Barham, K. (1994). Being an international manager. *European Management Journal, 12*(1), 49–58.

Wise, C. R. (2006). Organizing for homeland security after Katrina: Is adaptive management what's missing? *Public Administration Review, 66*(3), 302–318.

Yukl, G. A. (1999). An evaluation of conceptual weaknesses in transformational and charismatic leadership theories. *Leadership Quarterly, 10*(2), 285–305.

Chapter Twelve

The Role of Culture and History in the Applicability of Western Leadership Theories in Africa

Deanne de Vries

Does a black African who believes in and lives by values stemming from his or her African culture experience any dissonance between those values and the ones that characterize Western business practice, and which are thus part of the ethos of the corporation he or she is part of? If so, what are the differences in values, how serious are they, and what can be done to reduce them (Prozesky, n.d.)?

Africa is one of the fastest-growing economic regions in the world. The World Bank states that since the mid-1990s, the fifteen fastest-growing African countries (excluding the oil-rich countries) have had an average growth rate of at least 4.5 percent (Broadman, 2007). With more than 60 percent of the population below the age of twenty-five, Africa is expected to be home to 1.1 billion working-age people by 2040, more than either China or India (Leke, Lund, Roxburgh, & van Wamelen, 2010); however, much of the labor is unskilled. Those who are educated tend to lack practical management experience. Leadership matters in these challenging environments. An intimate knowledge of the local reality, the ability to navigate risk, and a talent for building effective relationships are crucial to a company's success when entering markets—particularly emerging markets. Africans have been leading kingdoms, tribes, companies, and community projects in a variety of contexts for as long as there has been civilization in Africa. However, 85 percent of US Fortune 500 company executives said they do not have enough globally competent executives (Gregersen, Morrison, & Black, 1998). Is this because the dissonance between a black African's culturally influenced values do not resonate with Western business practices?

As the world evolves into one global market, the need to understand how leaders are viewed, trained, and developed in different cultural and national contexts has become increasingly important (Ardichvili & Kuchinke, 2002; Rhodes et al., 2005; Yukl, Gordon, & Taber 2002). Cross-culturally competent leaders give companies a competitive advantage because their ability to effectively work in different cultures is a strong contributor to profitability (Caligiuri, 2006; Javidan, Dorfman, Sully de Luque, & House, 2006). However, the inability of companies and their leadership to adapt to foreign cultures has been a major cause of business failures (Johnson, Lenartowicz, & Apud, 2006). If we assume that leadership is important in global companies, then a question emerges: what makes a leader effective in different countries and diverse cultures?

Much work has been done—predominantly in the United States—identifying various types of leadership theories. With trait leadership theory, for example, scholars teach that effective leaders are born leaders. At birth they already have the innate personality and skills that guarantee they will be leaders later on in life. Again, questions emerge: do scholars on various continents identify the same sorts of traits or, for that matter, even ascribe to trait theory? Additionally, if a person is born with specific identified traits in one country, what happens if he or she moves to a different country as a child or after university? Will the leadership attributes they were born with still apply? A leader in the United States or Europe is quite different than the average leader in Senegal, Uganda, or Ghana. Furthermore, the style theory of leadership emphasizes the behavior of leaders; it is a leader's style that determines his or her effectiveness. Thus, does a leader's behavior vary from country to country? For that matter, should one's behavior vary or should it remain constant? Is situational leadership important, for example?

In this chapter, I first provide a basic overview of the role of culture in leadership. A discussion of the influence of historical events on culture and leadership is followed by a review of the evolution of leadership development in Africa to understand how the changing culture of Africa has affected the view of leadership in Africa. I conclude this chapter with recommendations on next steps for the development and enhancement of African leadership theories.

Leadership in a Cultural Context

Leadership is a popular topic of discussion in scholarly research, magazines, books, boardrooms, on university campuses, and around the dinner table. A commonly agreed-on definition of leadership, however, is still lacking. Adding to the complexity is the multicultural world in which we currently live and work. House, Hanges, Javidan, Dorfman, and Gupta, (2004) described leadership as "an enigma—a puzzle within a puzzle [that becomes] even more fascinating, complex, and daunting if looked at through a cross-cultural lens" (p. 54). So what is culture? How does it affect the definition of leadership? Why should we look at leadership through a cultural lens?

Culture manifests itself in two ways: the visible—skin color, a country's boundaries, manner of dress—and the invisible—values, morals, traditions, personality (Ayman & Korabik, 2010). The former is easy to see. The latter is much more nuanced. Understanding culture is paramount to understanding leadership because "the cultural values surrounding the leader determine which leader behaviors tend to be most effective" (Dickson, Den Hartog, & Mitchelson, 2003, p. 755). Many assume that culture is the same as nationality. Some from the United States may define themselves as "Americans" and then go into details, for example "We are from Texas, the Dallas area." Rarely would an American from the United States start off by saying "I am a Hernandez" or "I am Hispanic" or "My ancestors hailed from the Mayans." Conversely, when an African first meets someone, he or she tells his or her last name. (One may only discover a first name if one asks.) When one asks where an individual is from, the African will tell the village and then the tribe. It is not as important to say "I am Ugandan" or "I am Senegalese," because the idea of a "national culture" or a "country culture" was only introduced to (some might say "forced" on) Africa when the European colonialists gathered for a conference in Berlin, Germany, in 1884 to divide Africa among all the European nations, thereby creating "countries" where none had previously existed. Because no Africans were present in Berlin and Africans had never known national borders, most were not even aware of any "official boundaries" until much later, some not until independence in the 1960s. Hence, national culture, at least for Africans, may not be the best or most correct way to understand cultural differences (Bolden & Kirk, 2009).

A question then arises because 98 percent of research conducted on leadership originates in the United States (Bryman, 2004): to what extent do leadership models developed in the nation and culture of the United States apply to people from other countries and cultures? Research has shown that national culture is not a reliable way of understanding cultural differences and therefore leadership differences. Ayman and Korabik (2010) illustrate the influence of a leader's nationality through an experiment they conducted in which a Japanese leader in the United States behaved first as a stereotypical American leader and then as a typical Japanese leader with his American team. His staff considered him more trustworthy when he behaved as a Japanese leader than as an American leader.

Hence, I propose that to understand leadership, one must first understand culture. To understand culture, one must first understand the history of the area (in this case, Africa) one is interested in researching. Before progressing further, it should be noted that Africa is a continent, not a country. Africa is actually fifty-six very diverse countries each with its own collection of tribes, languages, religions, traditions, economic organizations, and leadership arrangements (Zoogah, 2009). However, for the purposes of arguing the principle that only through knowledge of history can one understand the culture and thereby leadership of a particular area, leeway is taken here and Africa is viewed as one collective culture.

History and Its Effect on Leadership in Africa

Trompenaars and Hampden-Turner (1998) tell the story of a frustrated Dutch manager in Ethiopia whose students left his course on how to manage change and went right back to their old ways. After speaking with his Ethiopian colleagues, he decided to study Ethiopian history books to identify modern management practices that may have played a role in earlier times. Having learned of Ethiopia's rich history, the Dutch manager then posed the need for change through examples of what Ethiopia had done right in the past that led to its reign as a center of trade, religion, and education. Suddenly, the management of change seminar captured everyone's enthusiastic support.

The history of leadership in Africa, I propose, can be divided into three phases. The first period is the historical or precolonial in which traditional African leadership was established; this period basically started from the beginning of civilization in Africa and lasted until the fifteenth century. The second period is the colonial period wherein European leadership ideas and methods were imposed on the Africans; this period transpired from the 1600s to the 1960s. The third and current period is what Gordon (2002) calls the "two souls" phase or postcolonialism with Africans torn among their own traditional leadership, colonialist leadership, and modern Western leadership theories, from the 1960s to the current time.

The few times historians write about leadership in Africa, it is usually only with a passing reference to the building of the pyramids in Egypt and is usually accompanied by "an undertone of astonishment in the degree to which management existed in Egypt" (Nkomo, 2006, p. 7). Little did the colonialists know when they first arrived on the shores of Africa in the fifteenth century that the world they "discovered" already had a multitude of vibrant cultures, flourishing trade, universities, political stability, and a well-established leadership culture (Gordon, 2002). Africa at the time was a conglomeration of clans, tribes, and kingdoms ruled by chiefs and kings whose longevity in office was dependent on listening to and meeting the needs of their people (Nkomo, 2006). Traditionally, leadership in Africa was based on kinship, religion, age, and tribe. Mangaliso (2001) summarized that sub-Saharan Africa "is characterized by the norms of reciprocity, suppression of self-interest, the virtue of symbiosis, and human interdependence" (p. 24).

African leadership changed dramatically with the arrival of colonialism. During the colonial period of leadership history in Africa (from the 1600s to the 1960s) much of what the Africans had known was uprooted. The influx of European values and the imposition of European leadership methodologies and organizational hierarchies had a tremendous and detrimental impact on Africa (Gordon, 2002). New power structures were introduced. New ways of influencing people to cooperate were introduced. Loyalty was no longer bound by clan but could be bought with guns or money. The value of community was pushed aside in favor of stressing individual gain, individual power, and individual accumulation of wealth. Borders were drawn. Fences were erected. Land shared for centuries among all tribes and kingdoms was now cordoned off and only the privileged few could access it. Most battles in Europe were fought over land as there was a very finite quantity of land. In Africa, however, where land was plentiful, a tribe would just move to a new location when skirmishes broke out between two tribes (usually over women or cattle). By forcing Africans into separate and distinct nation-states (many of which were too small to be viable, all of which divided preexisting kingdoms and tribes), the continent and its people were destabilized.

Europeans arrived in Africa and assumed leadership because they presumed Africa had no leadership, thereby laying the seeds of a leadership (and political and economical) crisis. Colonialism took leadership out of the Africans' hands. Africans were subject to new types of leaders who had other ways of thinking, different methods of obtaining power, and a different judicial system. No longer was leadership equated with listening to and meeting the needs of one's people or in the number of cows or wives a man had. A leader's tribe, religion, status in the community, and age started to matter less and less. There was a small but new group of African leaders that thrived in this environment: the "taker," an African who knew "how to manipulate Westerners and how to use, to their own ends, their once-upon-a-time tribe" (Boon, 2007, p. 48). Having turned their backs on traditional African values, the "takers" usually adopted the worst values of the first world colonialists and became self-serving, power-hungry, and ruthless. Many African leaders however were, and still are, caught between their traditional values and the new European values, hierarchies, and institutions.

Being caught between African and European cultures brings us to the third and current period that Gordon (2002) describes as leaders operating with two souls: one African traditional, one European colonial. Toward the middle of the twentieth century, native African leaders began rising up against and within the colonial governments. Kwame Nkrumah in Ghana, Jomo Kenyatta in Kenya, and Julius Nyerere in Tanzania all directly opposed the colonialist governments and promoted nationalism as the reason the colonialists needed to return leadership to the natives. In French-speaking West Africa, Leopold Senghor of Senegal and Houphouet-Boigney of the Ivory Coast worked within the colonial system to reintroduce native leaders and eventually lead their countries to independence from the French colonialists (Gordon, 2002). Today, technology, ease of transportation, and the influx of multinational companies have brought even more leadership traits and styles to the shores of Africa. Consequently, leadership in Africa is currently entrenched in a challenging mix of multiple cultural, political, economic, and social contexts that are complex, multilayered, and inter-woven with historical events (Nkomo, 2006).

With this brief historical overview, I show the influence that historical events can have on culture and on how leadership is viewed and learned. Without this background knowledge, I argue that it is difficult to implement any Western leadership theory effectively in Africa. In the first paragraph to this chapter, I highlight the fact that an African's cultural experiences influence his or her leadership and business ethos, causing dissonance with Western business practice. With a basic appreciation for and knowledge of Africa's history, I now consider some specific exam-ples of how African and Western leadership differ.

Western Versus African Approaches to Leadership

Leaders in Western and African countries approach leader-ship from some very different paradigms. Understanding these diversities is vital to understanding the applicability of leadership theories in Africa. Prozesky (n.d.) identifies seven differences between African values and those of Western business:

- Community above individualism
- External versus internal locus of control
- Supporting opposed to competing
- Employees as people first, then as workers
- The divergent definition of and sense of time
- Leadership through care and integrity versus power and status
- Wealth as something holistic, not just financial or material

Five of these differences are discussed in the next sections.

Community Above Individualism

A Westerner, influenced by Greco-Roman philosophy and Judeo-Christian religious beliefs, sees humans as rational beings responsible for their own actions (Boon, 2007). The African philosophy, however, is often summed up in one word: *ubuntu*. Ubuntu is from "*umntungumntu ngabanye* (a person is a person through others), which implies that the relationship and recognition by others is at the core of a person's identity" (House, Hanges, Javidan, Dorfman, & Gupta, 2004, p. 187). There is no one word that sums up ubuntu in the English language. Rather, ubuntu encompasses community, togetherness, interdependence, teamwork, mutual respect, and a participative way of working and decision making (Bolden & Kirk, 2009; Nkomo, 2006).

External Versus Internal Locus of Control

A Westerner believes in an internal locus of control, that everything is within his or her control, that decisions are made from one's self rather than by others to oneself. An African, by contrast, believes in an external locus of control, that certain things are just not in one's self-control. For most Africans, this control is in the hands of their ancestors. As an example, a Westerner might say "I missed the bus," whereas an African might say "the bus left me." The Westerner sees missing the bus as one's own fault; one should have done something different so as not to miss the bus. An African understands that catching the bus was not meant to be. The African did not purposely miss the bus; some external force just did not intend for that bus to be caught.

Employees as People First, Then as Workers

Boon (2007) relates how a Western leader with all the right leadership traits in a Western environment could be very ineffective in Africa. He gives an example of the underperforming African worker who has been warned a few times by his

Western-trained leader. When the worker does not change after three or four warnings, the leader dismisses the African. In the African paradigm, however, everyone who works with the underperformer would know he is the sole breadwinner at home, his wife is very sick, and that he financially supports the families of unemployed family members. Rather than firing the worker, the Africans might say, "Let's talk to him . . . it's our responsibility to keep him employed and to move him into a different environment where he will be useful" (Boon, 2007, pp. 62–63).

Leadership Through Care and Integrity Versus Power and Status

African leaders, though respected for their age and accomplishments, are there to serve their people, to pass on the values of their religion, and to build up the village (Masango, 2003; Nyerere, 1962). Although in some cultures royal birth was a prerequisite for being a chief, royal birth alone did not guarantee leadership; the community had to approve the chief because "the kingdom was more important than the king" (Hale, 2004, p. 6). If the chief or king or traditional leader was not acting in the best interest of his people or was not upholding the community's values, he was removed.

Wealth as Something Holistic, Not Just Financial or Material

In African society, an individual's wealth is not one's wealth alone. Wealth (whether in cattle, crops, money, or wisdom) is seen as the family's or the tribe's. Everyone is expected to use the collective wealth to better the entire community. Wealth in traditional African society does not translate into power or prestige (Nyerere, 1962).

As these examples illustrate, individual leadership traits, behaviors, and values are often different between Westerners and

Africans. Western management, for example, emphasizes individual traits and behaviors whereas Africans desire to maintain their traditional and community-oriented values. How important are these differences? How can African leaders and scholars of African leadership benefit from the years of research done in a predominantly Western context on leadership theories? What lessons can Western leaders and scholars learn from the African context of leadership?

Increasing the Knowledge Base of Leadership Theories in Africa

Multiple leadership theories have come out of the Western world: trait, behavioral, style, contingency, charismatic, servant, path-goal, and transformational to name just a few. The question is how can Africans benefit from the years of research conducted on these leadership theories, albeit from and related to a purely Western (and mostly male) frame of reference. Can these leadership theories apply to Africa? I would assert yes. As long as one starts from a base of a comprehensive knowledge of Africa's history and culture, it is possible to identify how best to augment African traditional leadership with pertinent elements of modern or Western leadership theories.

Western Leadership Theory in an African Context

In *Leadership in the African Context*, Van Zyl (2009) highlights four studies undertaken in Africa that illustrate particular traits that are important for leaders within the African context. In one study, Makgoba (1997) found that hospitality, friendliness, consensus, a common framework-seeking principle, ubuntu, and an emphasis on community characterized African leaders. Nyasani (1997) additionally published research that found sociality, patience, tolerance, sympathy, and acceptance were the important traits found among leaders in Africa. Khoza (2006) first highlighted the external locus of control that typifies African leaders as well as honesty, humbleness, integrity, empathy, humanity, and ubuntu. Van Rensburg (2007) also identified ubuntu as a key trait of leaders along with leaders being seen as trustworthy, inspirational, courageous, powerful, wise, role models, and community focused. Another scholar, Lassiter (2000), believes that there are five identifiable sub-Saharan African leadership characteristics that set African leaders apart from leaders in other parts of the world: psychological characteristics, influential role of society over that of the individual, importance of family and community, their worldview, and response to foreign influences.

Regarding the style leadership theory, Chhokar, Brodbeck, and House (2008) identified two studies conducted on leadership style in South Africa that were part of the GLOBE research project that looked at leadership in sixty-one countries. Booysen and van Wyk (2008) "found that outstanding leaders in South Africa are perceived to show a strong and direct, but democratic and participative, leadership style . . . sensitive to their followers' needs and are expected to reflect their followers' ideas, satisfy their needs, and be respectful and understanding" (pp. 452–453). These outcomes were corroborated by Charlton (1993), who found that the leading South African executives understand the current reality, exhibit excellent communication skills, have uncompromising standards of excellence, and a clear focus and vision for the future.

The GLOBE project team also concluded from their research that certain leader behaviors can be seen as universally accepted regardless of culture. Using this data from GLOBE as their starting point, Den Hartog, House, Hanges, Ruiz-Quintanilla, and Dorfman (1999) further researched the notion that certain leader behaviors can be seen as universally accepted regardless of culture. They discovered that attributes such as integrity (trustworthy, just, honest), charisma (inspirational and visionary leadership), as well as team-oriented, excellence-oriented, decisive, intelligent, and a win-win problem solver were indeed universally endorsed as representing outstanding leadership. Conversely, leaders who were viewed as irritable, noncooperative, egocentric, a loner, or ruthless were deemed ineffective.

African Leadership Theory

There is a growing body of research on the topic of "African leadership" or "leadership in Africa." Some take the view that the more Africans adhere to Western practices the more effective and efficient Africa will become. Others are tired of the endless Western countries' donor-funded management programs that well-meaning but ineffective groups are trying to enforce in Africa. "The fact that many African managers have the intellectual capacity to understand the logic underlying Western management principles and practices but revert to their pre-training behavior after participating in several training programs indicates fundamental weaknesses in the Western management-oriented training programs themselves" (Kuada, 1994, as quoted in Kuada, 2010, p. 10).

Nkomo (2006) advocates for Africa to embrace globalization while Zoogah (2009) urges leaders in Africa to find a way to combine modernism with traditionalism. Kuada (2007) urges African leadership to import only those Western practices that support African cultural values. Zaccaro (2007) argues for a combination of traits and styles (behaviors) as his research has shown an integrated approach is the most effective prediction of leadership success. One of the more interesting and practical suggestions comes from Prozesky (n.d.) who suggests a convergence; combining the best of both worlds and focusing on what they have in common. For example, while African culture values community and Western culture values individualism, social investment is valued by both cultures. Success is another value shared by both cultures—even though an African sees their success as holistic, something to be shared by the entire community and a Westerner sees it as an individually owned commodity. Whereas tradition is highly valued in Africa and Westerners value enterprise and innovation, both cultures agree that whatever is created should be sustainable. "Commitment to sustainability means that the creation of future viability simultaneously creates a new history to look back on with pride, and thus also a tradition—while also fostering enterprise" (Prozeksy, n.d., p. 5). It is a fact that cultural differences exist and that these can have a negative impact on business and a leader's effectiveness. Rather than focusing on the differences, Prozesky is urging leaders of multicultural teams to converge, to focus on shared values.

The multiplicity of opinions and a growing list of research studies show there is an interest in and desire for the identification of African leadership theories. As the Dutch manager noted earlier learned in Ethiopia, there are many relevant examples of leadership in Africa's history—Abu Bakr II and Mansa Musa of Mali, Cleopatra, the Queen of Sheba, Imhotep (the "father of medicine"), Shaka Zulu, and Emperor Haile Selassie I of Ethiopia—as well as modern-day icons such as Nelson Mandela, Archbishop Desmond Tutu, former UN secretary general Kofi Annan, president Ellen Johnson-Sirleaf of Liberia, and Nobel prize winner Wangari Maathai. Africans can learn from these "Great (Wo)Men" not only effective leadership traits but leadership styles as well. These leaders have led in Africa, on a global scale, as politicians, activists, in the business community, and in the church. Each of these leaders has retained respect for and adherence to the traditional ways of leadership in Africa while operating in a heavily Western-influenced world. They have found a way to lead with "two souls"—one African and the other their European colonial and neocolonial soul (Gordon, 2002).

Conclusion

To return to the opening question in the chapter, "Does a black African who believes in and lives by values stemming from his or her African culture experience any dissonance between those values and the ones that characterize Western business practice, and which are thus part of the ethos of the corporation he or she is part of?" (Prozesky, n.d., p. 1). Because cultural values of a black African often differ from Western business practices and leadership traits and styles, a black African would indeed experience dissonance between the two cultures of one's home and one's career. The dissonance, however, is not so serious that it cannot be overcome. To bridge the gap between African values and Western business practices, three processes must occur. Westerners must acknowledge that their leadership styles are not universal because their research has been limited primarily to one country, the United States. Africans must stand up, capture, and promote their own history, their culture, their values, and their beliefs. In this chapter, I have demonstrated that the trait and style leadership theories have contributed to the overall understanding of leadership, albeit primarily focused from the perspective of Western society. Thus, together, in the third process, Western and African scholars need to use the foundations of these Western leadership theories and the methods by which these theories were developed (or invent new methods) to identify the personality characteristics and behaviors that make leaders effective in Africa within the context of African history and culture. These three processes together will create a unique leadership approach whose foundations are the African traditional and cultural values but that learns from and borrows those applicable practices from Western and other non-Western (for example, Asian, Arab, or Hispanic) cultures. Here is a story to summarize my conclusion:

> Some Americans landed their plane in the middle of a Turkana village in rural Kenya. Expecting the Turkana to be amazed, the

Americans were perplexed that the Turkana reacted with shrieks of laughter not at the plane but at the Americans. Thinking the Turkana did not understand the power of this "beast," the Americans flew off and landed—this time on water. Still no sense of awe from the Turkana who just went and sat under the plane's wings enjoying the shade. The Americans even took one of the men for a flight, but on their return he stepped out as if nothing whatsoever had happened. (Graham & Beard, 1990)

Clearly, the Americans failed to realize that "the tribal Turkana's sense of self-esteem is well developed and completely intact, and that he has no need to go chasing after First World toys" (Boon, 2007, pp. 52–53) . . . or leadership theories.

References

Ardichvili, A., & Kuchinke, K. P. (2002). Leadership styles and cultural values among managers and subordinates: A comparative study of four countries of the former Soviet Union, Germany and the U.S. *Human Resource Development International, 5*(1), 99–117.

Ayman, R., & Korabik, K. (2010). Why culture and gender matter. *American Psychologist, 65*(3), 157–170.

Bolden, R., & Kirk, P. (2009). African leadership: Surfacing new understandings through leadership development. *International Journal of Cross Cultural Management, 9*(1), 69–86.

Boon, M. (2007). *The African way: The power of interactive leadership* (3rd ed.). Cape Town, South Africa: Zebra Press.

Booysen, L.A.E., & van Wyk, M. W. (2008). Culture and leadership in South Africa. In J. S. Chhokar, F. C. Brodbeck, & R. J. House (Eds.), *Culture and leadership across the world: The GLOBE book of in-depth studies of 25 societies* (pp. 433–474). New York: Psychology Press.

Broadman, H. G. (2007). *Africa's silk road.* Washington, DC: The International Bank for Reconstruction and Development/The World Bank.

Bryman, A. (2004). Qualitative research on leadership: A critical but appreciative review. *Leadership Quarterly, 15*, 729–769.

Caligiuri, P. (2006). Developing global leaders. *Human Resource Management Review, 16*, 219–228.

Charlton, G. D. (1993). *The human race: Leadership* (2nd ed.). Cape Town, South Africa: Rustica.

Chhokar, J. S., Brodbeck, F. C., & House, R. J. (Eds.). (2008). *Culture and leadership across the world: The GLOBE book of in-depth studies of 25 societies.* New York: Psychology Press.

Den Hartog, D., House, R. J., Hanges, P. J., Ruiz-Quintanilla, S. A., & Dorfman, P. W. (1999). Culture specific and cross-culturally generalizable implicit leadership theories: Are attributes of charismatic/transformational leadership universally endorsed? *Leadership Quarterly, 10*(2), 219–256.

Dickson, M. W., Den Hartog, D. N., & Mitchelson, J. K. (2003). Research on leadership in a cross-cultural context: Making progress, and raising new questions. *Leadership Quarterly, 14,* 729–768.

Gordon, J. U. (2002). *African leadership in the twentieth century.* Lanham, MD: University Press of America.

Graham, A., & Beard, P. (1990). *Eyelids of morning* (Reprint ed.). San Francisco: Chronicle Books.

Gregersen, H. B., Morrison, A. J., & Black, J. S. (1998). Developing leaders for the global frontier. *Sloan Management Review, 40*(1), 21–32.

Hale, J. R. (2004, August). *A contextualized model for cross-cultural leadership in West Africa.* Paper presented at the Servant Leadership Research Roundtable. Retrieved from www.regent.edu/acad/global/publications/sl_proceedings/2004/hale_contextualized_model.pdf

House, R. J., Hanges, P. J., Javidan, M., Dorfman, P. W., & Gupta, V. (2004). *Culture, leadership, and organizations: The GLOBE study of 62 societies.* Thousand Oaks, CA: Sage.

Javidan, M., Dorfman, P. W., Sully de Luque, M., & House, R. J. (2006). In the eye of the beholder: Cross cultural lessons in leadership from project GLOBE. *Journal of Management Perspectives, 20,* 67–90.

Johnson, P. J., Lenartowicz, T., & Apud, S. (2006). Cross-cultural competence in international business: Toward a definition and a model. *Journal of International Business Studies, 37,* 525–543.

Khoza, R. J. (2006). *Let Africa lead: African transformational leadership for 21st century business.* Johannesburg, South Africa: Vezubuntu Publishing.

Kuada, J. E. (1994). *Managerial behavior in Ghana and Kenya—A cultural perspective.* Aalborg, Denmark: Aalborg University Press.

Kuada, J. E. (2010). Culture and leadership in Africa: A conceptual model and research agenda. *African Journal of Economic and Management Studies, 1*(1), 9–24.

Lassiter, J. E. (2000). African culture and personality: Bad social science, effective social activism, or a call to reinvent ethnology? *African Studies Quarterly, 3*(3), 1–21.

Leke, A., Lund, S., Roxburgh, C., & van Wamelen, A. (2010, June). What's driving Africa's growth. *McKinsey Quarterly.* Retrieved from www.mckinseyquarterly.com/Whats_driving_Africas_growth_2601

Makgoba, M. W. (1997). *The Makgogo affair: A reflection on transformation.* Florida Hills, South Africa: Vivlia Publishers and Booksellers.

Mangaliso, M. P. (2001). Building competitive advantage from Ubuntu: Management lessons from South Africa. *Academy of Management Executive, 15*(3), 23–33.

Masango, M. (2003). Leadership in the African context. *The Ecumenical Review, 55*(4), 313.

Nkomo, S. M. (2006). *Images of African leadership and management in organisation studies: Tensions, contradictions and re-visions.* DOI: 10.1.1.118.2297.

Nyasani, J. M. (1997). *The African psyche.* Nairobi, Kenya: University of Nairobi and Theological Printing Press.

Nyerere, J. K. (1962). *Ujamma—the basis of African socialism.* Retrieved from www.jpanafrican.com/edocs/e-DocUjamma3.5.pdf

Prozesky, M. (n.d.). *Tensions between Western business values and African traditional values—a pilot study.* Retrieved from www.benafrica.org/downloads/martin_prozesky.pdf

Rhodes, D. L., Emery, C. R., Tian, R. G., Shurden, M. C., Tolbert, S. H., Oertel, S., & Antonova, M. (2005). A cross-cultural comparison of leader ethics. *Journal of Organizational Culture, Communications and Conflict.* Retrieved from http://findarticles.com/p/articles/mi_m1TOT/is_1_9/ai_n25121982/

Trompenaars, F., & Hampden-Turner, C. (1998). *Riding the waves of culture: Understanding cultural diversity in global business.* New York: McGraw-Hill.

Van Rensburg, G. (2007). *The leadership challenge in Africa.* Pretoria, South Africa: Van Schalk Publishers.

Van Zyl, E. (2009). *Leadership in the African context.* Cape Town, South Africa: Juta & Co.

Yukl, G., Gordon, A., & Taber, T. (2002). A hierarchical taxonomy of leadership behavior: Integrating a half century of behavior research. *Journal of Leadership & Organizational Studies, 9*(1), 15–32.

Zaccaro, S. J. (2007). Trait-based perspectives of leadership. *American Psychologist, 62*(1), 6–16.

Zoogah, D. B. (2009). Cultural value orientation, personality, and motivational determinants of strategic leadership in Africa. *International Journal of Leadership Studies, 4*(2), 202–222.

Chapter Thirteen

A Tao Complexity Tool

Leading from Being

Caroline Fu and Richard Bergeon

From ancient times to the present, inspired leaders make sage decisions amid confounding complexity. Those decisions emerge from diverse thinking paradigms of multiple frames of reference to guide people from all walks toward sustaining success. Perhaps intuitively, such leaders seem able to discern essential constituents for success obscured in complex circumstances to navigate through turbulence, leveraging nature's dynamism,[1] and human responsiveness.

This chapter is a narration of our search for, and development of, a practice tool that explicates such leadership perspicacity so that success can be within the grasp of every leader and any collective. Disclosing epiphanies that transpired and invoked our paradigm shift during our discovery, we share how we use an ancient tool in a novel way, which correlates leadership phenomena to energy abstractions.[2] Commonsense leadership relies on knowledge of the past to make decisions for the future, whereas uncommon sense extracts understanding from the present being energy to find patterns we overlook. Through telling our search experience, we introduce our new tool, an uncommon sense approach, which consists of an ancient Tao concept, a basic leadership language to describe activating force interactions that form complex patterns in situations, and a simple way of using the tool. We demonstrate how employing the tool as a language for communicating thoughts to better understand at-the-moment *being* in leadership incidents as they unfold enables leaders from multiple viewpoints to arrive at a new state of *knowing* in complex or chaotic situations. Via real-world examples, we illustrate how to self-teach using the tool. Finally, we impart through reflection how the tool is used to assess being while engaging in our experience.

Comprehending Complexity: Our Quest for a Tool

Decades ago, we began a search for a telltale analysis tool to assess the nonobvious realm, at a deep level of knowing, in complex situations that would help us with our corporate change efforts. Many leadership initiatives brought us accumulated knowledge about systems of dynamic interacting forces (Forrester, 1990; Senge, Kleiner, Roberts, Ross, Roth, & Smith, 1999; Sterman, 2000). Noted theories (Axelrod, 1997; Briggs & Peat, 1989; Holland, 1995; Prigogine, 1997; Shanahan, 1997) and our practice experiences in leading social and technological changes brought awareness of the emergent perplexity racing ahead of our understanding of complexity. We envisioned a tool that offers ways for finding key ingredients in leadership acumen to increase the odds of maintaining progress and the momentum of success at multiple, individual to global, levels of complexity.

Our explorations ultimately led us into ancient philosophy as we sought fundamental understanding of complexity and the perpetual essences of leadership knowing. The writings of Confucian and Taoist sages revealed a universal, philosophical grounding for assessing leadership reality (Confucius, 450 BCE/1959; Lao-Tze, 500 BCE/1891), whether during war or peace, in sickness or health (Sun Tzu, 350 BCE/1988). The sages appropriated nature's endless cycles of change and its dynamic forces and energies to explain reality as energy abstractions of the being. In Tao leadership philosophy, synchronizing with nature's life-giving *power* brings balance and well-being. In his lecture on constancy and change, H. Wilhelm explained nature's relevance to human affairs: "This is a power with a definite rhythm and with a definite direction, and with the attribute of being closed within itself. An entelechy in this sense is like a small self-contained world system. All of Chinese thinking—Confucianism, Taoism, as well as Buddhism—contains the idea that in the course of life, [hu]man will shape harmoniously those psychic and physical predispositions that [s/]he received as capital assets by unifying them and giving them form from within a center" (Wilhelm & Wilhelm, 1956/1995, p. 313). Wilhelm and Wilhelm's notion of power, rhythm, direction, and being explains the conceptual basis the Chinese use for assessing well-being at multiple levels of complexity. Using abstractions of nature's forces to represent constituents in complex situations, assessments range from diagnosing people's physical illness in Chinese medicine to dealing with human affairs and leadership decision making.

Influenced by Chinese philosophy, our first glimmer of what we grasped as the essential constituents of *being* and *living* appeared in original ancient Chinese texts and their translations. We found Yin-Yang-WuXing (pronounced "Yin-Yang-Wu-hsing") in the *Book of History (Shu-Ching)*, the oldest doctrine of the Chinese classics (Wilhelm & Baynes, 1950/1997). We decipher it literally as "Yin-Yang-five-walks," or the five essences of being and living, and think it is appropriate to use this ageless concept to fathom complexity. Yin-yang signifies nature's essence, the day-night change; an ancient glyph depicted the word *change*, with the symbols of sun (yang) on the left and moon (yin) on the right (Wilhelm & Baynes, 1950/1997, flyleaf, pp. i–ii). The word *walks* has unusual meaning; it is an abstraction of nature's energy and forces, connotes movement, direction, and existence—the essence of change. R. Wilhelm translated the concept as the yin-yang "five stages of change" (p. xlviii). H. Wilhelm rendered a more current interpretation as "the system" of five nature's "activating forces" in yin-yang complementarity (Wilhelm & Wilhelm, 1956/1995, p. 103).

The five activating forces constantly interact with and affect one another creating an energy state of presence or at-the-moment of being-in-motion. Being is never static; rather, being is the emergent collective yin-yang dynamics of energy, often appearing chaotic and complex. In any moment, there is a "state of transformation"—in "each moment the future becomes present and the present past" (Wilhelm & Wilhelm, 1956/1995, p. 26). "Generally, dynamic conceptualizations are prevalent in China. The Chinese do not emphasize 'substance' as mass; . . . rather [it is] conceived as a state of energy" (p. 293). Thus, being is a state of fluid flow of energy, indivisible into components for analysis. Attempts to divide energy abstraction distort the essence of the whole.

When we rediscovered this ancient Tao concept, we had an epiphany: success or failure of interventions in leadership phenomena relates to the awareness of the states of being, rather than just knowing. As knowing relates to the past, solely relying on knowing does not offer the essence of the present states of being. Thus, studying the states of being could lead to more knowing about the phenomena by uncovering the not-yet-attended complexity. Adopting this ancient concept helped us envision a mechanism for assessing complex leadership phenomena as they evolve from a formless vision and emerge into formed realities—a Tao leading.

Being and Knowing in Chaos with Tao

The Tao of Science (Siu, 1971) and its philosophical concept of paradox helped us reify our formless vision for an assessment mechanism and evaluate our being to inform our knowing in progress. The nature of being and existence, we grasped as the "Tao in the sense of ontology," is rooted in itself (Chuangtse in Fu, 1953, p. 6). Being, as in Tao, "has its inner reality and its evidences. It is devoid of action and of form. It may be transmitted, but cannot be received. It may be obtained, but cannot be seen" (p. 6). Being in chaos is best described as "appearance comes from non-appearance; Beginning comes out of non-beginning ([though] in accordance with Cosmology)" (p. 16). Tao tools are rooted in the cognitive yin-yang abstractions—if "we can penetrate the Tao of day [yang] and night [yin]" (Wilhelm & Wilhelm, 1956/1995, p. 31) then we understand how nature's primal change cycle affects the seasons. That is, longer days, exposure to the sun, and shorter nights, away from the sun, bring on summer, and shorter days and longer nights, winter. The day-night and seasonal changes are dependent on one another, wherein, if one constituent were to stop changing, all would come to a "standstill" (p. 23). Thus, as in nature, change is constant and inevitable; all nature's forces exist in complementarity.

Considering the yin-yang complementarity, then, when a leader or consultant enters into a situation, the entry marks a new state of change. The entry becomes a beginning of sensing being in chaos, as everything is in motion, standing still is only an illusion. H. Wilhelm described the initial situation:

> The holy men [leaders] of ancient times followed the yin and
> the yang and from them determined decay and growth; . . .
> formed things originate from the formless. . . . There is a primal
> change, a primal beginning, a primal origin, and a primal
> creation. The primal change is the state in which energy does
> not yet express itself. The primal beginning is the state in
> which energy originates; the primal origin is the state in which
> form originates; the primal creation is the state in which matter
> originates. When energy, form and matter are present, but not
> yet separate, we call this chaos. (Wilhelm & Wilhelm,
> 1956/1995, pp. 105–106)

Chaos, as a muddle of the indiscernible, is not only persistent, but also illusive and fluid. "Chaos means the state in which all things [forces] still exist mixed together and have not yet separated [distinct] one from another." Trying to assess the muddle in a commonsense way yields little progress. "If one looks at it, there is nothing to see; if one listens to it, there is nothing to hear; if one follows it, one obtains nothing" (Wilhelm & Wilhelm, 1956/1995, p. 105). Common sense regards nothing-ness as unworthy of interest.

Common sense demands that we know as much about the phenomenon as possible by analyzing the visible components, their relations, and behaviors to identify some order. Very often, when we think we perceive some semblance of order out of chaos (Prigogine & Stengers, 1984) that order reorders itself. The illu-siveness is like quantum encounters with multiple realities; "certain sense perceptions of different individuals correspond to each other, while for other sense perceptions no such correspon-dence [on a same event] can be established" (Einstein, 1922/2005, p. 2). Sense perceptions captured in thought differ in relations to reality (p. 39) forming "the very arena of reality" (p. viii). Reality perceived as chaos is emergent as "Jung's notion of 'chance' and 'observed moment,'" "Whitehead's 'specious present,'" "Siu's 'virtual presence,'" and "Maslow's 'unconscious impulse'" (Fu, 2008, p. 45). Whitehead (1938) explained the "specious present" as "the qualitative energies of the past are combined into a pattern of qualitative energies in each present occasion" (pp. 226–227) manifested as what Whitehead (1933/1961) called "an abstraction" (p. 186). Siu (1978) observed, the "virtual presence is something which is not real in the space-time sense, yet it exerts a practical effect as if it were" (p. 88). The virtual presence of being creates what we call energy-flow[3] (Fu, 2008) on a conceptual leadership playing field.

Whenever we enter a leadership playing field, we are obliged to act to overcome chaos. Jung advised that rather than look for certainty, we should exert energy "combating" perceived "danger" associated with "chance" (Wilhelm & Baynes, 1950/1997). Maslow (1987) viewed acting on an impulse as "an education in spontaneity and eager abandon, in being natural, nonvoluntary

[sic], noncritical, and passive in the Taoist style, trying not to try" (p. 66). In our opinion, any tool of value would assist leaders to "subsume" and "resonate" (Siu, 1978, p. 83) with the situation at hand to provoke thinking out of the box.

With this brief theoretical background on the Tao concept of being as states of energy-flow, we developed an uncommon sense tool for identifying and assessing the essential leadership constituents in complex situations that can lead to successful interventions. Tapping into the formless energy-flow abstractions and patterns to understand the at-the-moment being rather than basing interventions on the past knowing (perceived as common sense) requires uncommon sense assessments. Understanding the interplay of the contributing forces that emerge into a complex pattern of energy-flow can serve as a foundation for assessing the being to inform leadership knowing. Using our tool can help leaders discern the interaction of the activating forces in a seemingly chaotic situation, assess the manifested being, design interventions, and implement changes.

A Tool for Assessing Complexity

Our tool is based on the attributes of nature's five activating forces as conceived by ancient Chinese sages to represent symbolically all interactivity in human affairs. Complementarily, all five activating forces are neutral. However, human interactions and responses to changes alter the force intensities causing a shift in collective energy-flow. The shifts ripple change in the being fostering various observable complexity patterns in individuals and organizations. Using the tool, the patterns become visible on the leadership playing field and we can now perceive how the activating forces interact.

The five Chinese activating forces we translated from the ancient glyphs are water, plant, fire, soil, and metal. To use the forces as a tool, we had to find contemporary nomenclature to substitute for the symbolic terms. We consulted more than twenty translations of related literature and studied original ancient Chinese texts for words that we think describe our experiences with leadership phenomena. Summarized in Table 13.1 are the aspects of the nature's forces, their relevance to human affairs, Chinese scholarly interpretations, and action verbs. Those verbs chosen represent attributes of the activating force movements contributing to leadership energy-flow in our examples.

Table 13.2 is translated from the original Chinese text to explicate the interactions of the five activating forces that shape the two major cycles, constructive and destructive, and their respective shadow opposite cycles, decay and challenge.

Table 13.2 shows the interconnectivities of the five forces with each other. For example, water relates to plant—when water is strong, it nourishes plant (constructive cycle); however, when plant is strong, it saps water (decay cycle) depleting energy. Another example—when water is strong, it extinguishes fire (destructive cycle); but when fire is strong, it boils water (challenge cycle) and creates steam energy.

To relate how complex patterns emerge to form those cycles, we graphically illustrate interactions of the five activating forces. In Figure 13.1, we map the four cycles formed by nature's activating forces stated in Table 13.2 to show their intermingling relationships. The arrows denote the influence of one force on the other forces. The arrows do not imply a temporal process because all five forces act simultaneously and do so indivisibly; rather, they are indicative of how one force affects the others. There are four kinds of arrows on the map—curving, dotted curving, straight, and dotted straight—to represent how one force affects the others. The following describes the four cycles—two major cycles and two corresponding shadow cycles.

The constructive cycle (one major cycle) signifies that the entity is in a growth or generative state—a hopeful state without major obstacles. The curving solid arrows along the edge of the Tao symbol connect the five forces clockwise: water → plant → fire → soil → metal → water.

Table 13.1. The Attributes of the Five Activating Forces (Yin-Yang-WuXing)

Activating Forces	Water	Plant	Fire	Soil	Metal
Aspects of the forces relevant to nature's behavior	Water forms solid, liquid, or vapor; adapts to shape; seeks to level flowing to fill open spaces.	Plant endeavors to grow tall, wide, and deep, creating roots, branches, leaves, fruits, and seeds.	Fire appears spontaneously; spreads through; casts off embers; provides light and heat.	Soil provides grounding for its inhabitants; nurtures though ravaged by wind, sand, and water.	Metal, when melted, forms veins, nuggets, tools, machines, and alloys with other metals.
Relevance to human behavior	People and collectives work to meet needs; reach consensus; shape for growth; and adapt to conditions.	People and collectives seek to grow capability; add capacity; explore, discover, and conceive new ideas in response to challenges.	People and collectives seek, gain, expand, and absorb knowledge to enlighten; motivate to spark; compete, consume, and concur to win and shine.	People and collectives support efforts based on ideal, purpose, value, and goals with sustaining resources and knowledge.	People and collectives unite and form cohesive, capable, strong workforces to confront and learn from adversity.
Scholarly interpretation	Wisdom	Virtue	Etiquette	Trust	Integrity
Leadership action verbs	Balance	Strive	Spark	Ground	Bind

Table 13.2. Nature's Cycles of Five Activating Forces at Work— the Interactive Movements

Cycles of Energy-Flow States	Attributes and Effects on One Another
Constructive cycle (first major cycle) —Grow, generating	Energy-flow attributes: Nurture, reveal, illuminate, expand, energize • Water nourishes plant. • Plant fuels fire. • Fire fertilizes soil. • Soil nurtures metal. • Metal cultivates water.
Decay cycle (shadow of the constructive cycle) —Exhaust, consume	Energy-flow attributes: Neglect, undo, enervate, contract, unbalance • Water erodes metal. • Metal depletes soil. • Soil diminishes fire. • Fire burns plant. • Plant saps water.
Destructive cycle (second major cycle) —Decline, collapse	Energy-flow attributes: Discourage, prevent, separate, inhibit, dilute • Water extinguishes fire. • Fire melts metal. • Metal chops plant. • Plant loosens soil. • Soil muddies water.
Challenge cycle (shadow of the destructive cycle) —Agitate, compel	Energy-flow attributes: Enhance, stimulate, provoke, perturb, enable • Water quenches soil. • Soil nurtures plant. • Plant grasps metal. • Metal stirs fire. • Fire boils water.

The decay cycle (the shadow opposite of the constructive cycle) denotes the entity is in a state of exhaustion or overconsumption—a warning about excessive attention to growth. The curving dotted arrows connect the five forces counterclockwise: water → metal → soil → fire → plant → water.

The destructive cycle (the other major cycle) signifies that the entity is in decline or a collapsing state—an unfavorable

Figure 13.1. Yin-Yang-WuXing Energy-Flow of Nature's Five Activating Forces

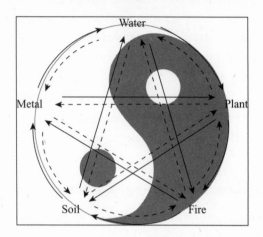

situation, all forces are destroying other forces. The straight solid arrows, forming a solid-line star shape inside the circles, connect the five forces in a sequence (the end of an arrow is the beginning of the next arrow): water → fire → metal → plant → soil → water.

The challenge cycle (the shadow opposite of the destructive cycle) denotes rising agitations in a situation, which compel interventions or rectifying actions. The straight dotted-line arrows alongside the straight solid-line arrows, but in the opposite direction, connect the five forces forming a dotted-line star: water → soil → plant → metal → fire → water.

The Tao symbol in the background reminds us that Tao, the yin-yang complementarity in nature, constantly influences and affects our decision making. Tao represents the light-shadow intermingling dynamics existing in every entity, person, organization, or country; shadow accompanies light and light creates shadow. Tao embodies the moment-to-moment shifting of being from one energy-flow state to another.

These descriptions illustrate how nature's five activating forces work to form the four interactive cycle structures. The language for the ancient tool consists of the five nouns representing the forces (Table 13.1)—*water, plant, fire, soil,* and *metal*—and four interaction structures (Table 13.2)—*constructive cycle, decay cycle, destructive cycle,* and *challenge cycle*—to describe the energy-flow of being. As the symbolic nouns in the ancient tool are placeholders intended for appropriate being descriptors (in time, situation, and purpose), we replace the nouns with leadership action verbs to give relevant meaning to stories that narrate the being in today's complexity.

A Leadership Language for the Tool

Using a language to communicate a story germane to a situation or environment makes it possible for leaders to collaborate on the playing field to narrate their own views from their positions and make informed decisions collectively. We superimpose corresponding selected leadership action verbs, noted in Table 13.1, on the five nature's forces. By adding the verbs on top of the forces in Figure 13.1, we formed Figure 13.2.

Figure 13.2. Leadership Energy-Flow Diagram Showing the Five Activating Forces

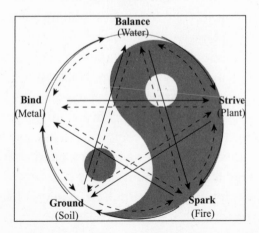

Those action verbs describe the activating forces we chose to illustrate leadership phenomena and became the language we communicate in writing our demonstrations.

Realizing leadership stories come in many forms, for instance, verbal, written, and expressive languages, we are called on to listen, grasp, unfold the stories, and enfold patterns into our thought flow. Our own experience in using this tool revealed that we communicate stories using many concepts to express and reason our points to each other. Thus, enfolding more stories requires more than just the five verbs used in Figure 13.2. Table 13.3, therefore, presents our recommendations, taken from translations, providing a broader selection applicable to more stories.

Using the Tool to Assess Being

To assess the being in complexity, one can employ the tool to graphically create a playing field where abstractions of the activating forces can be made visible. We recommend one start by establishing the playing field and positioning the activating forces graphically (in the abstraction) using Figure 13.1. One selects five verbs, one for each force, from Table 13.3 or creates his or her own verbs using the attributes described in Table 13.1 and the effects of the four nature's cycles explained in Table 13.2. The verbs should best represent the being in an ideal situation. The varying intensities of activating forces fashion full or partial energy-flow cycles, which emerge over time into complexity patterns in one's present moment of being. One can view the situation and find the pattern to discern which cycle is dominant to gauge a situational being. At any moment, one can examine the past, assess how the five activating forces are working in the present, diagnose a situation to look for the causality that derailed the progress, and intervene to influence the future. Understanding the causality can help the user of the tool identify ways to instigate a turnaround or redirection, intervene, and navigate back to progress.

Table 13.3. List of Suggested Action Verbs for the Activating Forces (Yin-Yang-WuXing)

Activating forces	Water	Plant	Fire	Soil	Metal
Movement descriptions selected from various translations to represent activating forces	Learn, placate, drown, flood, wear, bypass, flow, adapt, scour, change, balance, quiet, cleanse, still, nurture	Invent, grow, innovate, strive, absorb, expand, challenge, achieve, resist, bend, surround, surrender, yield	Energize, burn, warm, peak, enlighten, raise, spark, cheer, compel, force, lift, illuminate, yearn, destroy	Stabilize, endure, care, nourish, smother, ground, demand, alter, transform, transmute, provide, gravitate	Harvest, succeed, force, conduct, bind, rivet, cut, connect, enchain, consolidate, limit, determine, reform, solidify, enrich, contract, sink, melt

Embracing the feeling of being in chaos, those who use this tool can observe the energy-flow manifested in the present being as an emergence from past collective energy-flow caused by the dynamic effects of the activating forces. Each force contributes to the causality exerting intensity differently depending on human decisions, environmental influences, and responses from other forces engendering a perception of being in chaos. On the playing field, causality leaves tracks that form a pattern of chaos. The pattern may include aspects of more than one cycle.

Understanding causality of the energy-flow helps users of the Tao complexity tool intervene in any cycle that is not constructive. By matching the at-the-moment-being pattern to the constructive cycle, one may find the missing or weak force interactions. Alternatively, users may find unintentional emphasis on one or more activating forces deterring the desired purpose.

For example, effective interventions in an entropic decay cycle (the shadow) may return the situation to the constructive cycle (the light). Examining the situation in the destructive cycle could warn users to identify the causality and invoke renewal or transmutation. Users paying attention to the challenge cycle (the shadow) early on could stimulate organizational or individual potentials for breakthrough or transformation. Thus, being in the light during a constructive cycle, one should be cognizant of its shadow, the draining decay cycle. Similarly, being in the light during a destructive cycle, one should be aware of its shadow, the growth-stimulating challenge cycle, to tap innovation potential.

With our experience using the tool, we find users establish a baseline for assessing the entity of interest. This knowing process begins by identifying the entity's purpose, value, and its intended services or products. Users narrate a brief story on what the entity hopes or does to achieve its purpose, then choose five verbs from that story (refer to Table 13.1 and Table 13.3 for selection) that best represent the entity's activities and add them to Figure 13.1 to create the entity's own energy-flow diagram, akin to Figure

13.2. Those verbs should represent the five activating forces in the entity's hopeful situation. Retell the entity's hopeful story using the constructive cycle in the entity's diagram. This establishing baseline process may take several iterations until all the entity's stakeholders are satisfied with their choice of their five action verbs.

After the baseline is established, assessing the entity's being can be performed at any time. Users can assess the current (or at-the-moment) situations by narrating a reflective story of what has happened, using the entity's energy-flow diagram; focusing on derailment from the constructive cycle into other cycles; searching for missing, weakened, or overemphasized activating forces in the diagram; and then verifying the perceptions and assumptions associated with the story.

Once the entity's at-the-moment being is clear, users can understand the being and causality that led to the being and find ways to embrace complexity and deal with chaos. Users might imagine or design interventions and plan actions, and then bring them onto the playing field to see if the choice of mechanism matches the imaginary intervention result. One would gauge whether the constructive cycle is resumed; if not resumed, then one would reexamine assumptions and perceptions of the activating forces and interactions and repeat the procedure. Examples of intervention mechanisms include the Satir model (Satir, 1978), systems thinking (Senge, Kleiner, Roberts, Ross, Roth, & Smith, 1999), agent-based modeling (Holland, 1995), and the Tao model for leadership transformation (Fu & Bergeon, 2011).

Leadership Phenomena Assessment Demonstrations

As we understand, iteration of process increases the quality of knowing, which in turn informs how users evaluate the being. The being informs the knowing, whereas knowing increases the quality for assessing the being; they are in a reinforcing quality cycle. With Tao, quality can increase with positive and negative refinements. In the following three examples we demonstrate how the tool has helped us deepen our understanding of leadership complexity and allowed us to reveal energy-flow, causality, and the dynamics undergirding different situations.

Abbott Flywheel Effect: A Constructive Cycle Story. Our first demonstration, Abbott's intervention beginning in 1974 (Collins, 2001), shows how using leadership terms reveal the presence of a constructive cycle providing an overview being of an organization in an upward spiral to success. Fortuitously, we draw on a constructive cycle from our own experience. We met while working for Abbott Laboratories in 1979. At the time one of us was a first-level manager; the other was a project manager providing information technology support for pharmaceutical research. Abbott was in the early stages of a sustained growth spiral and was discussed in Collins's (2001) *Good to Great*. A flywheel effect graph of Abbott's investment performance success each year, 1974 to 1995 (p. 174), evidences that Abbott was in the constructive cycle.

In Collins's (2001) narrative, Abbott set out on its growth curve in 1974 when a "tremendous power [flywheel effect] exists in the fact of continued improvement and the delivery of results" took hold (p. 174). The CEO established a corporate baseline identifying "what they actually have the potential to be the best at and, just as important, what they *cannot* be the best at" (p. 99) and setting new values. Recognizing that other companies had a huge research lead in pharmaceuticals, Abbott focused on its strength in hospital nutritionals and diagnostics creating an attainable vision. Abbott, aligning with the vision, "reduced its administrative costs as a percentage of sales to the lowest in the industry . . . *and at the same time* became a new product innovation machine" (p. 123).

Abbott was an exciting place to work. The projects in our department included developing a molecular modeling system and a speech recognition system that cut the cost of data collection during research when huge volumes of data are hand-written, transcribed, and then redacted into meaningful data that can be analyzed using computers. Both systems aimed at reducing high cost factors involved in research. As a demonstration that Abbott searched for innovative products, we participated in evaluating the speech recognition system for potential commercial value.

Abbott recognized its place relative to the competition, its strengths, and opportunities available to it in the environment at that time, and leveraged that knowledge to pursue what it was best at—balance (water) force. It invested its energy in building on what it was best at to look for innovations and products that could enhance its market position—strive (plant). The company looked within to identify new products to market—spark (fire). It took those new products and aligned them with its goals—ground (soil). All employees subscribed to corporate goals in contributing their efforts to those new products—bind (metal). As part of the bind-force, we contributed to advancing Abbott's strengths to a higher level—balance (water). Our experience evidenced the beginning momentum of Collins's (2001) flywheel effect: a constructive cycle in an upward spiral.

The Nut Island Effect: When Good Teams Go Wrong. In our second example using the tool, we reference the Nut Island story (Levy, 2001). Paul F. Levy, an executive dean for administration at Harvard Medical School in Boston, conducted a case study on the Nut Island sewage treatment plant in Quincy, Massachusetts. He revealed a management lesson about a well-intentioned, thirty-year special task effort that made a wrong turn that led to catastrophic failure (pp. 51–59).

Levy (2001) described a self-forming task team that "performed difficult, dirty, dangerous work without complaint"; the team members "put in thousands of hours of unpaid overtime, and they even dipped into their own pockets to buy spare parts" (p. 51). The team handled its own staffing decisions, cross-trained themselves, and "ingeniously improvised their way around operational difficulties and budgetary constraints" (p. 52). Levy began: "In the first stage of the Nut Island effect, senior management, preoccupied with high-visibility problems, assigns the team a vital but behind-the-scenes task. This is a crucial feature: the team carries out its task far from the eye of the public or customers. Allowed a great deal of autonomy, team members become adept at organizing and managing themselves, and the unit develops a proud and distinct identity" (p. 52).

Retelling the first stage story using Figure 13.2, the task team built its reputation and gained senior management support—ground (soil). That support, extended into team autonomy, evidenced their synchronicity with management—bind (metal). The allowance of autonomy made the task team self-reliant in solving problems—balance (water). The self-reliance led the task team to raising their own standards and values—strive (plant). The new standards brought management recognition leading to fame and pride—spark (fire). The management recognition reinforced management trust in the task team—ground (soil). The constructive cycle thus spiraled upward.

Excesses in senior management trust and task team autonomy, bind (metal) reversed the energy-flow invoking the shadow decay cycle, derailing the task effort from the full constructive cycle into other undesirable cycles in the following stages:

> Second stage, the senior management team took "the team's self-sufficiency for granted" and ignored the team's needs for support. (p. 52)
>
> Third stage, the team, made it "a priority to stay out of management's line of sight," which led them to "deny or minimize problems and avoid asking for help." (p. 52)
>
> Fourth stage, the team began to "make up its own rules," told itself that the rules enabled it to "fulfill its mission." As a result, those rules masked "the deterioration of the

team's working environment and deficiencies in the team's performance." (p. 52)

Fifth stage, the team and senior management formed "distorted pictures of reality." Management told itself, "no news is good news" and was "unable to recognize the role it played in setting in motion this self-reinforcing spiral of failure." (p. 52)

During those four later stages, the story revealed many dynamic shifts caused by the fading linkages to management support. We use Figure 13.3 to describe the basic pattern that cultivated the effect. The grayed-out ground (soil) force and its associated to-and-from arrows illustrate the dynamics associated with management unresponsiveness to the task team's needs. Thus, without ground-force, the remaining four activating forces created a mixture of complex energy-flow patterns in each of the four stages.

In the second stage, the team attempted to maintain a constructive cycle without management participation by strengthening its internal bind-force, continued on the bind → balance →

Figure 13.3. Leadership Energy-Flow Diagram of the Nut Island Effect

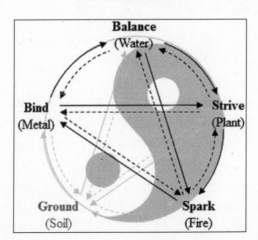

strive → spark → bind pattern; yet unaware of the missing linkage to ground-force, the spark → bind was lethal because it led to unintended complexity patterns.

In the third stage, attempts to sustain team independence from management created the spark → strive → balance → bind → spark pattern, which was a mixture of mostly decay cycle and a minor challenge cycle. The energy draining led the team to exhaustion, while the bind → spark led to building a stronger team.

In the fourth stage, the team was keeping up with the challenges, struggling to maintain momentum in fulfilling its mission, but, spending energy beyond its capacity, the team was deteriorating. The bind → spark → balance → bind pattern indicates a major challenging cycle and a minor decay cycle. The dynamics led to performance deficiency.

In the fifth stage, the team was unaware of the need to reverse the momentum of self-destruction and management was oblivious to its role in setting the team on a path to failure. The spark → bind → strive → spark pattern is a mixture of a major destructive cycle and a minor constructive cycle. The minor constructive strive → spark cycle strengthens spark force. Unintentionally, however, having a stronger spark force in a destructive spark → bind → strive cycle actually leads unerringly to destruction.

Ultimately, the "rickety Nut Island sewage treatment plant was decommissioned in 1997 and its core team was disbanded, after thirty years of efforts that left Boston Harbor no cleaner than it was when the team came together in the late 1960s" (Levy, 2001, p. 51). We often observed the Nut Island effect in corporate initiatives and transformation efforts. Observing these types of effects invoked our curiosity and motivated us to look for a complexity tool.

Reflection: Assessing At-the-Moment Being. We found the tool useful for narrating stories and designing interventions even as we were developing it. Reflection on experience in finding and determining the practicality of this tool provides an example of its use in shaping next steps. Although the constructive cycle was dominant in our journey, we admit being derailed numerous times into challenge and decay cycles. Those derailments stimulated our thinking as we referred to the tool often and thereby avoided treading into the destructive cycle. We began journaling our experience using the tool as a useful way of showing how it is applicable in day-to-day situations.

The reality of this journey has been complex. Without using Figure 13.2, our travels would be difficult to narrate. On the journey, we discovered the value of the chosen leadership terms to represent the five activating forces and to articulate our experience, and found maintaining a constructive cycle requires attentiveness. We discovered how overemphasis on any force unintentionally derailed us from the constructive cycle. Being anxious to prove an application to real-world cases, we unwittingly shifted to bind-force without going through spark-force and ground-force and we fell into a challenge cycle. Being cognizant of our position in the cycle allowed us to intervene and find our way back to the constructive cycle. When enervated, we returned to the balance-force, contemplating how reliance on commonsense translations had gotten us into the challenge cycle. Our diligence in checking into original Chinese text for enlightenment (or spark) prevented us from moving from strive to ground—which would have shifted us into a destructive cycle.

Summary

Our search for a practice tool led us to conclude that commonsense methods tend to direct us to view reality in the light of the obvious and assume that certainty is obtainable. We discovered that there is a shadow side of any action, or interaction, and certainty remains elusive no matter how hard we try to pin down the essence of a phenomenon. Turning to ancient Tao leadership philosophy and rediscovering an uncommon sense concept helped us conceptualize every situation as an interacting energy-flow whole and shun the practice of breaking phenomena into isolated components. The Tao complexity tool we developed reveals past and present states of being and the tracks of causality enabling us to identify appropriate interventions.

With the philosophical basis for the tool and reasoning behind how and why the tool works, we are able to approach a complex situation from multiple frames of reference and employ the tool to understand at-the-moment being and increase quality of knowing. Drawing on real-world examples, we have explicated our epiphanies as we used the tool and, most important, why interventions in leadership phenomena succeed or fail. We offer a basic language and invite users to employ the tool in complex situations to describe cycles and the interactive forces at work.

We believe our tool can invoke valuable insights to help leaders and consultants understand complexity in leadership phenomena and serve as a practical mechanism for anyone engaged in implementing change. This chapter is but a summary of a much larger and more detailed effort to illustrate how ancient wisdom can provide leadership tools for dealing with complexity.

Notes

1. Nature's dynamism describes nature's manifestation of the dynamics of all forces and energies that make up change in the world we humans inhabit.

2. Abstractions represent "concrete processes, factual extractions, thoughts, preoccupation, and conceptualization—explainable by laws of energy in physics" (Fu, 2008, p. 20). That is, the "notion of physical energy, which is at the base of physics, must then be conceived as an abstraction from the complex energy" (Whitehead, 1933/1961, p. 186). Abstractions differ in meaning and intention from

metaphors. Metaphors offer illusory, syllogistic comparisons without defined correlations with phenomena at hand.

3. Energy-flow—an abstraction denotes what Chinese call *ch'i* to represent energy in nature and human affairs. Ch'i signifies movements, interacting flows, and intermingling fluid attributes. There is ch'i in everything. Different kinds of ch'i are always interacting. Ch'i is the energy state that manifests the "being" or "presence" of a person, organization, enterprise, collective, or human affair (Fu, 2008, pp. 26–27).

References

Axelrod, R. M. (1997). *The complexity of cooperation: Agent-based models of competition and collaboration.* Princeton, NJ: Princeton University Press.

Briggs, J., & Peat, F. D. (1989). *Turbulent mirror: An illustrated guide to chaos theory and the science of wholeness.* New York: Harper and Row.

Collins, J. C. (2001). *Good to great: Why some companies make the leap . . . and others don't.* New York: HarperCollins.

Confucius. (1959). *Four books: The great learning, the doctrine of the mean, Confucian analects, and the works of Mencius* (J. Legge, Trans.). Taipei, Taiwan: Latitude Longitude Publishing. (Original work published 450 BCE)

Einstein, A. (2005). *The meaning of relativity, including the relativistic theory of the non-symmetric field* (Intro. by Brian Greene, 5th ed.). Princeton, NJ: Princeton University Press. (Original work published 1922)

Forrester, J. W. (1990). *Principles of systems.* Waltham, MA: Pegasus Communications.

Fu, C. (2008). *Energy-flow—A new perspective on James MacGregor Burns' transforming leadership: A new pursuit of happiness.* Doctoral dissertation, Antioch University, Yellow Spring, Ohio, LINK ETD. Retrieved from http://rave.ohiolink.edu/etdc/view?acc_num=antioch1218205866.

Fu, C., & Bergeon, R. (2011). A Tao model: Rethinking modern leadership for transformation. In J. D. Barbour & G. R. Hickman (Eds.), *Leadership for transformation* (ILA Building Leadership Bridges) (pp. 15–31). San Francisco: Jossey-Bass.

Fu, P. Y. (1953). *Philosophy of Chuangtse.* Master's thesis, National Taiwan University, Taipei.

Holland, J. H. (1995). *Hidden order: How adaptation builds complexity.* New York: Basic Books.

Lao-Tze. (1891). *The book of Tao* (Tao Te Ching) (J. Legge, Trans.). (Original work published 500 BCE) Retrieved from www.sacred-texts.com/tao/taote.htm

Levy, P. F. (2001). The nut island effect: When good teams go wrong. *Harvard Business Review, 79*(3), 51–59, 163.

Maslow, A. H. (1987). *Motivation and personality.* New York: Harper and Row.

Prigogine, I. (1997). *The end of certainty: Time, chaos, and the new laws of nature.* New York: Free Press.

Prigogine, I., & Stengers, I. (1984). *Order out of chaos: Man's new dialogue with nature.* New York: Bantam.

Satir, V. (1978). *Your many faces.* Berkeley, CA: Celestial Arts.

Senge, P. M., Kleiner, A., Roberts, C., Ross, R. B., Roth, G., & Smith, B. J. (1999). *The dance of change: The challenges to sustaining momentum in learning organizations.* New York: Broadway Business.

Shanahan, M. (1997). *Solving the frame problem: A mathematical investigation of the common sense law of inertia.* Cambridge, MA: MIT Press.

Siu, R.H.G. (1971). *The Tao of science: An essay on Western knowledge and Eastern wisdom* (Vol. 1). Cambridge, MA: MIT Press.

Siu, R.H.G. (1978). SMR Forum: Management and the art of Chinese baseball. *Sloan Management Review, 19*(3), 83.

Sterman, J. D. (2000). *Business dynamics: Systems thinking and modeling for a complex world.* Boston: McGraw-Hill/Irwin.

Sun Tzu. (1988). *The art of war* (SunJi BingFa) (T. Cleary, Trans.). Boston: Shambhala. (Original work published 350 BCE)

Whitehead, A. N. (1938). *Modes of thought.* New York: Macmillan.

Whitehead, A. N. (1961). *Adventures of ideas.* New York: Free Press. (Original work published 1933)

Wilhelm, H., & Wilhelm, R. (1995). *Understanding the I Ching.* The Wilhelm lectures on the *Book of Changes.* Princeton, NJ: Princeton University Press. (Original work published 1956)

Wilhelm, R., & Baynes, C. F. (1997). *The I Ching or Book of Changes* (R. Wilhelm, Trans., Foreword by Carl G. Jung, 3rd ed.). Princeton, NJ: Princeton University Press. (Original work published 1950)

Chapter Fourteen

The Leadership of Dr. Jane Goodall

A Four-Quadrant Perspective

Georgia Pappas

We live in a complex world with global warming, AIDS, geno-cide, natural disasters, violence against women and children, deforestation, animal cruelty, animal extinction, and so much more. Fortunately, there are many people who are working to address these challenges, often through nonprofit organizations. They share a common vision to change lives and create a just and sustainable world in which to live. People who choose to work and volunteer in the nonprofit sector demonstrate leadership and service that rise from a commitment to the common good. What does it mean to lead and become an effective leader to address these complicated social issues? Traditional hierarchical, role-based views of leadership are too simplistic for a world where nonprofits face unprecedented economic, demographic, technological, and social shifts (Gowdy, Hildebrand, La Piana, & Campos, 2009). Nonprofit organizations find themselves at the heels of a global financial crisis that has significantly altered donation patterns. Rapidly changing technologies have compressed time and space by quickly connecting people around the world. Changing demographics, particularly in the United States, are altering the face of the nonprofit workforce and communities served. Finally, there is blurring of lines between nonprofit and for-profit organizations addressing social issues that affects engaging younger generations into the nonprofit sector.

Leading in an uncertain world requires leaders of quality and character who authentically respond to the needs of the times. The focus of leadership in today's society can benefit from being more about who one *is* and less about what one *does* (Hesselbein, 1996). Leadership skills must also encompass more ethical, humane, and compassionate characteristics that arise from a deeper place within the individual. It is our values, intentions, and beliefs that define who we are and what we do as people and leaders committed to working toward healing the wounds of the world. The context in which leaders operate today requires a framework that expands the locus of leadership from the singular perspective of role-based behavior to focus on relational components among the individual and the collective (Lichtenstein, Uhl-Bien, Marion, Seers, Orton, & Schreiber, 2006). In this chapter, I view leadership holistically as I employ a multiperspective framework to better understand the dynamics of leading in a complex world.

A Multiperspective Framework of Leadership

There are a number of theories and models of leadership that include a focus on the behavior of leaders such as traits and styles (Jago, 1982; Popper, 2005), the relationship leaders have with followers depending on situation and motivation factors (Stogdill, 1974; Yukl, 2002), the psychological factors of the leader such as emotional intelligence (Goleman, 1995; Goleman, Boyatzis, & McKee, 2004), and the development of leaders (Day, Harrison, & Halpin, 2009; Torbert, 1991). Although these theories have stand-alone merit, their limitations are associated with the lack of integration and connection they have with each other. There is value in studying a variety of aspects of leadership, and a broader understanding of leadership can be gained also by examining the complexity of the nonlinear patterns of relationships between the parts needed to learn and develop (Bennet & Bennet, 2004; Laszlo, Laszlo, Romero, & Campos, 2003;

O'Connor & McDermott, 1997). A more integrated view of leadership requires a fundamental shift in ways of thinking about the dynamics of the leader, leadership, and leading.

In this chapter, I argue for a multiperspective view on leadership that includes behavioral and psychological aspects of leading from individual and collective perspectives. The multiperspective framework from which to explore leadership is provided by the integral philosophy of Wilber (2006). The four-quadrant framework shown in Figure 14.1 includes individual

Figure 14.1. Four Quadrants of Leadership

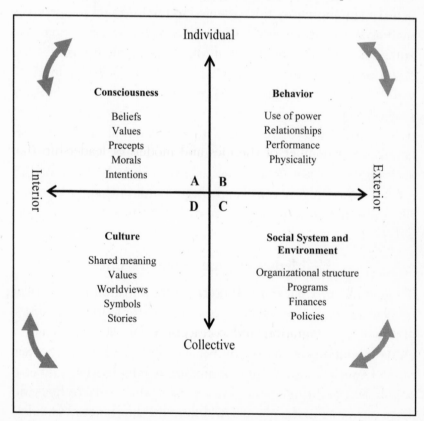

Note: This graph is an adaptation of Wilber's four-quadrant model.

consciousness, individual behaviors, collective social systems, and collective culture.

In Figure 14.1, the upper left, or A quadrant, is the subjective, interior perspective of the individual that echoes one's self-awareness and consciousness, reflected in a leader's beliefs, intentions, and moral development. The upper right, or B quadrant, represents the objective, exterior functions of the individual that are revealed through emotions, feelings, sensations, and behavior. Leader behavior would include characteristics such as one's use of power, developing relationships, and types of work performance. Quadrant B also includes the physical aspects of a leader, which can range from physical ability to how the brain works. The lower right, or C quadrant, is the exterior behavior of an organizational system reflected in institutional perspectives such as an organization's structure, programs, services, finances, and policies. The lower left, or D quadrant, is the interior of the group or collective consciousness. Quadrant D is the internal worldview of the collective represented in culture, values, or symbols shared by a group of individuals. Wilber (2006) asserts that modernity is concerned with the external (physical and behavioral world); however, to understand a phenomenon from an integral perspective all four quadrants are to be examined in relation to each other with an understanding that, over time, there is a mutual interaction among the parts.

Highlights of Jane Goodall's Life

To demonstrate the practical use of the four-quadrant theoretical framework, I have applied it to the life of ethologist, primatologist, and environmental conservationist Dr. Jane Goodall. I chose Goodall as a case study because she is a leader who has had an impact on a large community, is admired by a diverse population, and is recognized as a person who works to heal the deepest wounds of the planet. Additionally, the choice of Goodall presents an opportunity to add to the body of leadership literature by providing a case study of a female leader who is an agent of social change.

Valerie Jane Morris Goodall was born on April 3, 1934, in England, and is best known for conducting a fifty-year study of chimpanzees (humankind's closest living relative) in Gombe Stream National Park in Tanzania, Africa. It could be said that Goodall has fulfilled a predetermined destiny because her lifelong connection to chimpanzees began serendipitously when her father gave her a stuffed toy chimpanzee when she was just over one year old (Goodall, 1999). An internationally known primatologist and ethologist, she cofounded the Jane Goodall Institute (JGI) in 1977 to support her research in Gombe. The institute expanded its scope from supporting research efforts of chimpanzees to include the preservation of great apes and their habitats. Another focus of JGI is to create a worldwide network of youth, through its Roots & Shoots program, who are involved in community and environmental educational activities. The mission of the Jane Goodall Institute is to empower "people to make a difference for all living things" (Jane Goodall Institute, 2011, ¶1).

In 1957, Goodall began working as a secretary for Dr. Louis Leakey, world-renowned paleontologist and anthropologist. Under his mentorship, she began studying the chimpanzees of Gombe Stream National Park in Tanzania, Africa. Leakey knew she needed academic credentials for her research to be taken seriously by the male-dominated scholarly community after she began gathering unprecedented data on chimpanzee behavior. He arranged for Goodall to go directly into a doctoral program, even though she had no college experience, and she earned a degree in ethology from the University of Cambridge.

Goodall was the first person to make a recorded observation of an animal, other than humans, making and using a tool. She also observed chimpanzees eating meat, dispelling the belief they were exclusively plant eaters. Another shocking discovery was made when Goodall and her research team witnessed male chimpanzees brutally attacking and mortally wounding a female from another chimpanzee community. This aggressive behavior was not an isolated incident, and it would influence Goodall's thoughts and beliefs about the brutality of humans against each other (Goodall, 1988, 1999).

In her study of primates, Goodall set herself apart from the traditional scientific conventions of the time by naming the animals she studied rather than assigning each a number. The expectation was that information was recorded without empathy; however, Goodall claims that she was able to develop a deeper understanding of chimpanzees because of her empathetic approach to data gathering (Goodall, 1990). Her approach altered attitudes of scientists and others by raising awareness of the emotional capabilities of animals, which in turn raised questions about the ethics of animal experimentation. Her empathic approach became a catalyst for changing scientific practice with animals (Midgley, 1989). In 1986, at a conference in Chicago celebrating her book, *The Chimpanzees of Gombe*, Goodall became aware of the dire conservation issues involving chimpanzees. She was shocked by what she heard at the conference, saying, "It wrought in me a cataclysmic change. . . . When I arrived in Chicago I was a research scientist, . . . when I left I was already in my heart, committed to conservation and education" (Goodall, 1999, p. 206).

The programs of JGI reflect Goodall's shift in worldview when she expanded its focus to include chimpanzee protection, community development, and education programs. She began traveling three hundred days a year starting in the 1990s and continues to follow a tight schedule of lectures, fundraising events, business meetings, visiting JGI and Roots & Shoots sites around the world while keeping up with writing articles, books, and general correspondence (Peterson, 2006). She keeps this demanding schedule to share a message of hope for a better future in a world where people are suffering and the planet is being

Figure 14.2. Goodall's Leadership Interpreted Through the Four-Quadrant Integral Framework

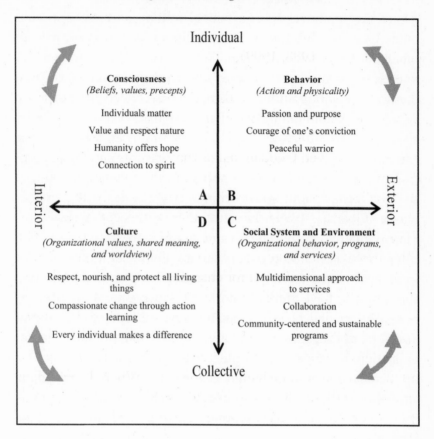

destroyed through pollution, deforestation, and so on, and to promote respect and compassion for all living things.

Although this description of Goodall's life is very brief,[1] it provides sufficient contextual knowledge for the ensuing leadership discussion within the multiperspective four-quadrant framework. My analysis of Goodall's life experiences is summarized in Figure 14.2, which highlights her beliefs and behaviors as well as the collective values and organizational behavior of the Jane Goodall Institute.

A Multiperspective View of Goodall's Leadership

There are four overarching beliefs, values, and precepts that guide Goodall's life and define her life purpose as identified in quadrant A (consciousness): individuals matter, value and respect nature, humanity offers hope to save the planet, and a spiritual connection among all living things. These beliefs are not to be viewed as separate from each other but as parts of a greater whole; these parts are intertwined and interwoven in all aspects of her life. Goodall's beliefs emerged through reflection and introspection of life experiences and are rooted in the values of courage, honesty, compassion, and tolerance that she learned from her family (Goodall, 1999). Her overarching precept is that individuals matter, both human and nonhuman individuals. She came to this conclusion after observing the social interactions of individual chimpanzees, confirming for her the understanding that animals have similar emotional and cognitive abilities as humans. Goodall believes that humans are part of the animal kingdom, not separate from it, and as such, humans have a moral obligation to respect and value nature. She reasons that our intellectual ability as humans does not give us the right to exploit animals and the environment but rather gives us the responsibility to protect them. Her hope for a better world lies with our humanity of care and concern for others. Goodall (1999) reminds her readers in her autobiography, *Reason for Hope*, that there are many positive attributes about the nature of humans who, unlike chimpanzees or other animals, have a more highly developed intellect. She believes that our intelligence combined with compassion gives us the ability to create positive change in the world through peaceful means. Finally, Goodall believes that connecting with our spiritual self is related to connecting with nature and the natural world. She believes that she came into this world to be a messenger of peace and hope and that she is following a higher purpose. She believes, after reflecting on her life, that she was following an overall plan and she was "being gently nudged or fiercely blown along a very specific route by an unseen, intangible Wind" (Goodall, 1999, p. 3). She also believes that all humans have a higher calling that includes the care and concern for all living things.

Goodall's actions and how she presents herself to the world are summarized in quadrant B of the framework (individual behavior). Goodall is a driven person with a large following of people who admire and respect her. There is a charismatic quality about her that has led to her being described as a "sage" and "messenger of peace" (Hunt, 2002). The behaviors described in this quadrant overlap and are aligned with the beliefs described in quadrant A (consciousness). There are several adjectives that describe Goodall's behavioral attributes or capabilities such as *visionary*, *agentic*, *optimistic*, *humble*, *disciplined*, *curious*, and *authentic*. These attributes are encompassed in the behaviors that dominate Goodall's life: passion and purpose, living the courage of her convictions, and being a peaceful warrior. Goodall's passion and purpose is related to her belief that she is destined for a greater purpose and is reflected in her focused pursuit of her goals, a strong work ethic, and the courage to withstand challenges that come with attaining her goals. The action Goodall takes to direct her passion and purpose is that of a peaceful warrior. She is unrelenting in her effort for change and does so through peaceful means such as collaboration, dialogue, and education. She fearlessly takes action that supports her beliefs, even in the face of doubt and opposing public opinion. When she takes action, it is persistent and nonviolent action. As a result of her leadership, there is a community of followers who share her worldview of respecting and protecting all living things through peaceful means and knowing that each person makes a difference in bringing about change to create a sustainable planet. Goodall is very vocal about her beliefs, but she also has the courage of her convictions to live her life in accordance with those beliefs. For example, Goodall gave up eating meat when she learned about the unethical treatment of animals in factory farming. Another sacrifice was to give up the peaceful existence of living in Gombe to use her celebrity to be the voice of nonhuman individuals who cannot speak for themselves.

The collective social system and environment represented in quadrant C describes organizational behavior of the Jane Goodall Institute in relation to its programs and services. The institute has grown from an organization that supports research of Gombe chimpanzees to an organization that reaches tens of thousands of individuals around the world with its programs and services to protect chimpanzees and their environment and to create environmental change for the common good. Over time, JGI has become a global organization that has expanded its programs to address the complex issues involved with animal and environmental conservation. The programs of JGI are designed to ensure long-term protection of great ape populations and their habitat while preserving biodiversity, cultural traditions, and livelihoods of communities. Environmental efforts of JGI include research and protection of chimpanzees, collaborative community-centered conservation measures, and a youth program (Roots & Shoots) that focuses on capacity building through education and leadership development.

There are three organizational characteristics that reflect the mission and operations of JGI: a multidimensional approach to services, collaboration, and community-centered and sustainable programs. The institute incorporates a multidimensional approach to services to address the complex issues surrounding conservation that include providing protection of chimpanzees through chimp sanctuaries, habitat protection, and community education. The complexity of environment, economics, conservation, people, and animals requires collaboration with diverse and sometimes opposing communities to comprehensively address these issues and to promote ownership in the solutions. For example, the institute provides support to villagers who identify and initiate projects that have meaning for them but also are activities that are economically and environmentally sustainable. The institute learned that it could not impose its values on local communities so they let villagers know that they will provide tools and resources for projects the villagers identify and initiate as long as there was a conservation component to the project. As a result, community activities range from growing cash crops such as coffee, coconuts, and mushrooms to infrastructure projects such as protecting water sources or planting fast-growing species of trees to be used for firewood and building poles (Peterson, 2006).

The culture of JGI (quadrant D) reflects Goodall's life experiences, her mission in life, and her personal worldviews. Goodall is the driving force of the programs and services offered by JGI as well as the values by which it operates. The programs of the Jane Goodall Institute are the vehicles for which Goodall enables others to act and create shared meaning regarding conservation and animal ethics. The individuals and groups who are involved with and are followers of JGI and Goodall share a culture and worldview that include respect for all living things, compassionate change through action learning, and the belief that every individual makes a difference. Africa is a prime example of what can happen when these collective worldviews of depth ecology do not govern a culture. The forest habitat of primates and other animal species is being destroyed with a growing population encroaching on virgin forests in their need for firewood for cooking, clearing land for subsistence farmland, hunting to the point of creating silent forests to meet a growing demand for animal protein in cities, and killing adult chimps to sell their infants as pets (Lindsey, 1999). These cultural practices are not sustainable, nor do they follow an ecological ethic. The institute's approach to address these issues is to change the worldview of its constituents through compassionate action, a concept described in *Compassion in Action: Setting Out on the Path of Service* (Dass & Bush, 1992). This way of service includes practices such as acts of the heart, stay awake to suffering, and opportunities for action, themes and ways of acting that resonate with how Goodall embodies her role as an agent of peaceful change and exemplifies the values of JGI.

The organization's values incorporate a deep ecology perspective that encourages the JGI community to respect, nourish, and protect all living things. One such effort is to prevent the abuse of animals for human benefit and to see them as individuals with personalities and emotions. Another organizational value is to create change compassionately through action learning, which is accomplished through the Roots & Shoots program by engaging youth to learn to be stewards of the planet by providing education and opportunities for practicing civic responsibility. Finally, the organizational value that "every individual makes a difference" gives credence to the belief that change is possible only when people are ready to challenge the existing system. Goodall believes that the changes one person makes will create a difference in the world, whether that change is something as simple as switching off lights, turning off water while brushing teeth, or buying eggs from free-range chickens. When enough individuals take action, there is a cumulative effect of bringing about change for the common good. The worldview that JGI is attempting to influence is that humans, as part of the animal kingdom, have a moral obligation because of our higher intellect to challenge existing shared meaning related to the environment and the use of animals for human benefit. When a mind-set of care and concern for all living things is adopted, then cultural change can occur in areas of traditional practices such as medical research and factory farming of animals for consumption.

Conclusion

A holistic understanding of leadership is needed that represents the complexities of leading in the rapidly changing and turbulent global society that we live in today. Integral theory allows us to view leadership perspectives that extend beyond rational actions to include the irrational forces of individuals and organizations.

A multiperspective view of leadership, when applied to Goodall's life, reveals a complex interplay of her beliefs, her behaviors, and in the programs and culture of the Jane Goodall Institute.

Goodall has had a tremendous, positive impact in the area of animal ethics, environmental conservation, and in bringing the message of hope and peace to the world. Witnessing her life, we can get a better understanding of how we, individually, influence our piece of the world knowing that who we choose to be and what we choose to do have a greater and further impact of which we may never be fully aware. Using Goodall as a case study of leadership can also provide an opportunity to look at our own lives and make choices in our thoughts and actions from a place of greater personal responsibility. Employing the four-quadrant perspective as a framework for analysis can provide us with greater insight into the relationship between interior motivations and exterior activities at the individual and collective level. The breadth and depth of understanding leading and leadership expands as we gain a deeper understanding of underlying beliefs, values, and precepts that influence behavior at the individual and collective levels. The culture of an organization is influenced by the spoken and unspoken values of its leaders. Policies and procedures of an organization and how they are carried out are a reflection of the beliefs and behaviors of individual leaders in relation to how work is accomplished. Using this four-quadrant perspective, we can begin to create a new understanding of leadership through the process of deconstructing life experiences in the context of beliefs and behaviors and in relation to community. Then we have a choice to construct new meaning that may lead to new behaviors that are more beneficial to us and to be "leaderful" to those around us.

With this chapter I provided the reader with an invitation to view leadership as an opportunity to be of service for the common good in a complex world filled with uncertainty. In a world of untapped human potential, we must understand the influence of our own beliefs and actions and encourage others to be agents of change by modeling the way. Although few of us may have the same achievements as Goodall, our efforts toward a better world, nonetheless, are just as important. By making the assumption that we are all leaders, and that leadership is not a position but a way of viewing our place in the world, we all have the capacity to make a difference in our own way and in our own sphere of influence. When we change ourselves, we change the world.

Note

1. An extensive biography of Goodall's life was published by Dale Peterson in 2006 titled *Jane Goodall: The Woman Who Redefined Man* that provides details of life events from her childhood through present day. He was given access to her personal letters, family, friends, and colleagues to collect comprehensive data of her life.

References

Bennet, A., & Bennet, D. (2004). *Organizational survival in the new world: The intelligent complex adaptive system.* New York: KMCI Press.

Dass, R., & Bush, M. (1992). *Compassion in action: Setting out on the path of service.* New York: Bell Tower.

Day, D. V., Harrison, M. M., & Halpin, S. M. (2009). *An integrative approach to leader development: Connecting adult development, identity, and expertise.* New York: Routledge.

Goleman, D. (1995). *Emotional intelligence: Why it can matter more than IQ.* New York: Bantam Books.

Goleman, D., Boyatzis, R., & McKee, A. (2004). *Primal leadership: Realizing the power of emotional intelligence.* Boston: Harvard Business School Press.

Goodall, J. (1988). *In the shadow of man.* Boston: Houghton Mifflin.

Goodall, J. (1990). *Through a window: My thirty years with the chimpanzees of Gombe.* Boston: Houghton Mifflin.

Goodall, J. (1999). *Reason for hope: A spiritual journey.* New York: Time Warner.

Gowdy, H., Hildebrand, A., La Piana, D., & Campos, M. N. (2009). *Convergence: How five trends will reshape the social sector.* San Francisco: The James Irving Foundation.

Hesselbein, F. (1996). The "how to be" leader. In F. Hesselbein, M. Goldsmith, & R. Beckhard (Eds.), *The leader of the future* (pp. 121–124). San Francisco: Jossey-Bass.

Hunt, S. A. (2002). *The future of peace: On the front lines with the world's great peacemakers.* New York: HarperCollins.

Jago, A. G. (1982). Leadership: Perspectives in theory and research. *Management Science, 28*(3), 315–336.

Jane Goodall Institute. (2011). Retrieved from www.janegoodall.org/about -jgi

Laszlo, K. C., Laszlo, A., Romero, C., & Campos, M. (2003). Evolving development: An evolutionary perspective on development for an interconnected world. *World Futures, 59,* 105–119.

Lichtenstein, B. B., Uhl-Bien, M., Marion, R., Seers, A., Orton, J. D., & Schreiber, C. (2006). Complexity leadership theory: An interactive perspective on leading in complex adaptive systems. *Emergence: Complexity and Organization, 8*(4), 2–12. Retrieved from http:// digitalcommons.unl.edu/cgi/viewcontent.cgi?article=1007&context =managementfacpub&sei-redir=1#search=%22complexity%20 leadership%22

Lindsey, J. (1999). *Jane Goodall: 40 years at Gombe.* New York: Stewart, Tabori & Chang.

Midgley, M. (1989). Are you an animal? In G. Langley (Ed.), *Animal experimentation: The consensus changes* (pp. 1–18). New York: Chapman and Hall.

O'Connor, J., & McDermott, I. (1997). *The art of systems thinking: Essential skills for creativity and problem solving.* Hammersmith, UK: Thorsons.

Peterson, D. (2006). *Jane Goodall: The woman who redefined man.* Boston: Houghton Mifflin.

Popper, M. (2005). *Leaders who transform society.* Westport, CT: Praeger.

Stogdill, R. M. (1974). *Handbook of leadership: A survey of theory and research.* New York: Free Press.

Torbert, W. R. (1991). *The power of balance.* Newbury Park, NJ: Sage.

Wilber, K. (2006). *Integral spirituality.* Boston: Integral Books.

Yukl, G. (2002). *Leadership in organizations* (5th ed.). Upper Saddle River, NJ: Prentice Hall.

If You Would Lead Me— Reflections on Leadership

Nigel Linacre

If you would lead me
Without knowing me
Who am I?

If you lead me now
Not knowing yourself
Who are you?

If I'll let you lead
And give of myself
What'll you take?

If you're my leader
And I wonder why
Is that OK?

If the vision's yours
And it is not mine
Where am I?

If you're going east
And I'm heading west
Who will lead?

If you are leading
And I have my truth
Will you hear?

If we share a dream
And it's truly ours
Who leads who?

If you need control
In order to lead
Can we trust?

If you're the leader
But I could lead now
May I lead?

If it gets too hard
And I trip and fall
Where are you?

If you are leading
But sense that you're lost
Will you ask?

If you talk your truth
And you walk it too
How will you?

If you lead strongly
Believing in you
Where am I?

If you have led me
And we have shared
What have I?

If you lead me well
And we've arrived
Will I know?

If we lead good lives
And imagine them
What is seen?

If your tomorrow
Has great potential
Can we lead?

If your vision includes
Room for me and mine
May I join?

Index

Page references followed by *fig* indicate an illustrated figure; followed by *t* indicate a table.

A

Abbott flywheel effect, 243–244
Abbott Laboratories, 243
Abrams, L., 68
Action research: description of, 140; gang leadership study approach of, 140–152
Adams, W. M., 52
Adler, R. P., 45, 49
Affective learners, 67
Africa: bridging the gap between Western leadership approach and, 223–224; fast-growing economy of, 209; history and effect on leadership in, 213–216; increasing knowledge base of leadership theories in, 219–222; Jane Goodall's study of chimpanzees in, 257–266; need for leadership in, 209–210; role of culture and applying Western leadership to, 210–211; "two souls" phase of postcolonialism in, 213–216; Western versus African approaches to leadership in, 216–219
African-American Affairs (National Youth Administration), 110
African leadership theories, 219–221
Alaedini, P., 1–2, 3, 5
Aldag, R. J., 193
Alexander, A., 110
Alexander, I. E., 119
Alger, H., 39
Allen, B., 109, 112, 113, 114
Allen, S. J., 2, 3, 79, 93
Allyn, P., 72
Amabile, T. M., 169
Amin, A., 51
Anderson, R., 180, 181
Anecdote circles: description of, 142; gang leader study use of, 142–143. *See also* Stories
Aper, J. P., 96
Appreciative inquiry, 53
Apud, S., 210
Arampatzis, G., 53
Ardichvili, A., 210
Argyris, C., 51
Armstrong, D. M., 64, 68

Arrow, K. J., 41
The Art of War (Sun Tzu), 38, 166
Assimacopoulos, D., 53
Auditory learners, stories for, 67
Avolio, B. J., 64, 75, 83, 190
Axelrod, R. M., 228
Ayman, R., 211, 212
"The Aztek Lesson" (Smerd), 22

B

Bagchi, S., 183
Bagley, W. C., 44
Baker, G., 139
Bandura, A., 48, 158
Bangsbo, J., 162, 163, 167
Barber, B., 24
Barham, K., 194, 203
Barker, R. A., 41, 50
Barnett, I.B.W., 123
Barr, R. B., 49
Barrett, E. J., 125
Barrett, F., 53
Bass, B., 84
Baynes, C. F., 229, 232
Beck, D., 144
Becker, G. S., 48
Beckstrom, R. A., 41, 50, 54
Behaviorism, 45
Bennet, A., 254
Bennet, D., 254
Bennis, W., 40, 192
Bergeon, R., 186, 227, 242
Berger, P. L., 48
Bethune-Cookman College, 126
Bethune, M. M., 110, 111, 126
Bjork, R. A., 46
Black, J. S., 210
Black women politicians: conception of politics by, 126–127; cultural legacy shaping, 122–124; developing a political consciousness, 124; education as conduit for leadership development of, 110–112; "personal is political" implications for, 124–126; reexamining leadership of,